Understanding and Teaching the Intuitive Mind: Student and Teacher Learning

The Educational Psychology Series
Robert J. Sternberg and Wendy M. Williams, Series Editors

Understanding and Teaching the Intuitive Mind: Student and Teacher Learning

Edited by

Bruce Torff
Hofstra University

and

Robert J. Sternberg
Yale University

LEA

LAWRENCE ERLBAUM ASSOCIATES, PUBLISHERS
2001   MAHWAH, NEW JERSEY   LONDON

Lawrence Erlbaum Associates, Inc., Publishers
10 Industrial Avenue
Mahwah, New Jersey 07430

Library of Congress Cataloging-in-Publication Data

Understanding and teaching the intuitive mind : student and teacher learning / edited by
Bruce Torff and Robert J. Sternberg.
    p.   cm. — (The educational psychology series)
    Includes bibliographical references and index.
    ISBN 0-8058-3109-6
    1. Concept learning.   2. Intuition (Psychology).   I. Torff, Bruce.   II. Sternberg,
Robert J.   III. Series.

LB1062 .U53   2000
370.15′23—dc21

                            00-030871

Printed in the United States of America
10 9 8 7 6 5 4 3 2 1

Contents

Preface

Many teachers have had the experience of teaching a lesson only to find that students' previously existing ideas have interfered with their learning. Experiences as such underscore the significant role played in the classroom by *intuitive conceptions*—knowledge or knowledge structures that individuals acquire and use largely without conscious reflection or explicit instruction. The intuitive mind sometimes works to facilitate learning in the classroom and other valued contexts. However, learning may also be impeded by intuitive conceptions, and they can be difficult to dislodge as needed. The intuitive mind is a powerful force in the classroom and often an undetected one.

Accordingly, the psychological literature includes a large and diverse body of theory and research on intuitive conceptions. This work has done much to investigate the psychological processes of the intuitive mind, but at present the literature is limited in certain respects. *Understanding and Teaching the Intuitive Mind: Student and Teacher Learning* moves into the breach in four ways. First, the literature is largely fragmented, especially between theorists and researchers investigating primary (innately specified and endogenously regulated) forms of intuition and secondary (socioculturally specified and exogenously regulated) forms. *Understanding and Teaching the Intuitive Mind: Student and Teacher Learning* pulls together diverse theoretical and methodological approaches to the origin, structure, function, and development of intuitive conceptions. Second, the book explores a diversity of academic disciplines. To date, intuitive conceptions have been studied most extensively in math and science. Here equal attention is paid to the sciences, arts, and humanities. Third, much of the psychological literature makes only limited contact with educational issues, leaving educators lacking a coherent account of how intuitive conceptions influence classroom learning and what can be done in response. *Understanding and Teaching the Intuitive Mind: Student and Teacher Learning* explicitly links theory and research to educational implications and classroom applications. Finally, recent theory and research in teacher education investigate the intuitive conceptions held by teachers—beliefs about teaching and learning that influence educational practices. This work has appeared largely in isolation from the literature on learners' intuitive conceptions. *Understanding and Teaching the Intuitive Mind: Student and Teacher Learning* focuses not only on students' intuitive conceptions, but also on teachers' intuitive beliefs about learning and teaching.

Understanding and Teaching the Intuitive Mind: Student and Teacher Learning supports psychologists, teacher–educators, educational administrators, teachers, prospective teachers, and others who seek to develop educational practices that are cognizant of (and responsive to) the intuitive conceptions of students and teachers. Diverse as are the viewpoints presented herein, they share the belief that educational practices have much to gain by systematic studies of the intuitive learner and teacher.

PLAN FOR THIS BOOK

Part II of this volume is devoted to theory and research on the intuitive conceptions employed by learners—inside and outside the classroom. In Chapter 2, Ben-Zeev and Star draw on the large literature on intuitive conceptions in math and science in a wide-ranging chapter that echoes the distinction between primary and secondary intuition. Here the authors suggest that the well-documented primary intuitive conceptions about mathematics held by learners are augmented by secondary ones as learners enter into formal schooling. Ben-Zeev and Star argue that intuitive conceptions can have mixed results, resulting in a predictable pattern of errors, in part due to dissonance between current instructional methods and learners' intuitive ideas about mathematics. Future research, the authors suggest, might well focus on the nature of secondary intuition in mathematics, especially as it involves postarithmetic quantitative operations.

In Chapter 3, Wertsch and Polman point out that history is a subject taught around the world, yet is largely absent from discussions about cognition and instruction, and in particular from discussions of the intuitive mind. Drawing a distinction between popular historical accounts (that arise in the absence of explicit instruction) and the formal history taught in schools, the authors locate popular historical knowledge in the realm of secondary intuition. Popular accounts have an intuitive appeal, they suggest, and individuals tend to slip back to compelling but often flawed popular accounts even after formal instruction that contradicts the popular version. Wertsch and Polman also suggest that the intuitive mind has been explored in greater detail in science and math than in the humanities because the narrative structure of knowledge in subjects such as history is qualitatively different from (and more difficult to operationalize than) the propositional (*paradigmatic* in Bruner, 1990) knowledge in science and math. A comprehensive understanding of intuition, the authors conclude, requires that paradigmatic and narrative forms of knowledge be brought together.

Freeman and Parsons (Chap. 4) suggest that learners construct a developing intuitive theory of art as they grow. Such a theory influences the way artistic judgments are made, the authors assert, yielding a form of bias that both supports and impedes individuals as they perceive or create art. With this view, learning to understand and make art requires learners to introspect on, evaluate, and ultimately revise an intuitive theory of art. As with intuitions in other areas, intuitive conceptions in the arts are a mixed blessing. Art education, the authors conclude, should stress the underlying conceptual development of students and not simply the products they make.

In her chapter on early-childhood education, Fromberg (Chap. 5) invokes complexity theory to account for patterns of classroom discourse in which teachers' and students' spontaneous reactions to comments and questions change the direction of a discussion, often in unforeseen but productive ways. Fromberg argues that the prevailing academic (curriculum-centered) model ill suits the learner, who benefits from both analytic and intuitive ways of knowing the world but finds the intuitive one underutilized and undervalued. With this view, it is a mistake for teachers to dominate classroom discussion to keep the focus on a particular set of learning objectives because such teacher-centered practices effectively cut off the intuitive mind. Here the call is for a paradigm shift to early-education practices that develop and integrate the analytic mind and the intuitive mind.

Part III of this volume focuses on teachers' intuitive conceptions about teaching and learning. In Chapter 6, Patrick and Pintrich describe developmental patterns in teachers' beliefs as teachers move from prospective teacher to novice to expert. The authors make the strong claim that the needed developmental changes constitute conceptual change—that is, learning to become an expert teacher involves the adoption of a new perspective that is incommensurable with the previous, outmoded one. At the heart of this change, Patrick and Pintrich assert, are motivational and epistemological factors. As such, the authors place into consideration a developmental form of primary intuition—based on epistemological development—and thus imply that both primary and secondary forms of intuition work to constitute teachers' beliefs. Patrick and Pintrich recommend that teacher–educators analyze prospective teachers' beliefs, encourage teachers to reflect on how such beliefs facilitate and constrain teaching, and provide instruction that facilitates needed conceptual change.

Chapter 7 by Woolfolk Hoy and Murphy describes teachers' implicit beliefs about teaching, beliefs that have their origin in the educational system and its cultural backdrop, and thus might be classified as secondary intuitive conceptions. The authors describe multiple sets of uncritically held implicit beliefs that teachers typically espouse, including beliefs about intelligence, sense of self, learning, teaching (and learning to teach), and assessment, as well as attitudes about (and expectations of) students. These beliefs converge to support a transmission-oriented model of education, and, like Patrick and Pintrich, Woolfolk Hoy and Murphy find teacher beliefs to be robust and resistant to change in favor of the learner-centered (constructivist) practices typically taught in teacher-education courses. At the same time, the authors suggest that teachers' beliefs can be amended in positive ways through curriculum designs and instructional strategies that encourage students to confront and analyze intuitive conceptions about teaching.

Chapter 8 by Anderson describes a qualitative study that examines the beliefs of individuals at different points along the path of a teaching career, from teacher-education student to practicing professional. The data reveal that beliefs about teaching are variable—not entirely anticonstructivist, as other teacher educators have asserted. Anderson also finds that teachers' intuitive conceptions of teaching are not necessarily obstacles to deeper understanding, but sometimes serve as stepping stones with the right kind of teacher education. Such progress, the author suggests, occurs at uneven rates among different individuals, may involve troubling-looking incidents in which teachers revert to naive views, and may be difficult to assess. A challenge facing teacher–educators, Anderson concludes, is to develop teacher-education practices that are responsive to the diversity of intuitive conceptions held by preservice and inservice teachers.

The chapter by Strauss (Chap. 9) summarizes a program of research exploring prospective teachers' intuitively held mental models of teaching and learning. Strauss suggests that teachers cling to a mechanical view of teaching in which right-sizing of information predicts successful knowledge transmission. Putting this claim in theoretical context, Strauss invokes the language of secondary intuitive conceptions. With this view, a culture's folk psychology and attendant folk pedagogy determine its educational practices (Bruner, 1996; Torff, 1999a, 1999b). Strauss suggests that Western culture's folk pedagogy tends to overemphasize the importance of subject-matter knowledge while downplaying teachers' mental models of teaching and learning. In accordance with other researchers of teachers' beliefs, Strauss argues that intuitions about teaching sometimes detract from teacher learning. The author concludes that teachers need to develop strong subject-matter knowledge to be sure, but that greater attention should be paid to the nature and development of teachers' intuitive conceptions about teaching.

In the volume's final chapter, Olson and Katz (Chap. 10) extend Strauss' emphasis on the impact of culture on intuitive conceptions about teaching. Building on prior work by Olson and Bruner (1996), Olson and Katz articulate four folk psychologies of education (or folk pedagogies)—each a worldview on what teaching is and what teachers should do. Of particular interest is the fourth folk pedagogy—the canon of knowledge, skills, beliefs, and values about education. The goal here is to determine whether this fourth folk pedagogy is distinct from the second (possession of knowledge) or the third (sharing beliefs). The authors' analysis reveals that the fourth pedagogy is evident in interviews with teachers in training. Like other authors in this volume, Olson and Katz call for reflective practices that help prospective teachers reconcile what is known about education with an equal concern for the subjective mental life of students.

At the end of the day, theory and research on the intuitive mind remain in a hazy state. There are different kinds of intuition, it seems, and it is far from clear how they relate, develop, and work. The following chapters further the debate by placing a diversity of views side by side. The intuitive mind remains a compelling, if difficult, topic for psychologists and educators alike.

ACKNOWLEDGMENTS

The editors would like to thank the authors who generously agreed to contribute to this book. We would also like to thank the following individuals for their assistance and encouragement: Laura Torff, Susan Rostan, Joseph Horvath, and Michel Ferrari. Production of this volume was made possible in part by funding provided by the Office of Educational

Research and Improvement of the Department of Education of the United States of America (OERI grant R206R950001).

REFERENCES

Bruner, J. (1990). *Acts of meaning*. Cambridge, MA: Harvard University Press.
Bruner, J. (1996). *The culture of education*. Cambridge, MA: Harvard University Press.
Olson, D., & Bruner, J. (1996). Folk psychology and folk pedagogy. In D. Olson & N. Torrance (Eds.), *Handbook of education in human development* (pp. 9–27). Oxford, England: Blackwell.
Torff, B. (1999a). Beyond information processing: Cultural influences on cognition and learning. In S. Ulibarri (Ed.), *Maria Montessori explicit and implicit in the 20th century*. Cancun, Mexico: International Montessori Congress.
Torff, B. (1999b). Tacit knowledge in teaching: Folk pedagogy and teacher education. In R. Sternberg & J. Horvath (Eds.), *Tacit knowledge in professional practice*. Mahwah, NJ: Lawrence Erlbaum Associates.

PART I

INTRODUCTION

CHAPTER ONE

Intuitive Conceptions Among Learners and Teachers

Bruce Torff
Hofstra University

Robert J. Sternberg
Yale University

In a high school physics class, Julie and her teacher, Mr. Ewing, are talking about the forces involved as he tosses a coin in the air. Julie suggests that Mr. Ewing's arm imparts a certain amount of force to the coin, and when this force dissipates the coin starts to fall. Julie's classmates indicate agreement with this commonsense analysis of the physics of a coin toss. Mr. Ewing is in his first year in the classroom and wants this matter cleared up, so he decides to inform the class about Newton's laws. Objects, he explains, do not collect and expend "force"—once the coin is set in motion, its path is influenced only by gravity and air resistance. During the lecture the students nod their heads, but a few days later they perform rather poorly on a physics test. The test results show that students can define and describe Newton's laws, but they continue to use naive notions to make sense of real-world problems (e.g., baseballs being thrown). Later an exasperated Mr. Ewing whispers to colleagues that this group of students is not especially strong in physics.

—Anonymous

This anecdote reveals the influence in classrooms of *intuitive conceptions*, which we define for the time being as preexisting knowledge or knowledge structures that predispose individuals to think and act in particular ways without much conscious reflection. Accordingly, the process of activating these conceptions might be called *intuition*. The domain of physics provides the "smoking gun" showing that students' learning in

3

the classroom is heavily influenced, and can be impeded, by intuitive conceptions. In this example, students hold fast to misconceived intuitive notions about force and agency (notions derivative of Aristotelian dynamics) even after successfully participating in a lesson featuring the prevailing scientific view of the physical world (Newtonian dynamics; e.g., diSessa, 1983; Larkin, 1988; McCloskey, Camarazza, & Green, 1980). Even students who perform in an exemplary manner in class revert to powerful yet inaccurate ideas about physics when tested on real-world problems due to previously existing ideas about physics that the typical course is apparently unable to dislodge.

Equally important in the prior anecdote are Mr. Ewing's intuitive conceptions—in this case, intuitive notions about how the mind works and how teaching should proceed. Implicit in Mr. Ewing's decision making is the intuitive view that learning occurs when students absorb information from the environment, so the best teaching occurs when the environment is made rich with information transmitted to students from teachers, books, and other sources. Studies of teachers' beliefs show that prospective teachers often hold fast to an intuitive transmission model of teaching despite the constructivist view (taught in most teacher-education programs) that knowledge is constructed individually by each learner based on environmental input and individual reflection (e.g., Anderson, 1994; Brookhart & Freeman, 1992; Bruner, 1996; Hollingsworth, 1989; Kagan, 1992; McLaughlin, 1991; Morine-Dershimer, 1993; Shulman, 1987; Strauss, 1993, 1996; Strauss & Shilony, 1994; Torff, 1998, 1999a, 1999b; Woolfolk Hoy, 1996; Zeichner & Gore, 1990). Even people who are trained in education hold powerful intuitive conceptions about teaching and learning, and these intuitive conceptions exert a great deal of influence on the way they think and act in classroom settings. Intuitive conceptions held by teachers, as well as those held by students, influence educational outcomes and not always for the better.

As we detail in the following, the literature in philosophy, psychology, and education set out a variety of approaches to theory and research in the workings of the intuitive mind. This diverse body of work addresses four sets of questions:

1. Defining *intuition* and *intuitive conceptions*:
What are intuitive conceptions? How are they structured? How do they work? Where do they come from? What factors facilitate and constrain their functioning?

2. Development of the intuitive mind:
How do intuitive conceptions change of over time? What factors facilitate and constrain this development?

3. Consequences of intuitive conceptions for learning in valued contexts:

What results do intuitive conceptions produce in classrooms and other learning environments? What factors facilitate and constrain the use of intuitive conceptions in classroom learning?

4. Implications for education:

What sorts of pedagogical recommendations have been made? What kinds of interventions are required to develop (or counter) intuitive conceptions in valued contexts of learning, especially in schools?

The present volume presents the viewpoints of nine sets of invited authors who were asked to discuss how their work relates to the notion of intuitive conceptions and what the educational implications of these intuitions might be. To set the stage for the remaining chapters, this chapter reviews the literature on intuitive conceptions. In what follows, to further define and conceptualize the slippery notions of intuition and intuitive conceptions, we provide a framework that brings together diverse approaches to the intuitive mind. We then employ the framework in a review of the literature on the influence of intuitive conceptions on learning. Finally, we take up a special case of intuitive conceptions with particular importance for education—teachers' intuitive beliefs about learners, learning, and teaching and the influence of these beliefs on educational practices.

CONCEPTUALIZING THE INTUITIVE MIND

Classicism and Interactionism, Past and Present

The notion of intuition has a long and disputatious history that begins in the discipline of philosophy, where there is vigorous debate centering on the origin and function of the intuitive mind. The classic view, identified with Spinoza and Bergson, holds that intuition is a form of intellectual process that is separate from conscious thought and that yields qualitatively different knowledge than the explicit reasoning of the conscious mind. With this view, intuition is a special human capacity that affords an experience of reality—a glimpse of ultimate truth precluded by reason. Opposing the classicists are the interactionists such as Dilthey and Wittgentein, who agree that intuition is conceptually distinct from reason but locate intuition in the person's interaction with the social world. With this view, what comes to an individual as intuitive depends on socially shared canons of knowledge and skill.

Psychologists have also devoted considerable attention to the notion of intuitive conceptions, especially in the decades since the cognitive revolution of the mid-20th century. Not surprisingly, the psychological literature tends to recapitulate the classicist–interactionist split in the form of the eternally vexing nature–nurture question. No single question has raised more attention than the relative contribution to human behavior of heredity (innately specified, biologically regulated factors) and environment (socially shared and culturally produced factors; see Sternberg & Grigorenko, 1997). On the one hand, views reminiscent of the classic tradition can be seen among a variety of branches of psychology, including cognitive psychology, cognitive-developmental psychology, and evolutionary psychology, where theory and research on intuitive conceptions have been presented as part of a more general quest to understand the innately specified universals of human cognitive structure and function. On the other hand, interactionist views of intuition also abound in contemporary psychology. Psychological anthropologists, cultural psychologists, and psychologists of the sociocultural school (i.e., psychologists focused on the influence of culture and context on cognition) see the origins of the intuitive mind in the interactions between the person and the cultural context. Here the focus is on the influence of processes of social interaction on the development of intuitive conceptions.

Large, diverse, and provocative as these bodies of literature on the intuitive mind are, they are thoroughly fragmented. In the main, the literature comprises a handful of separate pockets of theory and research, with limited communication both within and across the classicist–interactionist divide. This is no simple nature–nurture dispute. Theory and research on intuitive conceptions may be split along classicist–interaction lines, but it is misleading to cast these as opposing camps. Most theorists and researchers focus on one or the other but acknowledge the contribution of the opposite side, and some have made considerable contributions to both sides. As a theoretical matter, an individual could believe in 2 different kinds of intuition or 10. Needed is a framework for pulling together the diversity of views on the intuitive mind.

A Framework for Intuitive Conceptions

Defining Intuitive Conceptions

Intuitive is an intuitive notion. In common parlance, intuition is a handy notion for describing a way to make sense of the world—a form of perceiving and thinking that comes to people spontaneously and naturally without much deliberate conscious reflection, yielding uncritically held knowledge that resonates as truth. In most instances of use, the notion of intuition is suitably clear as a linguistic category and does not require a definition.

However, *intuition* quickly becomes problematic as a scientific term. Definitions of *intuition* and *intuitive conceptions* vary, leaving readers wondering how, if at all, the various terms and theories fit together. Wertsch and Polman (chap. 3, this volume) put it as such: "Although investigators have made headway in understanding what intuitive knowledge is, clarity about many basic terms remains elusive." Moreover, it remains unclear how intuition relates to other processes of cognitive representation.

One could argue that what is needed here is conceptual clarity in the form of a single definition for a single type of intuition. As a scientific matter, it seems impossible to develop a general theory of intuition that defines the term in a way that is palatable to theorists and researchers from differing viewpoints, given the current fragmentation of the intuitive-conceptions literature. As a practical matter, the single-definition model yields little promise for encouraging distant groups of theorists and researchers to the table.

A more pluralistic approach suggests that the human mind benefits from multiple ways to represent knowledge, and some of them operate outside of conscious reasoning and can therefore be considered intuitive. *Intuitive conceptions* are defined as knowledge or knowledge structures that need not be available to conscious reflection but that act to facilitate or constrain task performance. Intuitive conceptions are a subset of cognitive representations—those that can be invoked without conscious awareness. Accordingly, *intuition* is defined as the process through which intuitive conceptions are acquired and used. This agnostic and neutral definition promises to be inclusive of diverse approaches to the workings of the nonconscious mind.

Primary and Secondary Intuitive Conceptions

Positing multiple kinds of intuitive conceptions, not just a single kind, allows latter-day classicist and interactionist views to be accommodated. Indeed, the distinction can felicitously be drawn between primary and secondary intuitive conceptions. *Primary intuitive conceptions* are defined as innately specified knowledge or knowledge structures that are universal to the human species. This is our birthright for nonconscious thought—the portion of the human being's genetically specified hardware for cognition that works outside of conscious awareness. Primary intuitive conceptions appear to be in evidence in the opening anecdote of this chapter, wherein physics learners are guided by intuitive conceptions about force and agency not taught in or out of school.

In contrast, secondary intuitive conceptions comprise knowledge or knowledge structures that result from learner–environment interaction and are therefore particular to the sociocultural circumstances that produced them. Secondary intuitive conceptions are part of our cultural legacy—the nonconscious portion of the processes of enculturation through which individuals connect with the world around them. For example, people become able to conceptualize distances when they gain the use of culturally established measurement tools (e.g., the inch). Once a person has learned what an inch is and what it does, assessing distances becomes a task handled by invoking secondary intuitive conceptions.

Educational Implications of Intuitive Conceptions: The Facilitation Question

From the educator's viewpoint, the crucial questions concern the extent to which intuitive conceptions are helpful or harmful in valued contexts of learning (such as schools) and what educators should do in response. A further distinction is needed—one between intuitive conceptions that are supportive of learning in valued contexts such as schools (e.g., secondary intuitions about measurement seem unambiguously useful) and intuitive conceptions that are unsupportive (misconceived notions about physics may actively impede learning and require special efforts to dislodge).

Intuitive conceptions work both for and against educators, but it is important to note that determining the extent to which a particular one is helpful or harmful requires a detailed analysis of both the intuitive conception and the context in which it is used. In some cases, a particular intuitive conception may be consistently deleterious (e.g., notions about physics that are not correct). In other cases, intuitive conceptions may be consistently and unambiguously helpful (e.g., innately specified facial recognition capacities that operate nonconsciously have little in the way of a downside). In still other instances, intuitive conceptions have the power to assist or detract from learning depending on the context at hand. For example, primary intuitive conceptions about number and quantity make it seem intuitive to people that a larger number corresponds to a greater quantity. This intuitive conception makes decimals a breeze and fractions a nightmare because the latter counterintuitively decrease in quantity as the denominator grows larger. Only in context can it be determined when an intuitive conception is supportive or unsupportive. As such, what is needed is a situated model of intuitive conceptions that focuses on the person in context (rather than the person alone) as the relevant unit of analysis (Greeno, 1997; Putnam & Borko, 2000; Seely Brown, Collins, & Duguid, 1989).

Four Categories of Intuitive Conceptions

With two types of intuitive conceptions, primary and secondary, and two possible educational outcomes in valued contexts of knowledge use, a framework is established with four categories of intuitive conceptions:

(a) primary (innately specified) intuitive conceptions that are supportive of learning in valued contexts; (b) primary intuitive conceptions that work to impede learning; (c) secondary (culturally specified) intuitive conceptions of the supportive variety; and (d) secondary intuitions that interfere with learning.

The intuitive-conceptions framework affords a definition of *intuitive* that is broad enough to include diverse bodies of theory and research on the workings of the nonconscious mind. As such, the framework works to further the goal of vertical integration of the human sciences—the attempt to integrate various approaches to the human sciences, including various branches of psychology, anthropology, sociology, economics, and other disciplines concerned with human behavior (see Barkow, Cosmides, & Tooby, 1992). In what follows, this framework is used to review the literature on intuitive conceptions. We begin with a discussion of theory and research on primary intuitive conceptions, followed by work concerned with secondary intuitive conceptions.

PRIMARY INTUITIVE CONCEPTIONS

Implicit Learning

There has been a great deal of activity in cognitive psychology in the last three decades with aims to investigate the processes by which people acquire knowledge outside of conscious awareness. Most of this theory and research has been treated under the banner *implicit learning* (Berry & Dienes, 1993; Cleeremans, 1993; Reber, 1993; Torff, 1997). Implicit learning is "acquisition of knowledge that takes place largely independently of conscious attempts to learn and largely in the absence of explicit knowledge of what was acquired" (Reber, 1993, p. 5). The upshot of this large and vibrant body of work is that people benefit from a knowledge-acquisition mechanism that operates without the conscious awareness of the learner. Existence demonstrations of this phenomenon have been described in a variety of experimental settings, including artificial grammar, sequence learning, and control of complex systems.

Conceptual and methodological disputes have dogged this research area, especially concerning the extent to which the learning in implicit-learning experiments actually operates outside of conscious awareness. Absence of evidence makes weak evidence of absence, so there is always room for a methodological critique impugning a particular study's means of eliciting and assessing the extent of subjects' explicit knowledge. Moreover, the character of the knowledge representations yielded by implicit learning has been a contentious issue. Vigorous debate concerns the extent to which implicit learning yields abstract knowledge representations or situation-specific ones. There are also unresolved questions about the relationship between implicit and explicit processes of learning.

Implicit learning is thought to "give rise to the phenomenal sense of intuition. That is, people do not feel that they actively work out the answer" (Berry & Dienes, 1993, p. 14). For the present purposes, the implicit-learning literature describes the mechanisms through which the intuitive mind comes to produce nonconsciously held knowledge. Concerning the question of development, these mechanisms have been investigated primarily in a stable adult state, like many constructs in psychology, with little emphasis paid to possible developmental changes in their structure and function. The educational implications of this work have not been discussed extensively, but in general implicit learning is seen as a fundamentally positive process that supports learning in the laboratory, the classroom, and everyday situations.

Tacit Knowledge

The product of implicit learning is often called *tacit knowledge* (Sternberg & Horvath, 1999; Sternberg, Wagner, Williams, & Horvath, 1995; Torff, 1997, 1999b). Sternberg and colleagues define *tacit knowledge* as "procedural knowledge that guides behavior but is not readily available for introspection" (Sternberg, 1999, p. 231). Sternberg and colleagues have investigated tacit knowledge in several real-world disciplines, including academic psychology, business management, and military leadership. These studies have shown that tacit knowledge is a significant predictor of success (Sternberg, 1997; Sternberg et al., 1995; Sternberg & Horvath, 1999). Successful individuals, the argument goes, not only have a great deal of explicit knowledge about important tasks in a discipline, they also have a rich fund of tacit knowledge about the discipline. Tacit knowledge is a key component of practical intelligence, which is a component of Sternberg's Triarchic Theory of Intelligence (Sternberg, 1988; Sternberg, Torff, & Grigorenko, 1998a, 1998b). Practical intelligence is real-world know-how that is essential to adult success but is often not conceptually clear or taught explicitly, and thus often remains tacit. Sternberg's theory is singular among modern theories of intelligence in its explicit treatment of tacit knowledge—the cognitive representations created by the intuitive mind.

Sternberg and colleagues take primarily a domain-specific view that tacit knowledge varies across disciplines (in contrast to implicit-learning theorists, who argue that implicit learning functions in a domain-general manner). With this view, what counts as relevant and important tacit knowledge in, say, the field of classical music is largely although not totally different from the tacit knowledge germane to academic psychology. Sternberg and colleagues also suggested that tacit knowledge is best viewed with a developmental perspective. Accordingly, abilities are seen as forms of developing expertise, and acquisition and use of tacit knowledge are central components of the development of expertise (Sternberg, 1998).

Concerning the educational implications of the theory of tacit knowledge, Sternberg and colleagues concurred with implicit-learning researchers that tacit knowledge is a positive force that supports learning in valued contexts, in and out of school. That tacit knowledge supports the acquisition of expertise is most evident in instances of failure—that is, when tacit knowledge is not acquired and used as needed. With this view, failures in teaching and learning of tacit knowledge underlie many difficulties that people evince in school and on the job. Sternberg's group advocates educational practices that encompass not only the explicit knowledge required in a discipline (e.g., the formulas of physics), but also the tacit knowledge that is important in that discipline (e.g., how physicists conceptualize a project or get a paper published). A laudable goal for educators, then, is to make explicit as much knowledge as possible for the purposes of teaching. The first step is to analyze the tacit knowledge that is fundamental to a discipline, and the second step is to design vehicles for curriculum and assessment that teach the full range of knowledge and skill needed in the discipline, tacit as well as explicit.

Evolutionary Psychology

Theory and research in implicit learning and tacit knowledge investigate the way the modern human mind works. Evolutionary psychologists examine the adaptive pressures that have caused the mind to develop the way it has (see Barkow et al., 1992). This line of theory and research has included an explicit claim that the human mind is configured with a variety of modules—separate task-specific cognitive abilities—that evolved in response to the environmental challenges faced by the human species (Cosmides & Tooby, 1987; Tooby & Cosmides, 1990). Here the mind is considered to be something like a Swiss Army knife, designed with mechanisms specialized to meet the challenges that arise in particular environments. According to evolutionary psychologists, these modules are numerous, including innately specified capacities for facial recognition, spatial relations, rigid objects mechanics, tool use, social exchange, motion perception, and many others. A key feature of this theory is the claim that the conscious mind needs not be invoked for many modules to be activated. They also are thought to be content rich; that is, modules provide not only sets of procedures for solving problems, but also much of the information needed to do so. With this view, intuitive conceptions are a major component of the modern human's genetic heritage.

These modules are not thought to undergo significant developmental changes as the individual ages. Modules are seen as forms of innate hardwiring that are largely unaffected by environmental influences such as social norms or educational practices. As a result of this adevelopmental view, cultural contexts are not thought to initiate change of any kind in the cognitive activities of individuals. It is through culture, however, that people have responded to many of the evolutional pressures facing human beings, so it is useful to study cultures to see how they respond to different environmental challenges. With this view, cultures do not change individual minds, but culturally manifested responses to adaptive pressures direct the evolution of the human species.

Evolutionary psychology has become very popular since the 1980s, but the educational implications of this perspective remain largely undeveloped. Evolutionists have made one suggestion that is potentially of great importance to educators—the notion that not all of the innately specified modules serve the modern human well. Evolutionary pressures work slowly, but in the last several thousand years, human culture has moved at a fast pace. In that time, the genetic makeup of the human mind has not evolved significantly, but cultures have changed human life in countless ways. Although modern humans are adapted to be Pleistocene-era hunter–gatherers, most people live in a different sort of world—industrial society. The modern human is, on this view, fundamentally maladapted to the current environment. It follows, then, that modern humans should evince ways in which their behavior seems ill suited to contemporary challenges, intellectual and otherwise. For example, the spatial-relations module is well suited to keeping the hunter–gatherer's world in focus, but it is less suited to abstract uses like those found in geometry textbooks.

Hence, most people have the spatial ability needed to navigate around the neighborhood, but struggle to solve problems in Euclidean geometry. Evolutionary psychologists make clear that the adaptive legacy we have from our forebears does not always support our performance in the modern world. In the language of the intuitive-conceptions framework, we might call these *primary intuitive misconceptions*—innately specified intuitive conceptions that interfere with learning in valued real-world contexts.

Cognitive-Developmental Psychology

The notion that the individual's innately specified endowment might be a mixed blessing has been taken up in cognitive-developmental psychology, where there has been a great deal of interest in the intuitive mind. With behaviorist models and Piagetian theory in decline in recent decades, researchers have been emboldened to investigate entities that these influential theories explicitly proscribed—innately specified cognitive mechanisms that emerge early in life without interaction with the environment. Recent cognitive-developmental theory and research are rooted in part in the work of two colorful figures. The first is Chomsky (1968), whose nativist account of language acquisition dealt a devastating blow to both its behaviorist and Piagetian rivals. The second figure is Fodor (1983), whose theory positing a modular set of hardwired input systems ushered in a new era of skepticism about domain-general constructs such as Piaget's and a new focus on domain-specific processes. In the footsteps of Chomksy and Fodor, cognitive developmentalists have presented a variety of nativist constructs under such monikers as first principals, p-prims, constraints, and early developing modules. These innately specified structures are seen as guiding frameworks for specific types of cognitive activity, and they need not be called into conscious awareness to work.

With this view, human cognition, including its intuitive form, is domain specific rather than domain general to a significant extent (Hirshfeld & Gelman, 1994). Domains are separate components of an innately specified cognitive system and are thus not equivalent to culturally specified disciplines described elsewhere—more on that distinction later. Detailed studies of human performances rooted in innately specified structures have been reported in several domains: language (Pinker, 1994, 1998), psychology or theory of mind (Astington, 1993; Wellman, 1990), quantitative reasoning (Gelman & Brenneman, 1994), spatial cognition (Kellman, 1996; Spelke, 1991; Spelke & Hermer, 1996), and biology (Atran, 1994; Carey, 1996; Carey & Smith, 1993; Keil, 1989, 1994).

The extent to which these intuitive constructs develop in any meaningful sense of the word is a contentious issue among psychologists. Some see these innately specified constructs as guiding all subsequent cognition, throughout the life span, without evincing significant developmental changes (Spelke, 1991; Spelke & Hermer, 1996). This is mother nature's programming for intuitive thought, on this view, and it grows but does not significantly change, much like infants who have 10 fingers that grow larger and more dexterous but not fundamentally different in structure.

Other psychologists argue that profound developmental changes are evident in innately specified structures. Perhaps the leading proponent of the developing nature of intuitive conceptions is Carey, whose conceptual-change model has proved influential (Carey, 1985; Carey & Smith, 1993). Elements of the intuitive mind change significantly as the child develops, the argument goes, as a new set of beliefs replaces an old set, with the new one being qualitatively different and inconsistent (in Carey's terms, *incommensurable*). Educational interventions, Carey argued, have the power to usher along developmental changes that individuals need to make if they are to counter primary intuitive misconceptions and form accurate representations of the physical, mathematical, psychological, and biological worlds, and perhaps others as well.

The adevelopmental view also was criticized by Karmiloff-Smith (1992), who put forth a general theory of developmental changes in psychological structure and function called *representational redescription*. With this view, representations of knowledge in their initial form are implicit (unavailable to conscious awareness), but they become available to conscious awareness and reflection as the individual develops. Moreover, as this developmental progression occurs, knowledge from one module becomes available to other modules, and thus knowledge that begins as domain specific becomes generalized. Developmental change therefore involves a process of increasing connections (mapping) across domains as implicit knowledge becomes available to conscious awareness.

As noted, the primary intuitive conceptions described by cognitive developmentalists do not always support learning in valued contexts. For example, the domain of biology seems to involve intuitive conceptions that are misleading or inadequate. Research by Keil (1989, 1994) revealed that children are born with an understanding that living things and inanimate objects are fundamentally different. At the same time, children tend to believe that anything that moves is alive—including blowing sand and other inanimate objects. The human being's intuitive understanding of biology is in some ways lacking, requiring new learning for an accurate set of conceptions to hold sway. With this view, the significant challenges facing cognitive developmentalists and educators are to frame an account of when and how primary intuitive conceptions impede learning, and to develop educational practices that build on them, counter them, or both as needed to strengthen learning in valued contexts.

Taking Stock: Primary Intuitive Conceptions

At first blush, the research previously described seems to cohere into an integrated model. Adaptive pressures over the millennia have produced a set of mental structures universal to the modern human, as evolutionary psychologists describe. These structures operate in specific domains, as cognitive developmentalists insist, and draw on processes of implicit and explicit learning as they are developed and used. The result is expertise in specific domains and in cross-domain mapping abilities; such expertise comprises both tacit and explicit knowledge.

However, this unified model disintegrates on closer analysis. Major differences are evident with respect to the conceptualization, structure, development, consequences, and educational implications of intuitive conceptions. Moreover, differences of opinion are in evidence concerning the extent to which sociocultural contexts influence the intuitive mind. These are the focus of the following section.

SECONDARY INTUITIVE CONCEPTIONS

Alongside researchers investigating primary intuition—the latter-day classicists who locate intuitive conceptions in the genome—are contemporary interactionists who insist that to understand the intuitive mind one must take account of the culture in which the mind is situated. With this view, interactions in a particular cultural context influence the development and use of nonconscious cognitive processes, resulting in secondary intuitive conceptions.

Cultural Psychology and Psychological Anthropology

A notion along the lines of secondary intuition has a long history in anthropology, and in particular in psychological anthropology and cultural psychology—two closely related disciplines focused on the study of the psychological characteristics of members of a particular culture, with implications for studies of the universal elements of human cognition (Geertz, 1983; Shweder, 1991; Stigler, Shweder, & Herdt, 1990). Cultural psychologists have presented detailed case studies of the pervasive role of culture in the formation of the intuitive mind. For example, consider a type of interpersonal-space norm—conceptions of the appropriate distance between newly introduced people engaged in a conversation. Imagine a party with American and Arabic guests. Americans feel comfortable when there are 3 feet or so between interlocutors, so that the American guest takes up a position opposite her Arabic companion. Arabic people tend to like the distances to be less, so the Arabic guest, sensing the distance from the American to be too great, steps closer. The American now feels crowded and steps back. Across the room they travel, each compelled to act by interpersonal-space norms given to them by culture. These norms provide a clear example of the cultural formation of the intuitive mind—cultures teach their members such things as interpersonal-space norms, and individuals learn these although they seldom think about how comfortable they feel with interpersonal distances, at least not until such norms are violated. It is through culturally specified notions such as this one, the argument goes, that people accomplish valued objectives in part by invoking secondary intuitive conceptions.

Cultural psychologists explore the ways in which cultures place their stamp on the cognitive activities of individuals. The other group of psychologists concerned with culture, evolutionary psychologists, work the other way—examining cultures to determine how culturally manifested responses to adaptive pressures have shaped the evolution of the human intellect. The key difference here is that only cultural psychologists believe that cultural participation meaningfully changes the human mind as the individual develops. With this view, there is no difference among *learning*, *socialization*, and *enculturation*. All three terms denote the process by which individuals encounter and engage with elements of the surrounding culture. To learn about, for instance, interpersonal-space norms is to be socialized into the way one's community does things, and to be enculturated into the way members of a culture conceptualize the world and organize action in it. The term *communities of practice* has been used to describe the various groups in a culture (also known as subcultures) that influence the cognitive activities of individual members (Brown & Campione, 1990).

From this perspective, the key implication for educational practices is the recognition that all lessons are extensions of culture, and that teaching and learning in schools and elsewhere are tantamount to a program of socialization or enculturation. Such a view calls for care to be taken in curriculum design and instructional delivery because what is taught eventually becomes part of the individual student's psychological makeup. Accordingly, cultural psychologists emphasize contextualization of educational practices—making certain that vehicles for curriculum, instruction, and assessment correspond appropriately to the real-world challenges posed in communities of practice.

Sociocultural Psychology

A separate branch of psychology concurs with many of the positions taken by cultural psychologists, but emphasizes the processes of interaction through which the intuitive mind is constituted through culture. Often identified with Vygotsky (1978), this approach has been found under headings including sociocultural psychology, sociohistorical psychology, cultural-historical psychology, and sociocognitive psychology (Bahktin, 1981; Bruner, 1990, 1996; Cobb, 1996; Cole, 1971, 1996; Forman, Minick, & Stone, 1993; Hutchins, 1990; Lave, 1985; Luria, 1976; Rogoff, 1990; Torff, 1999a, 1999b; Wertsch, 1985, 1998). Vygotsky's theory of cognitive development has gained influence in recent decades, although it was first formulated in the 1930s. Vygotsky and his successors explore how social interactions—and thus culturally shared systems of meaning—work to constitute the development of the individual mind. Central to this theory is the assertion that social interaction yields secondary intuitive conceptions; through interaction in a cultural context, individuals acquire and use knowledge outside of conscious awareness.

Among the constructs of Vygotsky's theory is a distinction drawn between spontaneous and scientific concepts. Scientific concepts are the categories and procedures created by culture in a particular discipline (or community of practice); for example, consider the formal constructions of music theory such as chords and scales. (This example highlights that scientific concepts are not relevant only to science, but to any formal system, including concepts remote from science such as music.) Opposite to scientific concepts are spontaneous ones—concepts generated by individuals to accomplish goals and solve problems when left to their own devices. Continuing the musical example, a self-taught pianist develops a range of idiosyncratic concepts and strategies individually crafted to support piano playing. Spontaneous concepts are closely linked to the intuitive mind because many spontaneous strategies are deployed with little conscious reflection. Scientific concepts may be intuitive as well; consider Sternberg and colleagues' tacit-knowledge work previously discussed. Research shows how even the careers of scientists rely on tacit knowledge. In the end, both spontaneous concepts and scientific ones can involve intuitive conceptions.

Culturally provided conceptions, intuitive and otherwise, are described by Bruner (1996) as a sort of cognitive tool kit—a set of culturally manifested affordances and constraints through which people accomplish valued goals. Here the theoretical premise is that all human thought and action are fundamentally mediated, and therefore the study of mediational means is central to understanding the intuitive mind (Wertsch, 1985, 1998). Mediation is thought to have many forms, and chief among them is interpersonal interaction between individuals and their caregivers (e.g., parents and teachers; Rogoff, 1990). With this view, processes of guided participation in shared activity help individuals to gain knowledge and skills valued in a community of practice.

Since 1990, two theoretical movements have emerged from this work, each relevant to investigators of secondary intuitive conceptions. Theory and research in socially shared cognition examine how individuals come to share an understanding about a situation (such as a math lesson) that enables them to participate successfully (Resnick, Levine, & Teasley, 1991). A related line of work under the heading *situated* (or *distributed*) cognition investigates how individuals interact with (and depend on) the affordances and constraints embedded in symbolic, social, and physical aspects of the cultural environment (Greeno, 1997; Lave & Wenger, 1993). With this view, at the heart of the intuitive mind lie patterns of social interaction and tool use created by culturally manifested communities of practice.

The educational implications of sociocultural psychology have been gaining increased attention among researchers (Bruner, 1996; Forman et al., 1993; Gallimore & Tharp, 1990; Moll, 1990; Newman, Griffin, & Cole,

1989). With this view, secondary intuitive conceptions vary in the extent to which they are deliberately taught. Some of the culture's intuitive cognitive tools require little deliberate teaching effort, such as the interpersonal-space norms previously described. People seldom teach explicitly about these norms, and young people do not set out to learn them; yet through everyday interactions individuals end up with an intuitive and socially shared understanding of appropriate distance. Other intuitive conceptions are the focus of deliberate efforts to teach at home, at school, and in the world. Units of distance help make the point; individuals learn to understand distance using culturally produced measurement tools (e.g., the mile), and only though the use of the appropriate tool can they conceptualize distance. With enough teaching, modeling, and guided practice, individuals come to internalize culturally manifested elements such as units of distance, and for a lifetime thereafter the mile works as an intuitively meaningful conceptual tool. As such, some secondary intuitive conceptions are part of our society's deliberate teaching efforts, and some are part of our culture's more general effort to enculturate its members. Observations as such have prompted researchers to examine the patterns of interpersonal interactions in which learning takes place outside the classroom as well as in it (see Rogoff & Lave, 1984). With this view, teaching is best seen as a cognitive apprenticeship in which teachers coparticipate with learners and make their own work (and thinking about their work) evident to learners (Collins, Brown, & Holum, 1991).

As with primary intuitive conceptions, secondary intuitive conceptions yield mixed results for individual learners (in terms of supporting task performance in culturally relevant activities). Secondary intuitive conceptions constrain as well as facilitate valued cognitive activities. The term *secondary intuitive misconceptions* applies to instances of knowledge use in which secondary intuitive conceptions act to decrease task performance. To begin with, secondary intuitive conceptions may result in limited thinking. The kinds of mathematical thinking children develop, for example, depend not only on their individual ability and adult efforts to teach them mathematical concepts, but also on adults' own knowledge of mathematics, which in turn depends on their cultural heritage. An Oksapmin child in New Guinea appears to have the same universal ability in the domain of mathematics as a child in the West. However, the system of counting used among the Oksapmin—counting by body parts—does not support the development of algebraic thinking (Saxe, 1981). Secondary intuitive conceptions are not always transferable across contexts. Brazilian-market children, who do not attend school but who grow up in a country where modern mathematics is part of the cultural heritage, develop remarkable mathematical skills in the context of everyday buying and selling, but experience difficulties when given the same problems in a school-type format (Carraher & Carraher, 1981). In other cases, secondary intuitive conceptions take the form of oversimplifications that obscure fine-grained truths. Baron (1998) pointed to culturally specified notions (such as "myside bias" that runs counter to tolerant attitudes and constructive dialog) that are fundamentally misguided, resulting in errors in a variety of areas of public decision making. Overall, sociocultural psychology depicts an intuitive mind rooted in culture that serves as both bane and boon to the individual.

The Symbol Systems Approach

In general, little has been said about the relationship of primary and secondary intuitive conceptions. However, there is a theoretical possibility that at least some secondary intuitive conceptions are explicitly built on primary ones, and that primary ones evince developmental changes as cultures build on them. The fact that primary intuitive conceptions might be changed by development in a particular cultural context is a notion put forth by Gardner (1991; Torff & Gardner, 1999). Gardner posited that there are two kinds of symbols involved in human cognition: internal symbols in the form of cognitive representations guided by a set of innately specified modules (intelligences) and external symbols—the products of culturally manifested disciplines and communities of practice. Unlike other theorists, Gardner argued that the innate modules are subject to developmental change in symbol-processing structure and function as internal mechanisms that come into contact with external, culturally manifested ones. With this view, the course of development in a cultural context changes the way the innately specified modules work. Gardner agreed with the cognitive developmentalists and evolutionists, however, that primary intuitive conceptions may sometimes interfere with task performance and can be difficult to dislodge, but they are open to modification through educational interventions.

Taking Stock: Secondary Intuitive Conceptions

Investigators of secondary intuitive conceptions locate the intuitive mind—the world of thought not open to conscious reflection—in cultural patterns learned by individuals. At present, additional research is needed to frame an account of when and how secondary intuitive conceptions facilitate and constrain performance. At present, educators have little to go on to determine when and how intuitive conceptions are assisting or impeding students' learning. Additional theory and research in the educational connections of secondary intuitive conceptions will also address another central goal of educators—to develop educational interventions that respond to the intuitive mind of the learner, especially in cases where intuitive conceptions are difficult to amend as needed and thus require deliberate efforts on the part of educators.

There are also vexing issues concerning the relationship of primary and secondary intuitive conceptions. As noted, only Gardner (1991) suggested that innately specified systems are changed in the course of development in a cultural context, and little research evidence is available on this point. Moreover, there is a disjuncture between the domains posited by researchers of primary intuitive conceptions and the disciplines or communities of practice considered by investigators of secondary intuitive conceptions. Many secondary intuitive conceptions come packaged in disciplines, communities of practice, or both, with their own canons of valued knowledge and skill. This seems similar to the domain-specific view pursued by cognitive developmentalists, but it is not clear that the domains in this work correspond to the discipline (e.g., math and science) created by culture. Most likely, culturally valued disciplines such as science involve multiple sets of innately specified intuitive conceptions. Psychologists and educators interested in the intuitive mind must one day come to grips with how the domain-specific structures of primary intuition relate to the secondary intuitive conceptions fostered by disciplines and communities of practice.

INTUITIVE CONCEPTIONS ABOUT TEACHING

Theory and research investigating learners' primary and secondary intuitive conceptions generate some powerful educational implications, but these are not the only intuitive conceptions involved in classroom activities. Also at issue are intuitive notions about teaching and learning (held by teachers and other educators) that come into play as teachers and learners interact in classrooms. Intuitive conceptions about teaching have attracted less interest than those about learning, but this area is drawing increased attention as educators and psychologists seek solutions to vexing educational-reform challenges. Two related issues have been considered: the intuitive notions about teaching held by teachers with different levels of experience and education and the relationship between these intuitions and the professional pedagogy taught in teacher-education programs (Strauss, 1994; Torff, 1999b).

Of particular interest are the views of prospective teachers (individuals who plan to enter the teaching profession but have yet to do so) because these views come into contact with the formalisms of educational practice when the teacher-to-be enters a teacher-education program. Hence, a large body of literature in teacher education focuses on previously existing ideas that prospective teachers hold about education (e.g., Anderson, 1994; Brookhart & Freeman, 1992; Bruner, 1996; Hollingsworth, 1989; Kagan, 1992; McLaughlin, 1991; Morine-Dershimer, 1993; Shulman, 1987; Strauss, 1993, 1996; Strauss & Shilony, 1994; Torff, 1999b; Woolfolk Hoy, 1996; Zeichner & Gore, 1990). Far from being blank slates with little knowledge about education, prospective teachers' prior beliefs, expectations, and knowledge influence what they come to understand, value, and use from courses in teacher education.

Recent theory and research on teacher education seem to reflect a consensus concerning the specific positions that are held by this intuitive pedagogy (Anderson, 1994; Hollingsworth, 1989; Strauss, 1993, 1996; Strauss & Shilony, 1994; Woolfolk Hoy, 1996; Torff, 1999b; Zeichner & Gore, 1990). Prospective teachers tend to believe that knowledge is a property that is created outside people's heads, and learning occurs when people absorb knowledge. The right thing for educators to do, then, is to transmit as much knowledge as possible to students and see that they memorize it. With this view, knowledge should be crafted to fit the learner depending on the volume-of-processing capacity that children of a particular age can handle (Strauss, 1993, 1996). As noted, this view of teaching and learning has been dubbed the *transmission model*.

A number of chapters in this volume and elsewhere compare teacher beliefs and expert practices and find the former wanting (Torff, 1998, 1999a, 1999b; Woolfolk Hoy, 1996). Most contemporary psychologists believe that learning is a process of constructing knowledge, not simply receiving it, and thus the transmission model might well be replaced with a constructivist model that encourages learners to participate actively in sense making or knowledge constructing. Many expert teachers agree with psychologists that teaching is not transmission as much as facilitation of students' meaning making. Psychologists and expert teachers view teaching differently from prospective teachers, requiring the latter to undergo significant changes in perspective to obtain expertise in teaching.

Unfortunately, these changes are not always easy to make. Intuitive conceptions have proved robust—resistant to changes as a result of education or experience (Strauss, 1994; Torff, 1999b). Topics in education courses are often presented in the form of abstractions framed in terms of principles and strategies, whereas teacher knowledge is typically framed in terms of specifics such as events and stories (Doyle & Carter, 1996). Intuitive conceptions seem grounded and concrete, as if to speak with the voice of common sense. Applying intuitive notions in the classroom (e.g., in lesson planning) is rarely difficult, especially in comparison to teaching, according to the abstractions and formalisms of the discipline of education.

Most of the theory and research in this area is somewhat noncommittal about the relative contributions of primary and secondary forms of intuition in the formation of teachers' beliefs. Much of this work takes the position, tacitly or explicitly, that cultural constructions go a long way to determine the sorts of teaching that prospective teachers find to be intuitive, so it is under the rubric of secondary intuitive conceptions that much of the work on teachers' beliefs can be categorized. Bruner (1990, 1996; Olson & Bruner, 1996) described the processes by which cultural products become intuitively held educational beliefs. At issue here is *folk pedagogy*—a set of commonsense ideas about teaching and learning that grows out of our culture's *folk psychology*, a shared set of notions in a culture about how the mind works. With this view, folk pedagogy predisposes individuals to think and teach in particular ways, some of which are inconsistent with the concepts and practices characteristic of expert teaching.

As with intuitive conceptions in other domains, intuitive pedagogy may tend to persist despite successful participation in teacher-education programs (Strauss, 1993, 1996; Torff, 1999b). Becoming an expert teacher, then, is not simply a matter of gaining new knowledge or replacing inadequate preconceptions in a straightforward manner. With this view, explicit efforts by teacher educators are needed to counter these uncritically held beliefs, principally by encouraging prospective teachers to engage in activities that facilitate relevant forms of cognitive change. In particular, prospective teachers can be encouraged to reflect on their intuitive conceptions about education and explore instructional techniques that fall outside this intuitive understanding. Additional theory and research are needed to develop an account of how intuitive conceptions influence teaching, how such beliefs develop, and how they influence curriculum, instruction, and assessment—and ultimately students' learning.

THE COMPLEXITY OF INTUITIVE CONCEPTIONS

A quick review of the literature on the impact of intuitive conceptions on learning and teaching reveals the complex sets of factors involved. The previous section suggests that intuitive conceptions held by teachers (as well as those held by students) influence educational practices. In the classroom, the intuitive conceptions activated by both students and teachers involve, in all probability, both primary (innately specified) and secondary (culturally specified) forms of intuition. Intuitive notions of all kinds sometimes work in a supportive manner, boosting task performance, but sometimes work to interfere with learning.

At least three sets of issues emerge from this framework. First, little has been said about the interaction of teachers' and students' intuitive conceptions. At issue are how these sets of intuitions relate, and with what results, and with what implications for curriculum, instruction, and assessment. Second, it is far from clear how primary and secondary forms of intuition relate. Are the latter simply built on the former? Are the former changed by the latter? Are they simply separate forms of cognition? Finally, because intuitive conceptions both support and impede learning in valued contexts, an account is needed when intuitive conceptions operate for and against educators. Theory and research are needed to enable educators to capitalize on intuitive conceptions when possible and counter them when necessary. Intuition remains an elusive quarry.

REFERENCES

Anderson, L. (1994). *Reforming our courses and rethinking our roles*. Paper presented at the meeting of the Midwestern Association for the Teaching of Educational Psychology, Chicago, IL.

Astington, J. (1993). *The child's discovery of the mind*. Cambridge, MA: Harvard University Press.

Atran, S. (1994). Core domains versus scientific theories. In L. Hirschfeld & S. Gelman (Eds.), *Mapping the mind: Domain-specificity in cognition and culture*. Cambridge, England: Cambridge University Press.

Bahktin, M. (1981). *The dialogic imagination*. Austin: University of Texas.

Barkow, J., Cosmides, L., & Tooby, J. (Eds.). (1992). *The adaptive mind: Evolutionary psychology and generation of culture*. New York: Oxford University Press.

Baron, J. (1998). *Judgment misguided*. New York: Oxford University Press.

Berry, D., & Dienes, Z. (1993). *Implicit learning: Theoretical and empirical issues*. Hillsdale, NJ: Lawrence Erlbaum Associates.

Brookhart, S., & Freeman, D. (1992). Characteristics of entering teacher candidates. *Review of Educational Research, 62*, 37–60.

Brown, A., & Campione, J. (1990). Communities of learning and thinking, or a context by any other name. In D. Kuhn (Ed.), *Developmental perspectives on teaching and learning thinking skills*. Basel, Switzerland: Karger.

Brown, J., Collins, A., & DuGuid, P. (1989). Situated cognition and the culture of learning. *Educational Researcher, 33*, 32–42.

Bruner, J. (1990). *Acts of meaning*. Cambridge, MA: Harvard University Press.

Bruner, J. (1996). *The culture of education*. Cambridge, MA: Harvard University Press.

Carey, C. (1985). *Conceptual change in childhood*. Cambridge, MA: Bradford/MIT.

Carey, S. (1996). Perceptual classification and expertise. In R. Gelman & T. Au (Eds.), *Perceptual and cognitive development*. New York: Academic Press.

Carey, S., & Smith, C. (1993). On understanding the nature of scientific knowledge. *Educational Psychologist, 28*(3), 235–251.

Carraher, T., & Carraher, D. (1981). Do Piagetian stages describe the reasoning of unschooled adults? *Quarterly Newsletter of the Laboratory of Comparative Human Cognition, 3*, 61–68.

Chomsky, N. (1968). *Language and mind*. New York: Harcourt Brace.

Cleeremans, A. (1993). *Mechanisms of implicit learning: Connectionist models of sequence processing*. Cambridge, MA: MIT Press.

Cobb, P. (1996). Where is the mind?: A coordination of sociocultural and cognitive constructivist perspectives. In C. Fosnot (Ed.), *Constructivism: Theory, perspectives, and practice* (pp. 34–54). New York: Teacher's College Press.

Cole, M. (1971). *The cultural context of learning and thinking.* New York: Basic Books.

Cole, M. (1996). *Cultural psychology: A once future discipline.* Cambridge, MA: Harvard University Press.

Collins, A., Brown, J., & Holum, A. (1991). Cognitive apprenticeship: Making thinking visible. *American Educator.*

Cosmides, L., & Tooby, J. (1987). From evolution to behavior: Evolutionary psychology as the missing link. In J. Dupre (Ed.), *The latest and the best: Essays on evolution and optimality* (pp. 227–306). Cambridge, MA: MIT Press.

diSessa, A. (1983). Phenomenology and evolution of intuition. In D. Gentner & A. Stevens (Eds.), *Mental models.* Hillsdale, NJ: Lawrence Erlbaum Associates.

Doyle, W., & Carter, K. (1996). Educational psychology and the education of teachers: A reaction. *Educational Psychologist, 31*(1), 51–62.

Fodor, J. (1983). *The modularity of mind.* Cambridge, MA: MIT Press.

Forman, E., Minick, N., & Stone, C. (Eds.). (1993). *Contexts for learning.* New York: Oxford University Press.

Gallimore, R., & Tharp, R. (1990). Teaching mind in society. In L. Moll (Ed.), *Vygotsky and education.* New York: Cambridge University Press.

Gardner, H. (1991). *The unschooled mind.* New York: Basic Books.

Geertz, C. (1983). *Local knowledge.* New York: Basic Books.

Gelman, R., & Brenneman, K. (1994). First principles can support both universal and culture-specific learning about number and music. In E. Hirschfeld & S. Gelman (Eds.), *Mapping the mind: Domain specificity in cognition and culture.* New York: Cambridge University Press.

Greeno, J. (1997). A perspective on thinking. *American Psychologist, 44*(2), 134–141.

Hollingsworth, S. (1989). Prior beliefs and cognitive change in learning to teach. *American Educational Research Journal, 26,* 160–189.

Hutchins, E. (1990). *Culture and inference.* Cambridge, MA: Harvard University Press.

Kagan, D. (1992). Implications of research on teacher belief. *Educational Psychologist, 27,* 65–90.

Karmiloff-Smith, A. (1992). *Beyond modularity.* Cambridge, MA: MIT Press.

Keil, F. (1989). *Concepts, kinds, and cognitive development.* Cambridge, MA: MIT Press.

Keil, F. (1994). The birth and nurturance of concepts by domains: The origins of living things. In E. Hirschfeld & S. Gelman (Eds.), *Mapping the mind: Domain specificity in cognition and culture.* New York: Cambridge University Press.

Kellman, P. (1996). The origins of object perception. In R. Gelman & T. Au (Eds.), *Perceptual and cognitive development.* New York: Academic Press.

Larkin, J. (1983). The role of problem representation in physics. In D. Gentner & A. Stevens (Eds.), *Mental models.* Hillsdale, NJ: Lawrence Erlbaum Associates.

Lave, J. (1985). *Cognition in practice.* Cambridge, England: Harvard University Press.

Lave, J., & Wenger, E. (1993). *Situated learning.* Cambridge, MA: Cambridge University Press.

Luria, A. (1976). *Cognitive development.* Cambridge, England: Cambridge University Press.

McCloskey, M., Camarazza, A., & Green, B. (1980). Curvilinear motion in absence of external forces: Folk beliefs about the motion of objects. *Science, 210,* 1149–1151.

McLaughlin, J. (1991). Reconciling care and control: Authority in classroom relationships. *Journal of Teacher Education, 40*(3), 182–195.

Moll, L. (Ed.). (1990). *Vygotsky and education.* New York: Cambridge University Press.

Morine Dershimer, G. (1993). Tracing conceptual change in preservice teachers. *Teaching and Teacher Education, 9,* 15–26.

Newman, D., Griffin, P., & Cole, M. (1989). *The construction zone.* Cambridge, England: Cambridge University Press.

Olson, D., & Bruner, J. (1996). Folk psychology and folk pedagogy. In D. Olson & N. Torrance (Eds.), *Handbook of education in human development* (pp. 9–27). Oxford, England: Blackwell.

Putnam, R., & Borko, H. (2000, January–February). What do new views of knowledge and thinking have to say about research in teacher learning? *Educational Researcher, 29*(1).

Reber, A. (1993). *Implicit learning and tacit knowledge.* New York: Oxford University Press.

Resnick, L., Levine, J., & Teasley, S. (Eds.). (1991). *Perspectives on socially shared cognition.* Washington, DC: American Psychological Association.

Rogoff, B. (1990). *Apprenticeship in thinking.* Cambridge, MA: Harvard University Press.

Rogoff, B., & Lave, J. (Eds.). (1985). *Everyday cognition.* Cambridge, MA: Harvard University Press.

Saxe, G. (1981). Body parts as numerals: A developmental analysis of numeration among the Oksapmin in Papua New Guinea. *Child Development, 52,* 306–316.

Seely Brown, J., Collins, A., & Duguid, P. (1989). Situated cognition and the culture of learning. *Educational Researcher, 18*(1), 32–42.

Shulman, L. (1987). Reconnecting foundations to the substance of teacher education. *Teachers College Record, 91*(3), 300–310.

Shweder, R. (1991). *Thinking through culture.* Cambridge, MA: Harvard University Press.

Spelke, E. (1991). Physical knowledge in infancy: Reflections on Piaget's theory. In S. Carey & R. Gelman (Eds.), *The epigenesis of mind.* Hillsdale, NJ: Lawrence Erlbaum Associates.

Spelke, E., & Hermer, L. (1996). Early cognitive development: Objects and space. In R. Gelman & T. Au (Eds.), *Perceptual and cognitive development.* New York: Academic Press.

Sternberg, R. (1988). *The triarchic mind: A new theory of human intelligence.* New York: Viking.

Sternberg, R. (1997). *Successful intelligence.* New York: Viking.

Sternberg, R. (1998). Abilities are forms of developing expertise. *Educational Researcher.*

Sternberg, R., & Grigorenko, E. (Eds.). (1997). *Intelligence: Heredity and environment.* Cambridge, England: Cambridge University Press.

Sternberg, R., & Horvath, J. (Eds.). (1999). *Tacit knowledge in professional practice.* Mahwah, NJ: Lawrence Erlbaum Associates.

Sternberg, R., Torff, B., & Grigorenko, E. (1998a, May). Teaching for successful intelligence improves school achievement. *Phi Delta Kappan.*

Sternberg, R., Torff, B., & Grigorenko, E. (1998b, September). Teaching triarchically improves school achievement. *Journal of Educational Psychology.*

Sternberg, R., Wagner, R., Williams, W., & Horvath, J. (1995). Testing common sense. *American Psychologist, 50*(11), 901–912.

Stigler, J., Shweder, R., & Herdt, G. (Eds.). (1990). *Cultural psychology: Essays on comparative human development.* Cambridge, England: Cambridge University Press.

Strauss, S. (1993). Teachers' pedagogical content knowledge about children's minds and learning: Implications for teacher education. *Educational Psychologist, 28*(3), 279–290.

Strauss, S. (1996). Confessions of a born-again constructivist. *Educational Psychologist, 31*(1), 15–22.

Strauss, S., & Shilony, T. (1994). Teachers' models of children's minds and learning. In E. Hirschfeld & S. Gelman (Eds.), *Mapping the mind: Domain specificity in cognition and culture* (pp. 455–473). New York: Cambridge University Press.

Tooby, J., & Cosmides, L. (1990). On the universality of human nature and the uniqueness of the individual: The role of genetics and adaptation. *Journal of Personality, 58,* 375–424.

Torff, B. (1997). Into the wordless world: Implicit learning and instructor modeling in music. In V. Brummet (Ed.), *Music as intelligence.* Ithaca, NY: Ithaca College Press.

Torff, B. (1998). Thinking it over: Folk psychology, developmental research, and educational practice. In W. Cummings & N. McGinn (Eds.), *Education and development: Preparing schools, students, and the nation for the 21st century*. New York: Garland.

Torff, B. (1999a). Beyond information processing: Cultural influences on cognition and learning. In S. Ulibarri (Ed.), *Maria Montessori explicit and implicit in the 20th century*. Cancun, Mexico: International Montessori Congress.

Torff, B. (1999b). Tacit knowledge in teaching: Folk pedagogy and teacher education. In R. Sternberg & J. Horvath (Eds.), *Tacit knowledge in professional practice*. Mahwah, NJ: Lawrence Erlbaum Associates.

Torff, B., & Gardner, H. (1999). The vertical mind: The case for multiple intelligences. In M. Anderson (Ed.), *The development of intelligence*. London: University College Press.

Vygotsky, L. (1978). *Mind in society*. Cambridge, MA: Harvard University Press.

Wellman, H. (1990). *The child's theory of mind*. Cambridge, MA: Bradford/MIT.

Wertsch, J. (1985). *Vygotsky and the social formation of mind*. Cambridge, MA: Harvard University Press.

Wertsch, J. (1998). *Mind as action*. New York: Oxford University Press.

Woolfolk Hoy, A. (1996). Teaching educational psychology: Texts in context. *Educational Psychologist, 31*(1), 35–40.

Zeichner, K., & Gore, J. (1990). Teacher socialization. In W. Houston (Ed.), *Handbook of research on teacher education* (pp. 329–349). New York: Macmillan.

PART II

INTUITIVE CONCEPTIONS AND STUDENT LEARNING

CHAPTER TWO

Intuitive Mathematics: Theoretical and Educational Implications

Talia Ben-Zeev
Williams College

Jon Star
University of Michigan

What kinds of intuitions do people have for solving problems in a formal logic system? Studies on intuitive physics have shown that people hold a set of naive beliefs (Chi & Slotta, 1993; diSessa, 1982, 1993; McCloskey, Caramazza, & Green, 1980). For example, McCloskey et al. (1980) found that when people were asked to draw the path of a moving object shot through a curved tube, they believed that the object would move along a curved (instead of a straight) path even in the absence of external forces. Such an Aristotelian conceptualization of motion, although mistaken, may be based in part on forming an analogy to real-life examples, such as the Earth's circular movement around the sun (one does not see the forces that sustain such a movement).

Does there exist a similar body of knowledge that we can refer to as intuitive mathematics? That is, can we identify a set of naive beliefs that are applied to solving abstract mathematics problems? If so, how do these intuitions hinder or facilitate problem solving? The answers to these questions have implications for both psychology and education. By examining the nature of intuitive mathematics we could help (a) improve our understanding of people's formal and informal reasoning skills, and (b) create more effective instructional materials.

The focus of much research, to date, has been on the development of early mathematical cognition. A prime example comes from the work of R. Gelman and colleagues (e.g., Gelman, 1979, 1990; Gelman & Meck, 1983;

Starkey, Spelke, & Gelman, 1990) on implicit counting principles that enable preschool children to understand and perform addition. In contrast, there has been much less emphasis on intuitive understanding that develops as a result of learning mathematical procedures in later years. The largest lament on the part of the education community has been that an emphasis on learning procedures can lead to rote execution of problem-solving steps, resulting in a lack of correct intuition for these procedures. For example, students often learn how to execute a procedure, such as multicolumn subtraction, without understanding its underlying teleology (VanLehn, 1990). This finding has led to a proliferation of educational programs that emphasize the conceptual over the procedural (e.g., National Council of Teachers of Mathematics, 1989).

In this chapter, we examine the nature and origin of what we term as *symbolic intuition*, or the intuitive understanding of mathematical symbols that develops as a result of experience with formal and abstract school-based procedures. Before we define more formally what we mean by intuition, in general, and symbolic intuition, in particular, we would like the reader to try and solve the following five problems taken from a typical postarithmetic mathematics curriculum:

1. How many lines pass through any given two points in two-dimensional space?

2. A fair coin is flipped 10 times. The first nine flips all come up heads. What is the probability that the next, the 10th toss, will come up heads?

3. Which set has more members, the set of all rational numbers (numbers that can be expressed as one integer over another) or the set of all irrational numbers (nonrepeating decimals)?

4. What is 8% of 142?

5. Solve for x: $3x + 7 = 19$

Now try and introspect about your experiences. To what extent did you have intuitions about solving these problems and what were they like? Most high school students and adults have correct intuition about the first problem (only one line can pass through two points in two-dimensional space), incorrect intuitions about the second and third problems (erroneously assuming that there is a greater probability that the 10th toss will come up heads, and that all infinities are alike, respectively), and no intuitions about the fourth and fifth problems because computing percentages and solving polynomials can usually be done by employing procedures without understanding the concepts involved. We return to discussing the correct, incorrect, and lack of intuitions for solving these specific problems in more detail later.

In this chapter, we seek to extend the work on the mathematical cognition of preschool and elementary-school children to examining the symbolic intuitions that secondary-school students may have about problems such as the ones previously mentioned. Do secondary-school students have qualitatively different mathematical intuitions, and if so, how are these intuitions developed? As students move beyond the study of elementary arithmetic, what is the role of intuitions in their mathematics learning? In the remainder of this chapter, we discuss the nature and origin of correct and faulty intuitions in secondary school, in some detail, by identifying possible school-based and cognitive causes. We then provide some general prescriptions toward enhancing correct symbolic intuition.

First, however, we present a more formal definition of intuition. The term *intuition* is used in a variety of ways by scholars in different disciplines. Instead of listing each one, we divide intuitions according to two main views—the classical and the inferential—based on their philosophical origins. We then integrate these two viewpoints into our own conception of symbolic intuition.

WHAT IS MATHEMATICAL INTUITION?

What exactly is intuition? In general, the answer to this question is relevant to a variety of domains, including philosophy, mathematics, psychology, and education (Westcott, 1968). Philosophers such as Bergson and Spinoza have contrasted intuition with reason and logic, a view that can be found in some modern conceptualizations of mathematical intuition to be discussed later. Mathematicians have traditionally regarded intuition as a way of understanding proofs and conceptualizing problems (Hadamard, 1954). Psychologists have examined the role of intuitive thinking in a variety of domains including clinical diagnosis, creativity, decision making, reasoning, and problem solving. A growing body of research in cognitive psychology has been devoted to studying the process of insight, which is defined as a sudden understanding of something, an "Aha!" experience, after a period of trying to solve a problem unsuccessfully (e.g., Davidson, 1995; Gick & Lockhart, 1995; Seifert, Meyer, Davidson, Palatano, & Yaniv, 1995). This literature views intuition as a phenomenon that primarily occurs through implicit and non-analyzable processes. The psychological study of mathematical intuition has been mainly conducted in the area of statistical reasoning (e.g., Tversky & Kahneman, 1974). This work shows that people are susceptible to a variety of biases, such as ignoring base-rate information in making probable judgments. Finally, educators have been concerned with the question of how intuition affects the school-learning process. There has been recent focus in education on uncovering students' preexisting knowledge to make connections between school taught, formal knowledge, and students' informal intuitions (Mack, 1990; Resnick, 1986). A review of existing literature in the previously mentioned areas led us to identify two primary views of mathematical intuition. We call them the *classical-intuitionist* and the *inferential-intuitionist* views based on their philosophical origins.

The Classical-Intuitionist View

The main idea underlying the classical-intuitionist view is that mathematical intuition is dissociated from formal reasoning. That is, students represent a mathematics problem in such a way that the answer becomes self-evident immediately, without the need for justification or formal analysis. This view can be traced to a philosophical movement termed *classical intuitionism*, wherein philosophers such as Spinoza and Bergson argued that reason plays no role in intuition (Westcott, 1968; Wild, 1938). Classical intuitionists viewed intuition as "a special contact with prime reality, producing a sense of ultimate unity, true beauty, perfect certainty, and blessedness" (Westcott, 1968, p. 22). According to this viewpoint, intuition is antithetical to reason. The knowledge gained through intuition cannot be verified, supported, or even understood intellectually. Intuitive knowledge is not practical or applicable. It is considered to be a priori and independent of prior knowledge.

Some more modern conceptualizations in psychology and education embrace similar views on intuition. For example, Resnick (1986) viewed mathematical intuitions as cognitive primitives that can function without formal mathematical analysis. Similarly, Dixon and Moore (1996) defined intuitive understanding of a problem as a representation that is distinct from the representation of the formal-solution procedure for solving the problem. These intuitive representations, they argued, can be uncovered by using estimation tasks (see also Reed, 1984). Dreyfus and Eisenberg (1982) defined *intuitions* as mental representations of facts that appear to be self-evident. They operationalized mathematical intuition as the ability of the students to solve problems despite the absence of formal instruction on the topic. Finally, Fischbein and colleagues (Fischbein, Tirosh, & Melamed, 1981) defined *intuitive acceptance* as the act of accepting a certain solution or interpretation directly without explicit or detailed justification.

Where do such intuitions originate? A primary conjecture is that intuition that is unschooled and untutored is innate. An example of such an approach comes from R. Gelman and colleagues (Gelman, 1979, 1990; Gelman & Meck, 1983; Starkey et al., 1990), who delineated a set of what they believe are innate counting principles (this work is elaborated on in a subsequent section on primary intuitions). Other researchers, such as Wynn (1995), argued that infants have the ability to mentally represent numbers.

Furthermore, the studies by Wynn showed that infants tend to gaze longer at numerically incorrect versus correct outcomes of simple arithmetic calculations. Wynn (1995) argued that this finding demonstrates that infants can perform simple computations with positive integers that form the foundation of later numerical competence. The view that children possess intuitive or naive theories has been suggested in other domains as well, such as biology (Carey, 1995; Keil, 1981; Springer & Keil, 1989). The main relevance of the work on intuitive theories to the classical-intuitionist view is that it proposes that intuitive theories of numerosity, simple arithmetic, and other domains are preexisting and not learned, developed, or acquired by induction from experience (Wynn, 1992).

The Inferential-Intuitionist View

The inferential-intuitionist view departs radically from the classical-intuitionist view. The main idea underlying the inferential-intuitionist approach is that intuition is not a special mechanism but a form of reasoning guided by the interactions of people with the environment. This view can be traced to the writings of philosophers such as Ewing and Bunge (Westcott, 1968), who treated intuition as the product of prior experience and reason. In particular, Ewing felt that intuition was no more than a justified belief whose immediacy of apprehension (the Aha!) is only an illusion resulting from a series of rapid inferences unavailable to consciousness. Conceived in this way, intuitions could be subject to error depending on experience. Similarly, Bunge felt that intuitions are hypotheses that people test by performing probabilistic judgments.

An example of such a view in the education literature comes from Fischbein (1973). Fischbein argued that feelings of immediacy, coherence, and confidence about a mathematical solution may be the result of a minitheory or model that supports inferences based on implicit knowledge. In this framework, the processes that give rise to intuitions operate tacitly and without awareness, but they are suggested to be the same processes that support more explicit mathematical reasoning. Fischbein contended that, through a process of training and familiarization, individuals can develop new intuitions. Thus, this perspective implies that intuitions can be learned, acquired, and developed.

PRIMARY AND SECONDARY INTUITIONS

The classical-intuitionist view may be most useful for examining primary intuitions (Fischbein, 1973), which include the kind of informal everyday knowledge that preschool children use for performing simple arithmetic such as counting and addition. The inferential-intuitionist view, in contrast, may provide a more useful framework for examining secondary intuitions that are built up over long periods of formal training (Fischbein, 1973). This distinction between primary and secondary intuitions is important because it has the potential to reframe the types of questions one can ask about the development of mathematical intuitions of children.

Traditionally, research on mathematical intuitions of children have focused on articulating the principled knowledge that children have prior to formal schooling. R. Gelman and colleagues contended that principled knowledge appears very early in life before acquisition of language and assimilation of culture (e.g., Starkey et al., 1990). For example, R. Gelman and colleagues (Gelman, 1979, 1990; Gelman & Meck, 1983; Starkey et al., 1990) proposed that preschoolers have implicit counting principles before they are able to verbalize or state these principles explicitly. They offer five counting principles:

1. The one-to-one principle whereby every item in a display should be tagged with one and only one unique tag.

2. The stable order principle whereby the tags must be ordered in the same sequence across trials.

3. The cardinal principle whereby the last tag used in a count sequence is the symbol for the number of items in the set.

4. The abstraction principle whereby any kinds of objects can be collected together for purposes of a count.

5. The order-irrelevance principle whereby objects in a set may be tagged in any sequence as long as the other counting principles are not violated.

To show that children have implicit knowledge of this sort, R. Gelman and colleagues used ingenious experimental manipulations. For example, R. Gelman and Meck (1983) used an error-detection paradigm. In this paradigm, preschool children are asked to help teach a puppet to count by indicating whether a particular count sequence was correct. To examine knowledge of the one-to-one principle, for instance, the puppet either counts correctly, commits an error (counts an item twice or skips it altogether), or commits a pseudo error (counts correctly but by using an unusual sequence, such as skipping back and forth between items). Nearly all of the children tested detected almost all of the errors of the puppet. Most of the children offered some comment as to why the puppet was in error in each case. Although none of the children stated the one-to-one principle explicitly, their explanations indicated that they had acquired an understanding of the principle. Furthermore, children treated the pseudo errors as peculiar but not as erroneous. This work suggests that preschoolers not only possess general all-purpose abilities to sense and learn, but have capabilities to create and manipulate domain-specific representations.

In the early school years, children appear to rely on schemas for solving arithmetic word problems successfully. Schemas are mental structures that organize information from the environment in a useful way (Bartlett, 1932; Piaget, 1965; Schank & Abelson, 1977). For instance, Greeno (1980) and Riley, Greeno, and Heller (1983) suggested that children develop three types of schemas for solving arithmetic word problems. They include *change* (Joe had some marbles. Then Tom gave him five marbles. Now Joe has eight marbles. How many marbles did Joe have at the beginning?), *combination* (Joe has three marbles. Tom has five marbles. How many marbles do they have together?), and *comparison* (Joe has three marbles. Tom has five marbles more than Joe. How many marbles does Tom have?). At the basis of these schemas lies the part–whole schema (Riley et al., 1983). This schema allows children to distinguish the whole from its parts to successfully solve change, combination, and comparison problems.

Children appear to have intuitive theories that enable them to understand the world and make predictions beyond the domain of mathematics. For example, Carey (1995) demonstrated that even young children have a theory of living beings. A common underlying belief to this theory is the fact that living things can move on their own and are composed of internal biological matter. For instance, children often decide that a toy monkey is more similar to a human being than to a worm, but when they are told that people have spleens, children often decide that the worm had a spleen but the toy monkey does not. The phenomenon—where young children use naive causal theories for performing judgments that transcend surface-structural similarities—was also shown by S. Gelman and her colleagues (Gelman, 1988; Gelman & Markman, 1987).

Altogether, the previously mentioned studies demonstrate that children have principled knowledge that allows them to reason correctly and efficiently. Yet despite their mastery of certain fundamental mathematical ideas, children continue to have great difficulty with school mathematics. Thus, the driving question in much of the current research on mathematical cognition is, "Why should strong and reliable intuitions of the kind that have been documented in young children fail to reliably sustain school mathematics learning?" (Resnick, 1986, p. 161). One common answer to this question is that school mathematics overemphasizes rote manipulation of symbols. This overly procedural focus may discourage children from using their intuitions on school-learning tasks (Hiebert & Lefevre, 1986; Resnick, 1986, 1989).

However, if one accepts the idea that secondary intuitions exist, that it is possible to learn or develop intuitions, then it becomes plausible to imagine that mathematical concepts that are initially counterintuitive (or concepts for which we have no intuitions) may eventually become intuitive via correct reasoning. This idea constitutes a considerable departure from the ways in which mathematical intuition has been traditionally studied. Rather than focusing on how the primary intuitions of students can be applied to school-taught procedures, one can instead seek to establish how new intuitions can be developed.

Reconsider the five problems originally posed at the beginning of this chapter. The initial problem of how many lines pass through any given two points in two-dimensional space refers to the often intuitive fact that exactly one line can be drawn through any two points. Problem solvers who correctly answer this question are most probably utilizing their primary intuition. In contrast, consider the other four problems. The second problem presents a scenario where a fair coin is flipped 10 times and the first 9 flips all come up heads. The question regards the probability that the next, the 10th toss, will come up heads. The answer, .50, is not intuitive. Indeed, Kahneman and Tversky (1972) showed that people tend to judge sequences that have the same probabilities, such as HTTHTH and HHHTTT as being more or less random. The answer to the third problem is even less intuitive. It asks whether the set of rational numbers or the set of irrational numbers have more members. The reasoning of people usually leads to the mistaken conclusion that both sets are infinite and therefore have an equal number of members. Mathematics, however, suggests that the infinity of the set of irrational numbers is larger than the infinity of the set of rational numbers (the proof lies beyond the scope of this chapter, but the interested reader can consult Hofstadter, 1979, for an excellent discussion of the diagonal method of Cantor). Whereas many people find the mathematically correct solutions to the second and third problems to be counterintuitive, they may not have intuitions about the solutions to the fourth and fifth problems, but merely possess recipes for solving these problems rotely (what is 8% of 142? and solve for x: $3x + 7 = 19$).

The traditional approach to developing primary mathematical intuition would involve refining the instruction that accompanies Problems 2 through 5 to enable students to connect new material with their preexisting intuitions. An alternative view would be to foster the development of new, secondary intuitions. For example, Fischbein (1975) suggested that a student can develop the intuition that the probability of heads on the 10th flip is .50 by a process of experimentation and reflection (actually tossing a coin many times and observing the outcomes). The idea is that secondary intuitions can be distilled from engaging in active exploration and experimentation.

One reason that the primary intuitions of students may not support school mathematics learning is that the nature of the mathematics learned in middle and secondary school is different from that learned in elementary school. The initial exposure to postarithmetic mathematics for students is often abstract and symbolic. To perform successfully, students are required to demonstrate facility with mathematical symbols, both procedurally and conceptually (Arcavi, 1994; Fey, 1990), and to develop a new kind of symbolic intuition.

What is the nature of symbolic intuition and how can it be fostered? There are two possible approaches to examining this question. The first is to explore the correct intuitions of people. The second is to investigate the incorrect intuitions or misconceptions of people. Most of the work in this field has concentrated on the latter. The reason may be that misconceptions are particularly valuable for uncovering the ways in which people understand and represent problems internally. Piaget (1965) argued that by uncovering the origin of errors one can learn as much, or even more, about the mental representations of people than by examining correct performance alone. We take the same approach in the following discussion. We believe that by examining the nature of errors we may be able to shed some light on mathematical intuition. At the conclusion of this chapter, we return to the question of how correct symbolic intuitions may be developed as well.

MATHEMATICAL MISCONCEPTIONS
IN THE SCHOOL YEARS AND BEYOND

Problem-solving errors are intriguing. They are often rule based and internally consistent resulting in solutions termed *rational errors* (Ben-Zeev, 1995, 1996, 1998). Rational errors are misconceptions that result from an active construction of knowledge, in contrast to slips or careless errors that are produced from inadvertent actions in the execution of a procedure, such as omissions, permutations, and intrusions (Norman, 1981). For example, in the process of learning multicolumn subtraction, children often commit the following error:

$$\begin{array}{r} 23 \\ -\ 7 \\ \hline 24 \end{array}$$

On the surface, this error appears random. A closer look, however, reveals this underlying rule: "Subtract the smaller from the larger digit" (VanLehn, 1990). Specifically, the child subtracts the smaller digit (3) from the larger digit (7) irrespective of the position of the digits in the column (top or bottom). The rational basis for this error may stem from the previous experience of the student with single-digit subtraction, where the student was always taught to subtract smaller from larger numbers. The previously mentioned error seems to result from applying a correct rule in an incorrect context.

Studies have demonstrated that students possess a variety of mathematical misconceptions especially during the school years and adulthood (for a detailed review, see Ben-Zeev, 1996). Some of these misconceptions have been linked directly to flawed mathematical intuitions. Following are examples of several common misconceptions.

Geometrical Problem Solving

Dugdale (1993) described a geometry error that occurred in a high school class where students were asked to match polynomials to functions (i.e., they were shown a graph and asked to choose its corresponding equation from a set of given equations). The error consisted of confusing the y-intercept of a parabola with its vertex (i.e., the visual center of the graph). For example, students who commit this error would decide that the y-intercept in the parabola marked "a" that full out is "−1," instead of "−.6." Dugdale (1993) explained the confusion between the y-intercept and the vertex by pointing out that, in previous examples students were given, the y-intercept had always coincided with the vertex of the parabola (see the parabolas c and b in Fig. 2.1). The students had thus invented a functional invariance between the two features.

Exponential Growth

Mullet and Cheminat (1995) found that high school students tend to underestimate the rapidity of growth in exponential expressions. They provided students with examples of exponential expressions of the form a^x, where values of a were 5, 7, and 9, and values of x were 2, 3, 4, and 5. Students were explicitly told that the expressions 5^2 and 9^5 were the smallest and largest expressions, respectively. Students were then shown a sequence of exponential expressions, one at a time, and were asked to rate the magnitude of each expression on an equal-interval scale, where the small and large extremes corresponded to the expressions 5^2 and 9^5, respectively. Results show that almost all of the students exhibited difficulties in accurately estimating the value of a given exponential expression. In particular, students tended to believe that a linear increase in the exponent of an exponential expression (e.g., from 4^2 to 4^3 to 4^4) resulted in a linear increase in the entire expression (rather than an exponential

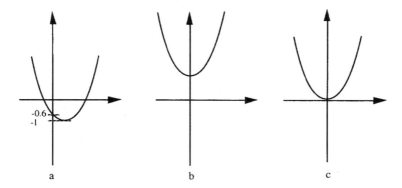

FIG. 2.1.   Examples of parabolas.

increase). Similarly, students believed that a linear increase in the base of an exponential expression (e.g., from 4^3 to 5^3 to 6^3) resulted in a linear increase to the entire expression.

Weighted Averages

Reed (1984) explored the intuitions of college students about the concept of weighted averages as represented in the estimation of solutions to standard distance–rate–time, work, and mixture problems. Reed found that students had great difficulty in using the weighted-average method to correctly estimate the solutions to all types of problems. Specifically, he found that students combined two numbers by calculating an unweighted average even when that average provided an unreasonable answer. For example, students were told that a pipe could fill a tank in 10 hours and another pipe could fill the same tank in 2 hours. When asked how long it would take to fill the tank if both pipes were used at the same time, about one third of the response of the students was 6 hours (the unweighted average of 2 and 10). The conclusion (Reed, 1984) was that many students lack an intuitive understanding of the weighted average concept.

Calculus

Several researchers have examined students' understanding of the concept of limit in calculus (Davis & Vinner, 1986; Dreyfus, 1990). They found that a common misconception was to erroneously assert that the terms in an infinite sequence get closer and closer to the limit but never reach it, such that for all n, $a_n \neq L$ (where a_n is the nth term of the sequence and L is the limit value).

LACK OF INTUITION OR (INADVERTENTLY) MISLEADING TEACHING PRACTICES: AN ANALYSIS OF THE COMMON MISCONCEPTIONS OF STUDENTS

Why do the correct intuitions that Resnick, Gelman, and others have found in young children fail to support mathematics learning in the school years? The answer to this question may lie in the interaction between the cognitive processing of the student, on the one hand, and the type of instruction the student receives, on the other. Central to this argument is the idea that errors often result from a systematic and logically consistent attempt to solve a new and unfamiliar mathematics problem (Ashlock, 1976; Brown & VanLehn, 1980; Buswell, 1926; Cox, 1975; VanLehn, 1983). An error often makes sense to the student who created it and agrees with the intuitions of the student. In this section, we focus on how teaching by using worked-out examples (Anderson, 1993; Ben-Zeev, 1995, 1996; Holland, Holyoak, Nisbett, & Thagard, 1986; VanLehn, 1986, 1990) and schemas (Davis, 1982; Hinsley, Hayes, & Simon, 1977; Mayer, 1982, 1985; Riley et al., 1983; Ross, 1984) can lead to the formation of correct and faulty intuitions, including the misconceptions previously described.

Induction From Worked-out Examples

Teachers use examples as concrete tools for illustrating concepts and procedures. The underlying assumption is that, by following the steps in a worked-out example, students would be able to induce or generalize the correct concept or procedure for the given skill, especially when the example is specific rather than general (Sweller & Cooper, 1985; VanLehn, 1990), and when students are encouraged to generate explanations during the learning process (Chi, Bassok, Lewis, Reimann, & Glaser, 1989; Chi & VanLehn, 1991; VanLehn, Jones, & Chi, 1992). For instance, in teaching the multicolumn-subtraction algorithm, teachers find it easier to illustrate concepts such as borrowing by using worked-out examples. It would be quite cumbersome to state the borrowing actions verbally and in the abstract. Similarly, when students are first introduced to the representation of fractions, teachers often provide concrete examples such as one third is one piece of a three-piece pie.

In providing students with concrete examples, teachers are actually catering to the preferences of the students. In fact, when students are given a choice between using worked-out examples versus written instructions or explanations, students overwhelmingly choose the former (Anderson, Farrell, & Saurers, 1984; LeFevre & Dixon, 1986; Pirolli & Anderson, 1985). This kind of learning, where the instruction by the teachers and the learning styles of the students match, has been termed *felicitous* (VanLehn, 1990).

When Worked-out Examples Lead
to the Development of Faulty Intuitions

Consider a common error that students produce in the process of adding fractions:

$$\frac{1}{3} + \frac{1}{2} = \frac{2}{5}$$

This error involves adding the numerators and denominators of the fractions directly. Silver (1986) suggested that it stems from instruction that illustrates fractions as parts of a pie, as mentioned in the previous section. Specifically, he claimed that students may reason that, because one third is one part of a three-piece pie and one half is one part of a two-piece pie, then altogether they make two pieces out of five pieces, or two fifths.

This finding generalizes to adult students as well. Consider the previous examples regarding misconceptions of exponential growth and the concept of a limit in calculus. Mullet and Cheminat (1995) showed that students tend to erroneously interpret linear growth in exponential expressions. The misconceptions of students may result from overgeneralization from the more familiar linear expressions. Similarly, the misconception that the terms in an infinite sequence get closer and closer to the limit but never reach it may be based on frequently encountered examples of infinite sequences—namely, monotonically increasing or decreasing infinite sequences such as .1, .01, .001, .0001, . . .

The idea that students systematically overgeneralize solutions from familiar problems has received empirical support as well. Ben-Zeev (1995) instructed Yale undergraduates on performing addition in a new number system called *NewAbacus*. She found that when students encountered new problems on the NewAbacus addition test, they produced systematic algorithmic variations on the examples they received during the learning phase.

Schemas

In the section on mathematical intuition in the early years, we presented the work of Greeno and colleagues (Greeno, 1980; Riley et al., 1983) on the use of change, combination, and comparison schemas for solving arithmetic word problems. In teaching more advanced algebraic word problems, students learn to develop schemas as well. Hinsley, Hayes, and Simon (1977) showed that college and high school students could categorize mathematics problems into different types by using the first words of the problem. For instance, problems that began with "A river steamer . . ." were categorized quickly as being part of the river current category. In essence, students were retrieving a schema for solving the problem by paying attention to particular salient features in the problem.

Additional evidence for schema use came from Mayer (1982), who presented students with a variety of word problems. They were either commonly encountered problems in algebraic textbooks or were of a less common type. Mayer asked students to first read and later recall a set of these problems. He found that when students tried to recall the less common problems, they often changed the forms of these problems into the more common versions. The common problems were associated with well-formed schemas and may have therefore formed the basis for the recall of less familiar problems.

When Schemas Contribute to the Development of Faulty Intuitions

A set of studies conducted by Reusser (reported by Schoenfeld, 1991) showed the negative effects of schema use as early as the first grade. Reusser provided first and second graders with the following problem: "There are 26 sheep and 10 goats on a ship. How old is the captain?" The majority of students were content to respond that the captain was 36 years old. In a similar vein, Reusser asked fourth and fifth graders to solve the following problem: "There are 125 sheep and 5 dogs in a flock. How old is the shepherd?" This time students performed more elaborate calculations to get to a reasonable solution. For instance, several students attempted solving the problem by calculating "125 + 5 = 130," and "125 − 5 = 120," first. They realized, however, that these results were too big. The students then had the insight of performing "125/5 = 25" and concluded that the shepherd was 25 years old.

Other instances of overusing schemas can be seen in more advanced mathematical domains. A particularly striking example came from Paige and Simon (1966), who gave college students problems that were logically impossible, such as the following:

> The number of quarters a man has is seven times the number of dimes he has. The value of the dimes exceeds the value of the quarters by two dollars and fifty cents. How many has he of each coin? (pp. 51–118)

This problem is logically impossible because if the number of quarters exceeds the number of dimes, then the value of the dimes cannot exceed that of the quarters. The majority of college students that were tested, however, were quite content to set up the formal equations ($Q = 7D$ and $.10D = 2.5 + .25Q$) for solving the problem. This kind of performance results from applying a rote schema for identifying variables and expressing the relationship between them in a formal way without paying attention to the actual meaning of the problem.

Operator Schemata and Deceptive Correlations

A group of schemas that involves the detection of correlations between the features of a problem and the operator or algorithm that is required for solving the problem has been termed *operator schemas* (Lewis & Anderson, 1985). The main idea underlying these schemas is that students learn explicitly or implicitly to associate a cue in a problem with the strategy for solving the problem. A particularly compelling example of this phenomenon comes from an elementary-school mathematics teacher (Schoenfeld, 1991) who taught students to explicitly search for a cue word in arithmetic word problems and then associate that cue with a particular solution strategy. Specifically, the teacher instructed the students to associate the word *left* with performing subtraction on problems similar to the following:

John had 7 apples
He gave 4 apples to Mary
How many apples does John have (left)? (p. 322)

However, when the same children were given the word *left* in nonsensical word problems with a similar surface structure (e.g., containing sentences such as "Mr. Left had 7 apples," p. 323), students proceeded to subtract the given quantities in the problem, signifying that what was a well-intended strategy on the part of the teacher fostered faulty learning.

This example provides anecdotal evidence, from a real-classroom environment, for what may be the effects of deceptive or spurious correlations on problem-solving performance (Ben-Zeev, 1996, 1998). These effects occur when a student perceives an association between an irrelevant feature in a problem and the strategy that is used for solving that problem (e.g., the association between the word *left* and the subtraction operator). When the student detects the irrelevant feature (the word *left*) in a new problem that requires a different solution algorithm, the student may, nevertheless, proceed to carry out the correlated solution strategy erroneously.

The confusion between the y-intercept of a parabola with its vertex, presented previously, may result from such a process of detecting and using deceptive correlations. Dugdale (1993) suggested that this confusion may occur from the fact that, in previous examples students were given, parabolas were symmetrical about the y-axis, resulting in a situation where the y-intercept and the vertex of the parabola lie on the same point.

Students may have encoded the correlation between the y-intercept and the vertex erroneously (e.g., When I am asked to find the value of the y-intercept, then I look for the lowest or highest point in the parabola).

There have been some empirical demonstrations of the effects of deceptive correlations on problem solving. For example, Ross (1984) taught college students elementary probability principles (e.g., permutation) by providing them with worked-out examples. Each example had a particular content (e.g., involving dice). When participants were tested on the probability principles, they tended to associate the particular problem content with the specific principle with which it had appeared in the worked-out example. When the same content appeared in a problem requiring a different probability principle, participants were reminded of the original principle with which the content was associated and proceeded to apply it erroneously.

More recently, Ben-Zeev (2000) demonstrated that deceptive or spurious correlations can affect the performance of even experienced problem solvers. Participants who received high scores on their Math SATs (700 or above) were instructed on how to solve problems that are frequently encountered on the Math SATs, called quantitative comparisons, by using two different algorithms: Multiply one side by n/n and multiply both sides by n (demonstrated in Fig. 2.2).

For half the participants in the study, multiply one side by n/n was correlated with a logarithm and multiply both sides by n was correlated with a radical. For the other half, the feature-algorithm correlations were flipped: Multiply one side by n/n was correlated with a radical and multiply both sides by n was correlated with a logarithm. During the testing phase, in one particular experiment, participants were given an implicit memory task where they were presented with a sequence of problem-algorithm pairs on the computer screen for a short duration (700 msec). Participants were then asked to rate the extent to which they would have liked or preferred solving the given problem by using the given algorithm on a 1 to 7 scale. Although most participants reported that they did not have enough time to see the stimuli on the screen, and they felt like they were guessing, results on the implicit memory task show that participants produced higher ratings in response to algorithms that were correlated with a problem feature during learning than when the algorithm was not.

This finding shows that, even on an implicit level, participants exhibited an intuitive preference for using the correlated algorithm even when there was no conceptual reason for doing so. The reason that students may come to rely on correlational structure may be that, in most cases, feature-algorithm correlations are predictive cues that lead students to the correct results (e.g., explicitly associate the word *left* in a word problem with subtraction).

Algorithm 1: multiply one column by n/n		Algorithm 2: multiply both columns by n	
$x > 0$		$x > 0$	
Column A	Column B	Column A	Column B
$\dfrac{x + 4}{log\,3}$	$\dfrac{2x + 6}{2log\,3}$	$\dfrac{x + 2}{\sqrt{2}}$	$\dfrac{2x + 4}{2\sqrt{2}}$

Determine whether the quantity in Column A is smaller than, larger than, or equal to the quantity in Column B, or whether the relationship cannot be determined.

Strategy: Multiply Column A by 2/2. This gives us $\dfrac{2x + 8}{2log\,3}$ in Column A. By comparing the denominators we find that because $2x + 8$ is larger than $2x + 6$, then Column A is larger.

Determine whether the quantity in Column A is smaller than, larger than, or equal to the quantity in Column B, or whether the relationship cannot be determined.

Strategy: Multiply both columns by $\sqrt{2}$. This action cancels the $\sqrt{2}$ in both columns, and leaves us with $x + 2$ in Column A and $\dfrac{2x + 4}{2}$ or $x + 4$ in Column B. Because $x + 4$ is larger than $x + 2$, then Column B is larger.

FIG. 2.2.   Features and algorithms counterbalanced over participants.

The review of the misconceptions literature suggests that the development of incorrect intuition may be related, in part, to instructional variables such as teaching by using worked-out examples and schemas. However, the ontogenesis of correct symbolic intuition is largely an unexplored issue.

CORRECT SYMBOLIC INTUITION

Examining the development of symbolic intuition is a significant departure from the ways in which mathematical intuition has been previously studied. Earlier research on intuition was concerned with primary intuitions and sought to determine why preexisting intuitions failed to support school mathematics. The modal recommendation that emerged from studies on primary intuition was for teachers, schools, and curriculum developers to change instructional practices so as to make better connections with the intuitive beliefs of students. The curriculum materials and new pedagogy that emerged from this program of research have made significant progress toward improving the state of mathematics learning and teaching in elementary schools and, to some extent, middle schools (e.g., National Council of Teachers of Mathematics, 1989).

Throughout this chapter, we have attempted to extend the discussion of mathematical intuition into the high school years, especially with respect to exploring the new symbolic intuitions that students develop or fail to develop in the study of postarithmetic mathematics. Given the significant differences in the nature of the mathematics that is learned in elementary school and high school, we believe that researchers should consider the possibility that intuitions about elementary and more advanced mathematics may be qualitatively different. A review of the current research on mathematical intuition has indicated that this issue is largely uncharted. However, we have identified two different perspectives that can inform the way in which our exploration of correct secondary intuition should proceed. Each of these perspectives may give some clarity to the study of secondary intuitions but also may raise difficult questions.

A Focus on Deep Understanding

One way to explore the development of secondary intuitions of students is to follow the trail of those who study primary intuitions. This viewpoint suggests that students develop or fail to develop secondary intuitions because of poor instructional methods and curricula. Teaching and learning should be reconceptualized, according to this view, so as to connect with and build on the primary intuitions of students.

Given the extensive use of symbols and procedures in secondary mathematics learning, the development of secondary intuition would necessarily be related to conceptual and procedural knowledge of students. Much has been written about the relationship between these two types of knowledge (e.g., Byrnes, 1992; Byrnes & Wasik, 1991; Hiebert, 1984, 1986). The main finding is that too often symbolic procedures are learned by rote and suffer from an impoverished conceptual knowledge base. The main idea is that if symbols and procedures could be imbued with and linked to conceptual knowledge, then students would be more likely to develop a deep understanding of symbolic procedures. It seems logical to assume that such deep understanding of symbolic procedures would be instrumental in the development of symbolic intuition.

This view shows promise in informing and guiding research into the development of secondary intuition. However, it also raises two difficult questions. First, the vast majority of research on conceptual and procedural knowledge has studied elementary-school mathematics learning. For the most part, the conceptual knowledge underlying the learning of arithmetic procedures (adding, subtracting, multiplying, and dividing) can be clearly delineated. For example, the borrowing procedure for subtraction is based on the idea of place value (Baroody, 1985), and the conceptual knowledge of fraction procedures involves understanding the part–whole relationship (Leinhardt, 1988; Mack, 1990; also see Lampert, 1986, for a discussion of conceptual knowledge for multidigit multiplication). However, it is more difficult to identify or specify the conceptual knowledge that underlies algebraic procedures. For example, what does it mean to have deep conceptual understanding of the procedure that is used to solve the equation, $3x + 7 = 19$? Most mathematics educators and researchers feel that they recognize deep algebraic understanding when they see it, but they find it difficult to articulate exactly what that deep understanding is or how to design curricula to foster its development. If the development of symbolic intuition is critically dependent on the establishment of links between conceptual and procedural knowledge of secondary-school mathematics, more effort needs to be devoted to explicitly defining what is meant by these terms, particularly with respect to algebra.

Second, the focus on deep understanding fails to consider how incomplete or incorrect primary intuitions may be implicated in the development of secondary intuition. As mentioned earlier, children have been shown to have some well-developed primary intuitions on entering school. Elementary-school mathematics instruction has sought to connect and strengthen these primary intuitions. To what extent is this approach generalizable to secondary-school mathematics? Is the construction of secondary intuition critically dependent on the existence of strong primary intuitions? In other words, can students develop intuitions about algebra when they have not developed intuitions about (for example) adding fractions? If instruction should seek to connect to and build on existing intuitions, how should secondary-school teachers and researchers proceed when primary intuitions are incomplete or incorrect? The relationship between existing primary intuitions and the development of symbolic intuitions has not yet been adequately examined.

A Focus on Doing

An alternative way to examine the development of secondary mathematical intuitions is more traditionalist. According to this viewpoint, students need to initially approach their learning of symbolic mathematics with the idea that mathematical meaning may be independent of intuition. It is through the doing of (and subsequent reflection on the doing of) symbolic procedures that students may come to develop deep understanding (and thus intuitions about) mathematical procedures (Baroody & Ginsburg, 1986).

The idea that correct learning may occur by first mastering procedures is consistent with a rich literature within the field of cognitive psychology on skill acquisition and learning by doing (e.g., Anzai & Simon, 1979). At times, this literature has been mischaracterized as advocating rote learning by proposing so-called *drill-and-kill* approaches to mathematics instruction. A more careful reading of research in this area indicates that not only does procedural practice play a vital role in the development of acquiring skills, but it may also be instrumental in promoting conceptual understanding. Anzai and Simon (1979) found that when individuals are able to successfully execute a procedural task, even in a crude, rote, or inefficient method, they are often able to use their correct solution to develop more efficient and thoughtful methods of problem solving. More recently, Simon and Zhu (1988) showed that students who were given examples of the factorization of polynomials [e.g., $X^2 + 5X + 6 = (X + 2)(X + 3)$], and were then asked to solve problems on their own [e.g., $X^2 + 9X + 18 = (\ )(\ )$], were able to generalize the underlying rules of factorization correctly [i.e., $X^2 + aX + b = (X + c)(X + d)$, where $c \times d = b$ and $c + d = a$].

Similarly, Resnick (1986) reported the following anecdote:

> The best high school math students I have talked with also have said that they are quite willing to suspend their need for 'sense' for a while while new rules are introduced, because they have found that after a period of just manipulating symbols in accord with the rules, the rules come to make sense to them. (p. 191)

The question of what it means to understand a symbolic algebraic procedure, therefore, is not trivial. It may be that suspending the need for sense in the execution of a procedure could have a beneficial role in the development of subsequent understanding and intuition. In the following section, we examine more closely the implications of intuitive mathematics for classroom learning and teaching.

IMPLICATIONS FOR THE TEACHING
AND LEARNING OF MATHEMATICS

How can teachers build on and foster mathematical intuition in the classroom? In an attempt to answer this question, it is important to consider the different roles that primary and secondary intuitions play in elementary- and secondary-school mathematics. The educational questions of interest with regard to primary intuitions is whether and how instruction should be redesigned so as to connect school mathematics with the preexisting intuitions of students. As mentioned previously, many educators feel that instruction does not connect to or build on preexisting understanding to the extent that it could.

In elementary-school mathematics, making connections with the primary intuitions of students can happen in at least two ways. First, students should be encouraged to generate and discover mathematical procedures on their own instead of only being taught the standard or most efficient problem-solving strategies by a teacher directly. This kind of a discovery approach can be used in the learning of formal mathematical algorithms, such as procedures for adding fractions and multiplying multidigit numbers. It can also be used in less algorithmic problem-solving contexts, such as the invention of procedures to determine the relative magnitude of rational numbers or the parity (odd–even) of integers. Second, school instruction can be redesigned to foster connections to preexisting knowledge through the use of manipulatives. Manipulatives (e.g., Geoboards, Cuisenaire rods, and base-10 cubes) allow students to contextualize or to make concrete the abstract concepts that numbers represent and to form abstract mathematical relationships based on familiar and more intuitive objects and relationships.

In the case of secondary intuitions, however, these two educational strategies (i.e., discovery learning and the use of manipulatives) seem more difficult to put into practice. The act of self-generating mathematical procedures and principles may not always be possible when one is working with complex symbolic expressions or equations. Also, despite some availability of manipulatives in teaching beginning algebra concepts (e.g., algebra tiles), it is uncertain how useful or practical these manipulatives are for learning more advanced algebraic or symbolic relationships.

Thus, at first glance, the task of how to redesign instruction so as to foster the development of secondary intuitions appears to be difficult. A second look, however, may give some hope for middle- and high school teachers. When students are encouraged to generate their own procedures for solving problems, what kind of reasoning do they engage in? During discovery learning, students cyclically go through the processes of experimentation followed by reflection (Fischbein, 1975). The value of the discovery approach lies not in the act of discovery, but rather in the thinking process that students engage in during discovery. Therefore, middle- and secondary-school teachers need not worry as much about whether students arrive at the right answer the first time they engage in discovery learning. Rather, teachers should try to incorporate instruction that emulates the processes that underlie discovery—experimentation and reflection.

What is meant by discovery is not always apparent even to well-intending instructors or textbook authors, however. Some high school discovery-oriented textbooks ask students to ascertain mathematical relationships that are obvious to them already. In the 10th-grade classroom of the second author, this situation occurred when students were solving a problem from a geometry text, which asked them to cut out triangles, measure each of the three angles, and find their sum. Most students already knew the answer to this exercise but many completed the activity anyway. Some students found a sum of 181 degrees or 179 degrees and yet filled in the blank on the worksheet with 180 degrees. By the end of this activity, perhaps a few more students had learned the fact that the sum of the angles in any triangle is 180 degrees. It is doubtful that this mathematical fact was any more intuitive to students as a result of their discovery. As this situation suggests, it is important that discovery is not divorced from experimentation and reflection. Discovery learning requires interest, motivation, and intrinsic reward.

The use of manipulatives may also enable students to go through a related cyclic process of experimentation (manipulation of concrete objects), attaining a sense of the underlying principles, and articulating the problem-solving process (Mason, 1996). Manipulation provides students with a means for getting a sense of patterns, relationships, and quantities. As students start to get a sense of the material, they begin to try to bring these patterns and relationships to articulation. The act of articulation—speaking, writing, or both—changes the way students see ideas; patterns and relationships that previously existed only in the concrete world of the manipulatives can become generalized or more abstract. This shift in the form of the ideas, from concrete to generalizable, allows what was previously abstract to become manipulable, repeating the cycle. Clearly it is not the use of manipulatives in and of itself that can lead to the development of intuitions. Manipulatives can help students see the general in the specific and the specific in the general (Mason, 1996). It is this process of iterative generalization that has the most potential to encourage the development of secondary intuitions.

This iterative generalization process can be found in the Curriculum and Evaluation Standards for School Mathematics (National Council of Teachers of Mathematics, 1989). For example, one problem involves determining the amount of money in the bank account of a person at the end of 10 years, given an initial deposit of $100 and 6% interest rate, compounded annually. Students often initially attempt to manipulate the patterns and relationships in this problem with a calculator; by engaging in repeated calculations involving multiplication and addition, students can get a sense of the problem situation and articulate a solution. Further generalization can be encouraged by what if questions (e.g., Brown & Walter, 1993), such as: What if the initial deposit is changed to $500? By using and manipulating a variable for the principal, students can begin to get a sense of the relationship between the initial deposit and the ending balance. This process can be repeated in a way that encourages students to continue generalizing and thus to develop secondary intuitions about the patterns and relationships in this particular problem.

In summary, our recommendations for incorporating primary and secondary intuitions into the classroom are to incorporate both discovery-oriented learning and the use of manipulatives in the ways that we have previously described these two instructional strategies. These teaching strategies can help connect new formal materials to preschool knowledge of students as well as to foster new intuitions about repeating structures and patterns. Intuition can and should be an integral part of the learning process.

CONCLUSION

In this chapter, we have attempted to explore the issue of mathematical intuitions of secondary-school students. We have argued that the study of such intuitions may require a different approach than ones that have been reported in the well-established literature on intuitions of students in elementary school. In summary, we make the following four main points.

First, we adopt the philosophical stance that intuitions can be learned. We argue that if one accepts the idea that secondary intuitions exist, one must also acknowledge that reason does play a role in intuition (the inferential-intuitionist viewpoint). Students enter formal schooling with a wide variety of mathematical abilities and intuitions. As schooling progresses, students not only construct mathematical knowledge and strengthen existing intuitions, but also build new secondary intuitions.

Second, the mathematics education and psychological communities have extensively examined the relationship between the informal and primary mathematical intuitions of students and their subsequent learning in elementary school. The constructivist perspective, which argues that instructional methods should focus on allowing students to strengthen existing intuitions by making connections between informal and formal mathematical understanding, has yielded promising results (e.g., Resnick, 1986). However, it is unclear how this approach relates to the development of higher level mathematical intuition.

Third, there has been a great deal of research devoted to the development of misconceptions. This research has shown us that systematic errors may be based on an internally consistent logic that is overgeneralized from worked-out examples and schemas. The logic underlying errors may lead to the development of incorrect intuitions. This finding highlights the importance of instructional variables, such as teaching by using worked-out examples and by schemas, in the process of forming (mis)understandings.

Finally, we believe that the relationship between instructional variables and the development of secondary intuition is quite complex. Students fail to develop reliable, sustainable secondary mathematical intuitions for different and interrelated reasons. Among these reasons is the presence of incomplete, incorrect, or both, primary intuitions, dissonance between current instructional methods and intuitive ideas about mathematics by students, and the ill-defined relationship between algebraic procedural skills and deep conceptual understanding.

Mathematical intuition may be a rubric for at least two different kinds of intuitions: primary and secondary. We have already gained some advances in understanding the nature of primary mathematical intuition. The future challenge is to identify the nature of secondary or postarithmetic mathematics intuition. Such a quest will shed some light on intuitive processes, in general, and will have important applications to education.

REFERENCES

Anderson, J. R. (1993). *Rules of the mind*. Hillsdale, NJ: Lawrence Erlbaum Associates.
Anderson, J. R., Farrell, R., & Saurers, R. (1984). Learning to program in LISP. *Cognitive Science, 8*, 87–129.
Anzai, Y., & Simon, H. A. (1979). The theory of learning by doing. *Psychological Review, 86*(2), 124–140.
Arcavi, A. (1994). Symbol sense: Informal sense-making in formal mathematics. *For the Learning of Mathematics, 14*(3), 24–35.
Ashlock, R. B. (1976). *Error patterns in computation*. Columbus, OH: Bell & Howell.
Baroody, A. J. (1985). Pitfalls in equating informal arithmetic procedures with specific mathematical conceptions. *Journal for Research in Mathematics Education, 16*(3), 233–236.
Baroody, A. J., & Ginsburg, H. P. (1986). The relationship between initial meaningful and mechanical knowledge of arithmetic. In J. Hiebert (Ed.), *Conceptual and procedural knowledge: The case for mathematics* (pp. 75–112). Hillsdale, NJ: Lawrence Erlbaum Associates.
Bartlett, F. C. (1932). *Remembering*. Cambridge, MA: Cambridge University Press.
Ben-Zeev, T. (1995). The nature and origin of *rational errors* in arithmetic thinking: Induction from examples and prior knowledge. *Cognitive Science, 19*, 341–376.
Ben-Zeev, T. (1996). When erroneous mathematical thinking is just as "correct": The oxymoron of rational errors. In R. J. Sternberg & T. Ben-Zeev (Eds.), *The nature of mathematical thinking* (pp. 55–79). Mahwah, NJ: Lawrence Erlbaum Associates.
Ben-Zeev, T. (1998). Rational errors and the mathematical mind. *Review of General Psychology, 2*(4), 366–383.
Ben-Zeev, T. (2000). *Spurious correlations in problem solving*. Manuscript submitted for publication.
Brown, J. S., & VanLehn, K. (1980). Repair theory: A generative theory of bugs in procedural skills. *Cognitive Science, 4*, 379–426.
Brown, S. I., & Walter, M. I. (1993). Problem posing in mathematics education. In S. I. Brown & M. I. Walter (Eds.), *Problem posing: Reflections and applications*. Mahwah, NJ: Lawrence Erlbaum Associates.
Buswell, G. T. (1926). *Diagnostic studies in arithmetic*. Chicago, IL: University of Chicago Press.
Byrnes, J. P. (1992). The conceptual basis of procedural learning. *Cognitive Development, 7*, 235–257.
Byrnes, J. P., & Wasik, B. A. (1991). Role of conceptual knowledge in mathematical procedural learning. *Developmental Psychology, 5*, 777–786.
Carey, S. (1995). On the origin of causal understanding. In D. Sperber, D. Premack, & A. J. Premack (Eds.), *Causal cognition: A multidisciplinary debate* (pp. 268–308). New York: Clarendon.
Chi, M. T. H., Bassok, M., Lewis, M. W., Reimann, P., & Glaser, R. (1989). Self-explanations: How students study and use examples in learning to solve problems. *Cognitive Science, 13*, 145–182.
Chi, M. T. H., & VanLehn, K. (1991). The content of physics self-explanations. *Journal of the Learning Sciences, 1*, 69–105.
Chi, M. T. H., & Slotta, J. D. (1993). The ontological coherence of intuitive physics. *Cognition and Instruction, 10*, 249–260.

Cox, L. S. (1975). Diagnosing and remediating systematic errors in addition and subtraction computation. *The Arithmetic Teacher, 22*, 151–157.

Davidson, J. E. (1995). The suddenness of insight. In R. J. Sternberg & J. E. Davidson (Eds.), *The nature of insight* (pp. 125–155). Cambridge, MA: MIT Press.

Davis, R. B. (1982). The postulation of certain specific, explicit, commonly shared frames. *Journal of Mathematical Behavior, 3*, 167–201.

Davis, R. B., & Vinner, S. (1986). The notion of limit: Some seemingly unavoidable misconception stages. *Journal of Mathematical Behavior, 5*, 281–303.

diSessa, A. A. (1982). Unlearning Aristotelian physics: A study of knowledge-based learning. *Cognitive Science, 6*, 37–75.

diSessa, A. A. (1993). Toward an epistemology of physics. *Cognition and Instruction, 10*, 105–225.

Dixon, J. A., & Moore, C. F. (1996). The developmental role of intuitive principles in choosing mathematical strategies. *Developmental Psychology, 32*(2), 241–253.

Dreyfus, T. (1990). Advanced mathematical thinking. In P. Nesher & K. Kilpatrick (Eds.), *Mathematics and cognition: A research synthesis by the International Group for the Psychology of Mathematics Education* (pp. 113–134). Cambridge, MA: Cambridge University Press.

Dreyfus, T., & Eisenberg, T. (1984). Intuitions on functions. *Journal of Experimental Education, 52*(2), 77–85.

Dugdale, S. (1993). Functions and graphs—Perspectives on student thinking. In T. A. Romberg, E. Fennema, & T. Carpenter (Eds.), *Integrating research on the graphical representation of functions* (pp. 101–130). Hillsdale, NJ: Lawrence Erlbaum Associates.

Fey, J. T. (1990). Quantity. In L. A. Steen (Ed.), *On the shoulders of giants: New approaches to numeracy* (pp. 61–94). Washington, DC: National Academy Press.

Fischbein, E. (1973). Intuition, structure, and heuristic methods in the teaching of mathematics. In A. G. Howson (Ed.), *Developments in mathematics education* (pp. 222–232). Cambridge, England: University Press.

Fischbein, E. (1975). *The intuitive sources of probabilistic thinking in children*. Dordrecht, Holland: D. Reidel.

Fischbein, E., Tirosh, D., & Melamed, U. (1981). Is it possible to measure the intuitive acceptance of a mathematical statement? *Educational Studies in Mathematics, 12*, 491–512.

Gelman, R. (1979). Preschool thought. *American Psychologist, 34*(10), 900–905.

Gelman, R. (1990). First principles organize attention to and learning about relevant data: Number and the animate–inanimate distinction as examples. *Cognitive Science, 14*(1), 79–106.

Gelman, R., & Meck, E. (1983). Preschoolers' counting: Principles before skill. *Cognition, 13*(3), 343–359.

Gelman, S. A. (1988). The development of induction within natural kind and artifact categories. *Cognitive Psychology, 20*, 65–95.

Gelman, S. A., & Markman, E. M. (1987). Young children's inductions from natural kinds: The role of categories and appearances. *Child Development, 58*, 1532–1541.

Gick, M. L., & Lockhart, R. (1995). Cognitive and affective components of insight. In R. J. Sternberg & J. E. Davidson (Eds.), *The nature of insight* (pp. 197–228). Cambridge, MA: MIT Press.

Greeno, J. G. (1980). Some examples of cognitive task analysis with instructional implications. In R. E. Snow, P. Federico, & W. E. Montague (Eds.), *Aptitude, learning, and instruction* (Vol. 2, pp. 1–21). Hillsdale, NJ: Lawrence Erlbaum Associates.

Hadamard, J. (1954). *An essay on the psychology of invention in the mathematical field*. New York: Dover.

Hiebert, J. (1984). Children's mathematics learning: The struggle to link form and understanding. *Elementary School Journal, 84*(5), 497–513.

Hiebert, J. (1986). *Conceptual and procedural knowledge: The case of mathematics.* Hillsdale, NJ: Lawrence Erlbaum Associates.

Hiebert, J., & Lefevre, P. (1986). Conceptual and procedural knowledge in mathematics: An introductory analysis. In J. Hiebert (Ed.), *Conceptual and procedural knowledge: The case of mathematics* (pp. 1–27). Hillsdale, NJ: Lawrence Erlbaum Associates.

Hinsley, D., Hayes, J. R., & Simon, H. A. (1977). From words to equations. In P. Carpenter & M. Just (Eds.), *Cognitive processes in comprehension* (pp. 89–106). Hillsdale, NJ: Lawrence Erlbaum Associates.

Hofstadter, D. (1979). *Godel, Escher, Bach: An eternal golden braid.* New York: Basic Books.

Holland, J. H., Holyoak, K. J., Nisbett, R. E., & Thagard, P. R. (1986). *Induction: Processes of inference, learning, and discovery.* Cambridge, MA: MIT Press.

Kahneman, D., & Tversky, A. (1972). Subjective probability: A judgment of representativeness. *Cognitive Psychology, 3,* 430–454.

Keil, F. C. (1981). Constraints on knowledge and cognitive development. *Psychological Review, 88,* 197–227.

Lampert, M. (1986). Knowing, doing, and teaching multiplication. *Cognition and Instruction, 3*(4), 305–342.

LeFevre, J., & Dixon, P. (1986). Do written instructions need examples? *Cognition and Instruction, 3,* 1–30.

Leinhardt, G. (1988). Getting to know: Tracing students' mathematical knowledge from intuition to competence. *Educational Psychologist, 23*(2), 119–144.

Lewis, M. W., & Anderson, J. R. (1985). Discrimination of operator schemata in problem solving: Learning from examples. *Cognitive Psychology, 17,* 26–65.

Mack, N. K. (1990). Learning fractions with understanding: Building on informal knowledge. *Journal for Research in Mathematics Education, 21,* 16–32.

Mason, J. (1996). Expressing generalities and the roots of algebra. In N. Debnarz, C. Kieran, & L. Lee (Eds.), *Approaches to algebra: Perspectives for research and teaching* (pp. 65–86). Dordrecht, Holland: Kluwer Academic Publishers.

Mayer, R. E. (1982). Memory for algebra story problems. *Journal of Educational Psychology, 74,* 199–216.

Mayer, R. E. (1985). Implications of cognitive psychology for instruction in mathematical problem solving. In E. A. Silver (Ed.), *Teaching and learning mathematical problem solving: Multiple research perspectives* (pp. 123–138). Hillsdale, NJ: Lawrence Erlbaum Associates.

McCloskey, M., Caramazza, A., & Green, B. (1980). Curvilinear motion in the absence of external forces: Naive beliefs about the motion of objects. *Science, 210,* 1139–1141.

Mullet, E., & Cheminat, Y. (1995). Estimation of exponential expressions by high school students. *Contemporary Educational Psychology, 20*(4), 451–456.

National Council of Teachers of Mathematics. (1989). *Curriculum and evaluation standards for school mathematics.* Reston, VA: Author.

Norman, D. A. (1981). Categorization of action slips. *Psychological Review, 88,* 1–15.

Novick, L. R. (1988). Analogical transfer, problem similarity, and expertise. *Journal of Experimental Psychology: Learning, Memory, and Cognition, 14,* 510–520.

Novick, L. R., & Holyoak, K. J. (1991). Mathematical problem solving by analogy. *Journal of Experimental Psychology: Learning, Memory, and Cognition, 17,* 398–415.

Paige, J. M., & Simon, H. A. (1966). Cognitive processes in solving algebra word problems. In B. Kleinmuntz (Ed.), *Problem solving: Research, method, and theory* (pp. 51–118). New York: Wiley.

Piaget, J. (1965). *The child's conception of number*. New York: Norton.

Pirolli, P. L., & Anderson, J. R. (1985). The role of learning from examples in the acquisition of recursive programming skill. *Canadian Journal of Psychology, 39*, 240–272.

Reed, S. K. (1984). Estimating answers to algebra word problems. *Journal of Experimental Psychology: Learning, Memory, & Cognition, 10*, 778–790.

Resnick, L. (1986). The development of mathematical intuition. In M. Perlmutter (Ed.), *Perspectives on intellectual development: The Minnesota Symposia on child psychology* (Vol. 19, pp. 159–194). Minneapolis: University of Minnesota Press.

Resnick, L. B. (1989). Developing mathematical knowledge. *American Psychologist, 44*(2), 162–169.

Riley, M. S., Greeno, G. J., & Heller, J. (1983). The development of children's problem solving ability in arithmetic. In H. P. Ginsburg (Ed.), *The development of mathematical thinking* (pp. 153–196). New York: Academic Press.

Ross, B. (1984). Remindings and their effects in learning a cognitive skill. *Cognitive Psychology, 16*, 371–416.

Schank, R., & Abelson, R. P. (1977). *Scripts, plans, goals, and understanding: An inquiry into human knowledge structures*. Hillsdale, NJ: Lawrence Erlbaum Associates.

Schoenfeld, A. H. (1988). When correct teaching leads to faulty results: The disasters of "well-taught" mathematics courses. *Educational Psychologist, 23*, 145–166.

Schoenfeld, A. H. (1991). On mathematics as sense making: An informal attack on the unfortunate divorce of formal and informal mathematics. In J. F. Voss, D. N. Perkins, & J. W. Segal (Eds.), *Informal reasoning and education* (pp. 311–343). Hillsdale, NJ: Lawrence Erlbaum Associates.

Seifert, C. M., Meyer, D. E., Davidson, N., Palatano, A. L., & Yaniv, I. (1995). Demystification of cognitive insight: Opportunistic assimilation and the prepared-mind perspective. In R. J. Sternberg & J. E. Davidson (Eds.), *The nature of insight* (pp. 65–124). Cambridge, MA: MIT Press.

Silver, E. A. (1986). Using conceptual and procedural knowledge: A focus on relationships. In J. Hiebert (Ed.), *Conceptual and procedural knowledge: The case of mathematics* (pp. 181–198). Hillsdale, NJ: Lawrence Erlbaum Associates.

Simon, H. A., & Zhu, X. (1988). Learning mathematics from examples and by doing. *Cognition and Instruction, 4*, 137–166.

Springer, K., & Keil, F. C. (1989). On the development of biologically specific beliefs: The case of inheritance. *Child Development, 60*, 637–648.

Starkey, P., Spelke, E. S., & Gelman, R. (1990). Numerical abstraction by human infants. *Cognition, 36*(2), 97–127.

Sweller, J., & Cooper, G. A. (1985). The use of worked examples as a substitute for problem solving in learning algebra. *Cognition and Instruction, 2*, 59–89.

Tversky, A., & Kahneman, D. (1974). Judgment under uncertainty: Heuristics and biases. *Science, 185*, 1124–1131.

VanLehn, K. (1983). On the representation of procedures in repair theory. In H. P. Ginsburg (Ed.), *The development of mathematical thinking* (pp. 201–252). Hillsdale, NJ: Lawrence Erlbaum Associates.

VanLehn, K. (1986). Arithmetic procedures are induced from examples. In J. Hiebert (Ed.), *Conceptual and procedural knowledge: The case of mathematics* (pp. 133–179). Hillsdale, NJ: Lawrence Erlbaum Associates.

VanLehn, K. (1990). *Mind bugs: The origins of procedural misconceptions*. Cambridge, MA: MIT Press.

VanLehn, K., Jones, R. M., & Chi, M. T. H. (1992). A model of the self-explanation effect. *Journal of the Learning Sciences, 2*, 1–59.

Westcott, M. (1968). *Toward a contemporary psychology of intuition*. New York: Holt, Rinehart & Winston.

Wild, K. W. (1938). *Intuition*. Cambridge, England: Cambridge University Press.

Wynn, K. (1992). Evidence against empiricist accounts of the origins of numerical knowledge. *Mind and Language, 7*, 315–332.

Wynn, K. (1995). Infants possess a system of numerical knowledge. *Current Directions in Psychological Science, 4*, 172–177.

CHAPTER THREE

The Intuitive Mind and Knowledge About History

James V. Wertsch
Washington University

Joseph L. Polman
University of Missouri–St. Louis

Claims about the intuitive mind and intuitive knowledge have come to occupy an important role in contemporary discussions of cognition and instruction. Scholars from a variety of theoretical perspectives have examined the nature and development of intuitive knowledge in several domain-specific areas, including psychology (Astington, 1995), biology (Keil, 1989), and physics (Carey & Spelke, 1994). Furthermore, the findings from this research have come to play an increasingly important role in the analysis and organization of formal instruction (e.g., Dykstra, Boyle, & Monarch, 1992; Posner, Strike, Hewson, & Gertzog, 1982). In this chapter, we briefly review some of the senses that the term *intuitive* takes on in relation to scientific conceptions, and then go on to examine an area that has been largely neglected in cognitive research: historical knowledge and instruction. We discuss some of the unique characteristics of knowledge and instruction in the discipline of history, such as narrative knowing and the importance of such instruction for national identity. Such factors complicate the direct application of research findings and instructional designs from the natural sciences to history teaching and learning, and necessitate the need for more research on intuitive conceptions in the history domain.

SENSES OF INTUITIVE KNOWLEDGE
IN SCIENTIFIC COGNITION

Although investigators have made important headway in understanding what intuitive knowledge is, clarity about many basic terms remains elusive. A review of the discussion does indicate, however, some consensus about the senses that the term *intuitive* can take on. Specifically, two related meanings seem to have emerged. The first stems from the fact that the term *intuitive* is often taken to stand in opposition to *schooled* or *scientific*. Indeed, in some early discussions, the issue was often not so much what intuitive knowledge is as what it is not. From this perspective, intuitive knowledge is understood in terms of being homegrown (i.e., spontaneous or everyday according to Vygotsky, 1987) and not grounded in the principles of abstract, logical organization that underlie schooled discourse and thinking.

Recent analyses, such as those concerned with conceptual change, have done much to rectify some of the weaknesses of this earlier tendency. Investigators working from this perspective reject a tabula rasa view of learning in which teachers are viewed as providing information through didactic instruction and students are viewed as absorbing correct (i.e., schooled) concepts. Instead, the focus has switched to the nature of conceptual change that starts with what are variously called *intuitive concepts*, *misconceptions*, and *preconceptions*. Among other things, this research has suggested that the intuitive conceptions students bring to a learning situation are quite robust and cannot easily be replaced through direct instruction (Confrey, 1989) due to the tendency to assimilate new ideas to existing ones.

Several studies in this line of research suggest that ignoring the intuitive concepts of students results in school knowledge about scientific phenomena that they are unable to apply in real-world settings (e.g., Lewis, Stern, & Linn, 1993; Reif & Larkin, 1991; Resnick, 1987). By explicating the intuitive knowledge of students in various domains, research in this field holds some promise for guiding instruction and the design of learning environments (Posner et al., 1982). For example, Dykstra et al. (1992) outlined ways that physics teachers could diagnose differing conceptions by students of the relationship between force and motion and then induce them to transform these conceptions. Similarly, research on models of heat and temperature by students has led to greater understanding of their naive ideas in this domain, which educators can then attempt to connect to understanding based on scientific concepts (e.g., Lewis & Linn, 1994). From this perspective, the task of the educator is to create cognitive disequilibrium that forces accommodation of existing concepts through differentiation, class extension, or reconceptualization.

While recognizing the caveats and complexities that such research has introduced into the picture, we would argue that intuitive knowledge from this perspective continues to be viewed largely in terms of its opposition to schooled or scientific knowledge. Specifically, it is viewed as not being characterized by abstract concepts that are subject to conscious reflection and as not being organized into logical systems. A correlate of this is that intuitive knowledge involves a level of thinking that is less developed and hence less adequate than scientific knowledge for approaching many problem-solving situations.

The second sense of the term *intuitive* is related to the first, but is sufficiently distinct to merit separate treatment. It has to do with the attractiveness, if not seductiveness, of intuitive reasoning. Many investigators have reported that it is no easy task to make the transition away from intuitive toward schooled knowledge. Furthermore, it has often been observed that even when individuals demonstrate a proficiency in scientific reasoning, they often find it difficult to avoid employing intuitive knowledge even in settings where it would clearly be more appropriate to employ the former.

For instance, Lewis and Linn (1994) showed that a physicist who has a formal understanding of the principles of conductance may cling to the notion that wrapping a soda can in aluminum foil will keep it cooler than wrapping it in wool. The relevant scientific principles entail that, because aluminum conducts heat better, a cold can wrapped in foil will more quickly equilibrate to the surrounding temperature (i.e., the cold can and liquid will get warmer). The reason that the foil-wrapped can feels so cold is precisely because of that same conductance. Nonetheless, this scientist continued to hold to the idea that aluminum foil keeps things cool and hot better than other materials in part because he recalled early experiences and advice from his mother. The everyday knowledge continues to hold sway even after more scientific knowledge has been acquired and even at times when the scientific principles are explicitly called for in the context (in this case, the prompting of an interviewer).

Such cases are striking because they provide a reminder of the power that intuitive knowledge often holds over human thought. At least in some instances, this allure of intuitive knowledge persists in the face of scientific knowledge that is well understood and that clearly yields superior explanation and prediction.

In summary, there are two related senses of intuitive that we detect in current discussions. First, something may be intuitive in the sense that it is not based on abstract, schooled concepts that are subject to conscious reflection. This is the sense we seem to have in mind when we say that we really cannot explain why we have arrived at some conclusion because it is just intuitive. In this sense, we either have not—or cannot—identify the abstract, systemically organized principles or concepts that support our conclusion. Second, when we say that something is intuitive, we often mean that it has great allure and is hard to ignore. This is the sense we seem to have in mind when we say things like, "I know that logic tells me something else, but I have to follow my intuition that. . . ."

CHARACTERISTICS OF HISTORICAL KNOWLEDGE
AND INSTRUCTION

An important fact about accounts of the intuitive mind that we have touched on so far is that they have been proposed primarily in connection with knowledge about natural science. In this realm, the distinction between intuitive and schooled knowledge and the advantages of employing the latter are clear—at least relatively speaking. In the following, we explore another area of formal instruction where some of these distinctions—and some of this consensus—break down.

The area of knowledge and instruction we have in mind is history. History is a subject that is taught in schools around the world, yet it has been largely absent from discussions about cognition and instruction, including discussions about the intuitive mind (one exception is the edited volume by Carretero & Voss, 1994). Is this simply an oversight, or are there other, more motivated reasons for this lacuna? We believe the latter is the case and that this derives from the fact that historical knowledge is characterized by some properties not necessarily found in other areas of instruction.

The Narrative Organization of Knowledge
About History

The most important way that historical knowledge typically contrasts with knowledge about natural science concerns its narrative organization. The distinction we have in mind has been the focus of a great deal of discussion in the philosophy of history (e.g., Mink, 1978; White, 1987). Recently, Bruner (1986, 1990, 1996) formulated a distinction between paradigmatic and narrative knowing that bears directly on discussions of cognition and instruction.

To argue for the centrality of narrative knowledge in the case of history is not to say that there is no role for non-narrative forms of representation and knowledge. Authors such as White (1987) and Wertsch (1998) noted that other forms of representation, especially annals and chronicles, may play a role, and investigators such as Carretero, Jacott, Limón, Lopez-Manjón, and León (1994) argued that scientific forms of discussion and thinking may be the object of instruction. Nonetheless, a review of discussions about historical knowledge reveals that it is widely recognized as taking a narrative form and that this form contrasts in crucial ways with scientific or paradigmatic forms of thinking.

Studies in the humanities (e.g., Scholes & Kellogg, 1966) and the social sciences (e.g., Bruner, 1990; Polkinghorne, 1988) provide important insights into some of the complexities of narratives and narrative knowing. As Ricouer (1984) noted, a crucial property of narratives is that they grasp together what otherwise might appear to be disparate information into an organized whole of a certain sort. In the view of Mink (1978), "the cognitive function of narrative form . . . is not just to relate a succession of events but to body forth an ensemble of interrelationships of many different kinds as a single whole" (p. 144). Thus, the entreaty to remember the Alamo does not simply beckon us to recall who was there and what series of events happened, but also to keep in mind the complex political and moral messages and interrelationships bodied forth by the story as a whole.

The process of grasping information together in narrative knowing is characterized by a particular set of organizational principles—especially principles concerned with the facts that a narrative involves a plot and is organized around temporality. As White (1987) noted, a narrative is characterized by a well-marked beginning, middle, and end that achieves closure, a conclusion, and a resolution. It is also characterized by an identifiable narrative voice and a central subject. Furthermore, by emplotting events and actors, narratives assign them a meaning, or interpretation, and this meaning typically revolves around the intentions of individuals and groups. Thus, the meaning of the events that took place at Pearl Harbor on December 7, 1941, take on one meaning if they are emplotted as part of the unprovoked Japanese sneak attack story and quite a different meaning if they are emplotted in a narrative about Japanese concern with how the United States was attempting to cut off Japanese resources in the Pacific Ocean and thereby threaten the well-being of Japan (White, 1995).

The fact that narratives are organized around plots rather than structures of abstract conceptual knowledge does not mean that issues of formal instruction and schooled knowledge are not relevant to them. As authors such as Bruner (1996) noted, in addition to the development of skills in explanation associated with scientific theory, the goals of formal instruction include the development of skills for interpreting narrative texts in search of understanding, which is "the outcome of organizing and contextualizing essentially contestable, incompletely verifiable propositions in a disciplined way" (p. 90). Illustrations of how this applies to history instruction can be found in the research of Wineburg (1991), who examined how students critically evaluate claims by testing them against textual evidence.

Narrative Truth and Emplotment

However, even the most rigorous efforts at interpretation cannot address another major issue in historical representation: what Mink (1978) termed *narrative truth*. The relationship between the accuracy of individual statements included in a narrative and the narrative truth of the whole is a complex one. Mink rejected the assumption that narrative truth can be reduced to the logical conjunction of assertions included in a text. If this were the case, then "the truth-value of the text [would simply be] a logical function of the truth or falsity of the individual assertions taken separately: the conjunction is true if and only if each of the individual propositions is true" (Mink, 1978, pp. 143–144). In the view of Mink, such approaches amount to attempts to reduce narrative to what Bruner termed *paradigmatic knowing*. Specifically, Mink (1978) argued that such attempts reflect the efforts of "philosophers intent on comparing the form of narrative with the form of [scientific] theories, as if [narrative] were nothing but a logical conjunction of past-referring statements" (p. 144).

The notion (Mink, 1978) of narrative truth touches on an essential issue that makes clear the distinction between narrative knowing, such as that involved in history instruction, and paradigmatic, scientific explanation. Specifically, it touches on the fact that one and the same set of events can sometimes be legitimately and convincingly emplotted in alternative ways. Even when agreement has been reached that all the propositions in a text are adequately supported by evidence, there often remains more than one way to grasp these propositions together into a narrative whole. For example, in reviewing two historical treatments of the Dust Bowl in the American Southwest in the 1930s, Cronon (1992) noted that both take the same basic set of events into account, but one emplots these from the perspective of a tragedy and the other emplots them from the perspective of human victory over adversity.

Making this point in no way suggests that historians are at liberty to emplot information about historical events in any way they like. There is widespread agreement about procedures for determining what constitutes evidence to support a narrative interpretation, and it is often the case that a piece of evidence clearly disconfirms a narrative account that one might otherwise be tempted to use. Because understanding involves "organizing and contextualizing essentially contestable, incompletely verifiable propositions in a disciplined way" (Bruner, 1996, p. 90), the relationship between evidence and narrative interpretation is complex and open ended. However, such interpretation can—and must—be carried out in accordance with clear standards and objective evidence.

Goals of History Instruction

The points we have made about narrative truth, emplotment, and so forth are related to another major property of history instruction having to do with its goals. In contrast to subjects such as science and mathematics, the goals of history instruction extend beyond the mastery of intellectual content and instrumental rationality (Habermas, 1984) and touch on issues of citizenship and the creation and maintenance of nation-states. As FitzGerald (1979) noted:

> History textbooks for elementary and secondary schools are . . . essentially nationalistic histories. The first American-history text was written after the American Revolution, and because of it; and most texts are still accounts of the nation-state. [History textbooks] are written not to explore but to instruct—to tell children what their elders want them to know about their country. This information is not necessarily what anyone considers the truth of things. Like time capsules, the texts contain the truths selected for posterity. (p. 47)

What FitzGerald called "truths selected for posterity" are typically motivated by goals other than disinterested scholarly inquiry. As Anderson (1991) noted, instruction about history is one of the means that modern societies employ to create imagined communities, especially nation-states. Nation-states utilize a variety of means such as history textbooks, museums, commemorations, and maps to make it possible for groups to be able to think about the nation. From this perspective, the narratives that students are intended to take away from history instruction serve as essential cognitive instruments in the formation and reproduction of nation-states and their citizens.

This point is sometimes formulated in terms of national memory and identity. For example, Schlesinger (1992) argued that:

> [H]istory is to the nation rather as memory is to the individual. As an individual deprived of memory becomes disoriented and lost, not knowing where he has been or where he is going, so a nation denied a conception of its past will be disabled in dealing with its present and its future. As the means for defining national identity, history becomes a means for shaping history. (pp. 45–46)

In such discussions, it is widely assumed that identity is much more than a cognitive issue. For example, in his critique of what he perceived as attempts to disunite America, Schlesinger (1992) was not simply discussing a range of value-free ways to emplot the past. Instead, his comments about depriving a nation of its history were part of a heated debate over which narrative of the past of America should be reflected in new history standards and textbooks.

The parties involved in such debates take it for granted that some emplotment of the past must occur; in this way, they all recognize the role of narrative knowing in our understanding of history. The nature of their argument is over which emplotment is to be used, which story students' "elders want them to know about their country" (FitzGerald, 1979, p. 47). All this points to the fact that historical narratives are being asked to do more than serve as neutral cognitive instruments. Indeed, scholars of the cultural resources nation-states employ to reproduce themselves speak of the "*attachment* that people feel for the inventions of their imaginations," an attachment associated with the fact that "nations inspire love, and often profoundly self-sacrificing love" (Anderson, 1991, p. 141).

MASTERY AND APPROPRIATION

Issues of attachment to historical accounts are often discussed under the heading of *internalization*. As Wertsch (1993, 1998) argued, however, there are several problems with this term. The first and most general concerns the assumptions that the notion of internalization makes about boundaries between external and internal Cartesian spaces. For our present purposes, however, another equally important problem emerges— namely, most notions of internalization fail to distinguish between two crucial, and sometimes crucially different, processes in instruction and knowledge about history.

The distinction we have in mind is that between the mastery and appropriation of cultural tools (Wertsch, 1998). These notions are part of an account of mediated action (i.e., human action that is fundamentally characterized by an irreducible tension between active agents and the cultural tools they use to carry out action). Examples of *cultural tools* or *mediational means* (terms we use interchangeably) are "language; various systems for counting; mnemonic techniques; algebraic symbol systems; works of art; writing; schemes, diagrams, maps, and mechanical drawings; [and] all sorts of conventional signs" (Vygotsky, 1981, p. 137). From the perspective of mediated action, forms of action such as speaking, reasoning, and calculating inherently involve agents actively using cultural tools. In this view, the cultural tool does not act by itself, somehow mechanistically causing action (e.g., language does not produce utterances), but neither do agents act in isolation from cultural tools. Instead, the irreducible tension between active agents and cultural tools comprises a basic unit of analysis.

In our case, the origins of this line of reasoning are to be found in writings by Vygotsky (1987), Bakhtin (1986), and Zinchenko (1985), but it is also a line of reasoning that has emerged elsewhere from quite different theoretical traditions. For example, several investigators in cognitive science have arrived at strikingly similar conclusions. For instance, Clark (1997) spoke of the "embodied, embedded agent acting as an equal partner in adaptive responses which draw on the resources of mind, body, and world" (p. 47). Regardless of theoretical genealogy and terminology, the general point is that forms of human action such as speaking, solving multiplication problems, and using visual imaging software to design a new aircraft are interpreted in terms of an irreducible tension between active agent and cultural tool.

The cultural tool that is of interest to us as we examine historical knowledge is language in general and, more specifically, narratives. One of the basic properties of these narratives is that they are socioculturally situated. Rather than being universal and rather than being independently or spontaneously constructed by individuals, they reflect and shape specific sociocultural settings. As the earlier comments by FitzGerald (1979) and Schlesinger (1992) suggested, nation-states and other social groups are deeply invested in promulgating their own particular interpretation of history, and this interpretation may differ quite strikingly from that provided by others. Unlike the case with knowledge about natural science, then, there may be no strong tendency for knowledge about history—at least history as taught in schools—to converge on a universal, commonly accepted set of truths or interpretations.

From the perspective of mediated action, mastery and appropriation are constructs used to examine the complex relationship that may exist between agents and cultural tools. Instead of focusing on knowledge of history in abstraction from human action, the focus is on the uses that agents make of cultural tools such as the narratives they find in textbooks in specific sociocultural settings to represent the past.

There is a body of research that already exists on what we are calling *mastery*—namely, research on how students comprehend and remember historical narratives. For example, Beck and her colleagues (Beck & McKeown, 1994; Beck, McKeown, & Gromoll, 1989; Beck, McKeown, Sinatra, & Loxterman, 1991) carried out extensive analyses of history textbooks and of the understanding of fifth and eighth graders of particular events in American history that these textbooks cover (see Wertsch, 1998, for a review from the perspective of mediated action). Although there are some grounds for optimism, these authors noted that "the single most striking pattern . . . was the amount of confusion" (Beck & McKeown, 1994, p. 250) in students' understanding of important events in American history. Indeed, they reported that in some cases instruction seemed to have exacerbated this confusion and that mastery of a basic narrative about the American Revolution was less advanced after fifth-grade instruction than it had been before.

Findings about how certain narrative forms but not others can serve as effective cognitive instruments, or cultural tools from the perspective of mastery, are central to any complete account of cognition and instruction about history. It is impossible to think about the nation if one does not have cultural tools with adequate affordances (Wertsch, 1998) for doing so. However, mastery of even the best organized narrative about the past does not guarantee that this cultural tool will be used as intended, and this is where issues of appropriation arise. In our usage, *appropriation* is a translation of the Russian term *prisvoenie* used by Bakhtin (1979). A literal translation of this term would yield something like, "to bring something into oneself, to make something one's own." As we understand it, appropriation is a process of making something like a historical narrative one's own—of taking ownership of it. As such, it stands in opposition to resistance or rejection.

In many instances, the mastery of a cultural tool is closely linked to its appropriation; indeed, it is widely recognized that one of the best ways to help students master an idea, concept, or narrative is to give them some ownership of it (e.g., Dewey, 1938/1950). However, there are important instances in which these two dimensions of the relationship between agents and the cultural tools they employ do not coincide. Particularly striking cases of this can be found in totalitarian states, where schools were charged with the task of promulgating historical accounts that large segments of the population did not believe. As Tulviste and Wertsch (1994) and Wertsch (1998) noted in the case of Estonia, for example, individuals could sometimes demonstrate a high level of mastery of the official history narratives provided by Soviet era schools, but they often actively resisted these accounts or rejected them outright. Although they could reproduce these narratives and even use them with great facility in argumentation, they clearly had not made them their own.

Less striking, yet quite clear cases of how appropriation may not coincide with mastery can be found just about anywhere. For example, Wertsch and O'Connor (1994) found that, in recounting the origins of their country, a group of U.S. college students revealed quite similar levels of mastering the basic official narrative, but they varied somewhat in the degree to which they appropriated it. Some seemed to accept it without question, whereas others were ambivalent. Such evidence again points to the need to differentiate the mastery and appropriation of cultural tools such as narratives.

In these cases, the issue is not simply one of appropriating or resisting an official historical narrative that exists in isolation. Rather, such appropriation or resistance inevitably occurs in the context of a set of narrative accounts about the same events, and typically these accounts compete and even conflict with one another. Furthermore, these competing narratives typically derive from different sectors of sociocultural context. For example, the official Soviet historical accounts that were resisted by Estonians in the Tulviste and Wertsch (1994) study had been presented in schools, whereas the unofficial history, which Estonians appropriated, typically were based on discussions among family and friends.

INTUITIVE KNOWLEDGE ABOUT HISTORY

As noted earlier, intuitive knowledge has been discussed primarily in connection with natural science. However, in our account of historical knowledge, which we have framed in terms of mediated action, mastery, appropriation, and so forth, we have argued that notions of intuitive knowledge come into play for it as well. In this connection, we are particularly concerned with what we earlier called the allure of intuitive knowledge. In what follows, we explore the idea that certain aspects of historical knowledge, especially those developed during childhood—typically in informal learning settings—continue to have a kind of power over imagination even after learning more elaborated and well-documented historical accounts in formal instructional settings.

An example of the kind of dynamics we envision can be found in research by Wills (1994). Using year-long observations in three eighth-grade classrooms, he conducted extensive analyses of instruction in U.S. history, especially as it touched on the presentation of Native Americans. His study was motivated in part by the fact that new, multicultural history textbooks were being introduced into the formal instructional setting that he examined. These new materials were at the center of a great deal of debate, and the teachers in this study expressed a desire to harness them to present new views of Native Americans that "challenge rather than perpetuate stereotypes" (Wills, 1994, p. 280).

Much of the analysis by Wills (1994) focused on an assumption of mainstream American culture about how Native Americans should be represented in history. This assumption, which is supported by popular media and other means, is that "the Great Plains during westward movement is where Native Americans belong in American history" (Wills, 1994, p. 290). According to Wills (1994), there is an associated tendency to "situate Native Americans in a particular period of American history, confining their presence to the Great Plains while virtually ignoring their presence throughout the rest of American history" (p. 290). From the perspective of the narrative tools provided by the sociocultural setting, this means that

Native Americans tend to be given a minimal role in the overall plot, and it means that they tend not to be represented as active agents (Wertsch, 1998) when they do appear. Instead, they are bit players in a Eurocentric narrative about progress and westward expansion.

The tendency to take Great Plains Indians as representing all Native Americans at all periods of U.S. history has important implications for the narrative presentation of the past. In outlining these implications, Wills (1994) focused in particular on the issue of whether Native Americans are viewed as settled farmers or nomadic hunters. The difference becomes crucial in the context of the cultural tool employed to represent the past: a narrative that is basically organized around notions of progress, westward expansion, and the Quest for Freedom (Wertsch, 1998). If Native Americans are understood as nomadic hunters (a perspective that derives from focusing on the Great Plains Indians), then the consequences of European settlers pushing them off the land are not as problematic as they would be if they were understood as settled farmers. Assuming that they were nomadic hunters minimizes conflict with the basic narrative tool being used to understand the past. If it is argued that many Native Americans during European expansion were settled farmers, then the negative consequences of pushing them off the land are much greater in the sense that it is more difficult to overlook the direct contradiction between this action and a narrative generally organized around themes of progress and the quest for freedom.

Wills (1994) argued that the nomadic-hunter account of Native Americans is pervasive and privileged in American popular culture. Furthermore, he noted that it can be acquired in a variety of informal learning environments such as watching television and films. In contrast, the settled-farmer account of Native Americans is something that is being introduced through new scholarship and the use of new multicultural textbooks. It apparently is not readily acquired in everyday or informal-learning environments, instead requiring formal instruction.

A few additional observations made by Wills add important elements to this picture. First, the teachers were familiar with both the nomadic-hunter and the settled-farmer accounts of Native Americans. Second, they expressed a desire to focus on introducing their students to the settled-farmer account. Third, despite this expressed intention, they employed the nomadic-hunter representation on several crucial occasions in classroom discussion. Perhaps the most obvious case of this in the study was Ruth, who specifically told her students early in the school year, "Not all Indians were nomadic. They didn't all travel around and follow buffalo herds. Some of them farmed. And they needed chunks of land to farm on" (Wills, 1994, p. 281). Later in the school year, however, Ruth argued against a student's presentation of Native Americans as settled farmers, saying, "Most of [the Native Americans] did not farm, most of them traveled around. . . . So it wasn't like they [i.e., European settlers] went in and they uprooted these guys' houses and stuff" (Wills, 1994, p. 282).

The interpretation is that Ruth "seemed to have forgotten her comments on Native Americans . . . , emphasizing [their] nomadic character . . . and stressing that Native Americans did not believe one could own the land because they thought the land belonged to everyone" (Wills, 1994, p. 281). He viewed this switch from the settled-farmer representation to the popular image of Native Americans as buffalo-hunting nomads as a subtle attempt not to "upset the 'celebration' of American expansion and progress that is at the heart of the narrative of American history present in classroom lessons and curricular materials" (Wills, 1994, p. 282).

In summary, the analysis (Wills, 1994) identified two accounts of the past in these classroom discussions: one grounded in the assumptions of popular culture (what we term *popular history*) and one reflecting formal classroom instruction (what we term *formal history*). His analyses indicated that the teachers were quite familiar with both accounts. This does not mean, however, that the two accounts had equal status or arose in the same way in spoken or written discourse. The teachers expressed a desire to focus on the formal history, giving it a special status in their instructional goals. In contrast, popular history in this case seems to have been something the students—and the teacher—acquired without the aid of formal instruction.

CONCLUSION

The observations we have made about popular and formal history suggest some interesting parallels with intuitive and schooled knowledge about natural science. First, as is the case with intuitive knowledge about natural science, students seem to become acquainted with popular history without the help of formal instruction. This knowledge about popular history is what Wills (1994) had in mind when he pointed to the assumption of mainstream American culture that Great Plains Indians are a prototype of Native Americans in general and hence that Native Americans were basically nomadic hunters. Second, formal instruction seems to be the place where knowledge about formal history as well as formal science is developed. Third, formal instruction in both cases occurs in the context of—and often in competition with—intuitive knowledge. Indeed, formal instruction is often in a position of having to overcome the influence of intuitive knowledge. Students come to formal instruction about history already equipped with popular history narratives; as a result, this instruction often must be geared to refuting or overcoming the impact of these narratives. In the case examined by Wills (1994), the fact that Ruth felt compelled to state what the Plains Indians were not, coupled with her tendency to slip back into relying on popular history, are both indications of a deep familiarity with this account and its continuing allure.

Perhaps the most striking point about all this is that, even when individuals have mastered the formal history presented in school, there is a tendency to forget this account and fall back on the popular one. Like Wills, we are struck by the fact that, although Ruth was quite familiar with the formal historical account (indeed, professing a desire to teach it in an attempt to displace old stereotypes), she displayed a tendency to slip back into using the popular account. As in the case of intuitive knowledge about natural science phenomena, the allure of popular history may remain even when someone knows, and professes a preference for, a formal historical account.

All this leaves us with a set of questions about the relationship between popular history as we have outlined it, on the one hand, and intuitive knowledge and the intuitive mind, on the other. In our view, popular history is similar to intuitive knowledge about natural phenomena in at least three ways: (a) both develop without the support of formal instruction; (b) both provide a context in which formal instruction occurs and schooled knowledge emerges; and (c) both continue to have a kind of allure in the face of formal knowledge. The first and third of these parallels correspond with the two basic senses of intuitive knowledge outlined earlier; the second has major implications for how history instruction might be formulated on sounder theoretical foundations. The second has also been the object of a great deal of research on science instruction, where a growing body of research attempts to specify how teachers can foster change from certain common intuitive concepts toward their counterpart schooled concepts. An example are the Dykstra et al. (1992) educational interventions aimed at transforming intuitive student conceptions of the relationship between force and motion into the schooled conception. Parallel research could involve the design and evaluation of educational interventions aimed at fostering change from common popular history narratives to their counterpart formal history narratives.

These parallels point to a set of issues that call out for further discussion. At the same time, however, we would emphasize that we see an important difference between knowledge about history and knowledge about natural science. This is the essential difference between narrative and paradigmatic knowing (Bruner, 1990). Hence, in addition to the parallels we have outlined, we believe a complete picture would have to take into account the distinct properties of cognition in these two domains. The fact that narratives are organized around temporality, emplotment, and human intention makes narratives, as well as their mastery and appropriation, different in essential ways from knowledge about natural phenomena. Hence, the parallels outlined herein need to be elaborated in the context of a framework that also recognizes the unique properties of cognition in the two domains. The resulting picture will undoubtedly go well beyond what studies from any single perspective have attempted to date.

REFERENCES

Anderson, B. (1991). *Imagined communities: Reflections on the origin and spread of nationalism*. London: Verso.

Astington, J. W. (1995). *The child's discovery of the mind*. Cambridge, MA: Harvard University Press.

Bakhtin, M. M. (1979). *Estetika slovesnogo tvorchestva* [The aesthetics of verbal creation]. Moscow: Iskusstvo.

Bakhtin, M. M. (1986). *Speech genres and other late essays* (C. Emerson & M. Holquist, Eds., V. W. McGee, Trans.). Austin: University of Texas Press.

Beck, I. L., & McKeown, M. G. (1994). Outcomes of history instruction: Paste-up accounts. In M. Carretero & J. F. Voss (Eds.), *Cognitive and instructional processes in history and the social sciences* (pp. 237–256). Hillsdale, NJ: Lawrence Erlbaum Associates.

Beck, I. L., McKeown, M. G., & Gromoll, E. W. (1989). Learning from social studies texts. *Cognition and Instruction, 6*(2), 99–158.

Beck, I. L., McKeown, M. G., Sinatra, G. M., & Loxterman, J. A. (1991). Revising social studies text from a text-processing perspective: Evidence of improved comprehensibility. *Reading Research Quarterly, 26*(3), 251–276.

Bruner, J. (1986). *Actual minds, possible worlds*. Cambridge, MA: Harvard University Press.

Bruner, J. (1990). *Acts of meaning*. Cambridge, MA: Harvard University Press.

Bruner, J. (1996). *The culture of education*. Cambridge, MA: Harvard University Press.

Carey, S., & Spelke, E. (1994). Domain-specific knowledge and conceptual change. In E. Hirschfeld & S. Gelman (Eds.), *Mapping the mind* (pp. 72–91). New York: Cambridge University Press.

Carretero, M., & Voss, J. F. (Eds.). (1994). *Cognitive and instructional processes in history and the social sciences*. Hillsdale, NJ: Lawrence Erlbaum Associates.

Carretero, M., Jacott, L., Limón, M., Lopez-Manjón, A., & León, J. A. (1994). Historical knowledge: Cognitive and instructional implications. In M. Carretero & J. F. Voss (Eds.), *Cognitive and instructional processes in history and the social sciences* (pp. 56–73). Hillsdale, NJ: Lawrence Erlbaum Associates.

Clark, A. (1997). *Being there: Putting brain, body, and world together again*. Cambridge, MA: MIT Press.

Confrey, J. (1989). A review of the research on student conceptions in mathematics, science, and programming. In C. Cazden (Ed.), *Review of research in education* (pp. 3–56). Washington, DC: American Educational Research Association.

Cronon, W. (1992). A place for stories: Nature, history, and narrative. *The Journal of American History, 78*(4), 1347–1376.

Dewey, J. (1938/1950). *Experience and education*. New York: Macmillan.

Dykstra, D. I., Boyle, C. F., & Monarch, I. A. (1992). Studying conceptual change in learning physics. *Science Education, 76*(6), 615–652.

FitzGerald, F. (1979). *America revised: History schoolbooks in the twentieth century*. New York: Vintage Books.

Habermas, J. (1984). *The theory of communicative action: Vol. 1. Reason and the rationalization of society* (T. McCarthy, Trans.). Boston: Beacon.

Keil, F. (1989). *Concepts, kinds, and cognitive development*. Cambridge, MA: MIT Press.

Lewis, E. L., Stern, J. L., & Linn, M. C. (1993, January). The effect of computer simulations on introductory thermodynamics understanding. *Educational Technology, 14,* 45–58.

Lewis, E. L., & Linn, M. C. (1994). Heat energy and temperature concepts of adolescents, adults, and experts: Implications for curricular improvements. *Journal of Research in Science Teaching, 31*(6), 657–677.

Mink, L. O. (1978). Narrative form as a cognitive instrument. In R. H. Canary & H. Kozicki (Eds.), *The writing of history: Literary form and historical understanding* (pp. 129–149). Madison: University of Wisconsin Press.

Polkinghorne, D. E. (1988). *Narrative knowing and the human sciences*. New York: State University of New York Press.

Posner, G. J., Strike, K. A., Hewson, P. W., & Gertzog, W. A. (1982). Accommodation of a scientific conception: Toward a theory of conceptual change. *Science Education, 66*(2), 211–227.

Reif, F., & Larkin, J. H. (1991). Cognition in scientific and everyday domains: Comparison and learning implications. *Journal of Research in Science Teaching, 28*(9), 733–760.

Resnick, L. B. (1987). Learning in school and out. *Educational Researcher, 16,* 13–20.

Ricouer, P. (1984). *Time and narrative* (K. McLaughlin & D. Pelauer, Trans.). Chicago: University of Chicago Press.

Schlesinger, A. M., Jr. (1992). *The disuniting of America: Reflections on a multicultural society*. New York: Norton.

Scholes, R., & Kellogg, R. (1966). *The nature of narrative*. London: Oxford University Press.

Tulviste, P., & Wertsch, J. V. (1994). Official and unofficial histories: The case of Estonia. *Journal of Narrative and Life History, 4*(4), 311–329.

Vygotsky, L. S. (1981). The instrumental method in psychology. In J. V. Wertsch (Ed.), *The concept of activity in Soviet psychology* (pp. 134–143). Armonk, NY: M. E. Sharpe.

Vygotsky, L. S. (1987). *The collected works of L. S. Vygotsky: Volume 1. Problems of general psychology. Including the Volume Thinking and speech* (N. Minick, Ed. & Trans.). New York: Plenum.

Wertsch, J. V. (1993). Commentary on J. A. Lawrence & J. Valsiner, "Conceptual roots of internalization: From transmission to transformation." *Human Development, 36*(3), 168–171.

Wertsch, J. V. (1998). *Mind as action*. New York: Oxford University Press.

Wertsch, J. V., & O'Connor, K. (1994). Multivoicedness in historical representation: American college students' accounts of the origins of the United States. *Journal of Narrative and Life History, 4*(4), 295–309.

White, G. M. (1995). Mythic history and national memory: The Pearl Harbor anniversary. *Culture & Psychology, 3*(1), 63–88.

White, H. (1987). *The content of the form: Narrative discourse and historical representation*. Baltimore, MD: Johns Hopkins University Press.

Wills, J. (1994). Popular culture, curriculum, and historical representation: The situation of Native Americans in American history and the perpetuation of stereotypes. *Journal of Narrative and Life History, 4*(4), 277–294.

Wineburg, S. S. (1991). On the reading of historical texts: Notes on the breach between school and academy. *American Educational Research Journal, 28,* 495–519.

Zinchenko, V. P. (1985). Vygotsky's ideas about units of analysis for the analysis of mind. In J. V. Wertsch (Ed.), *Culture, communication, and cognition: Vygotskian perspectives* (pp. 94–118). New York: Cambridge University Press.

CHAPTER FOUR

Children's Intuitive Understandings of Pictures

Norman H. Freeman
University of Bristol, UK

Michael J. Parsons
Ohio State University

Art remains one of our more mysterious activities. Philosophers continue to argue whether the significant qualities of artworks lie more in the intentions of the artist, the work, or the mind of the viewer. Individual artworks are notoriously ambiguous, and interpretations of them can differ greatly, often varying with culture, age, or education.

This presents problems to teachers. If, as we believe, the primary aim of art education is to teach an understanding of art, then it helps to know something of how students currently understand art. The thesis of this chapter is that children develop an intuitive theory of art as they grow up. They do this in an attempt to make sense of the domain, with all its complexities, and their intuitive theories respond to the nature of the domain. The chapter offers an analysis of intuitive theories of visual art by learners, with the hope that it will be useful to teachers.

An account of intuitive theories of art by learners is difficult to construct for several reasons. One reason is that art is complex. Theories of visual art must account for at least four different elements—the picture, what it pictures, the artist, and the viewer—and organize the relations among them. We offer a map of these elements later. A second reason is that artworks, like people but in their own peculiar way, trigger emotional responses even when the viewer cannot explain why. How they do so is a standard philosophical question. Our view is that an understanding of art is related to an understanding of people and their states of mind. A third reason is that a satisfactory mastery of the relations constituting the domain requires an awareness of one's own interpretive role as a viewer. That awareness is not easily achieved. Our account tracks the growth of this awareness.

In what follows, we discuss general intuitions about visual art by learners (i.e., their *framework theory*, their general worldview of possibilities in a domain, to use the notion of Wellman, 1990). This requires two kinds of tasks. One is to map the domain and the relations that any theory must try to coordinate. The other is to describe some of the typical intuitive conceptions that learners come to hold and in what sequences. The map helps one describe these conceptions and explain in what way they develop and become more complex. Our suggestion is that learners take a long time to work out a theory of art, and for most people that theory remains intuitive and largely unarticulated. If it were articulated and spelled out fully, it would be equivalent to a philosophy of art, covering much of the ground that philosophers of art normally cover.

In short, our topic is the development of the way learners interpret artworks: the elements and relations they attempt to coordinate, the assumptions they use to make sense of art, the sources and resources they call on, and the consequent kinds of understandings at which they arrive. We put together two analyses of the development of intuitive theories of art, each approaching the topic from a different angle. One analysis (Freeman, 1995) emphasized the domain involved, the elements that the learner has to coordinate in a theory of art. This analysis conceived a picture as lying at the center of a network of relations that involve an artist, a viewer, and something outside the picture (the world). In the case of a representational picture, that world is the scene represented. Freeman (1995) argued that children normally seem to acquire sufficient insight into the relations among these four elements to launch a conceptual revolution somewhere around middle childhood. The other analysis (Parsons, 1987) emphasized the increasingly reflective character of intuitive theories as they develop and their increasing insightfulness. The responses of a learner to art focus on different elements of the art situation in a predictable pattern. This basic pattern can be summarized as a focus first on the subject matter of the picture (Freeman's world), then on the artist, and finally on the self as viewer. In the most typical sequence, children interpret artworks first in terms of the world represented. Later they appeal to the expressive intentions of the artist. After that they become aware of their own interpretative activity as viewers (Parsons, 1987). This progression is one of increasing cognitive complexity and also, normatively, one of increasing adequacy to the artworks (i.e., it leads to better interpretations). In summary, where Freeman (1995) tended to focus on the breadth of the domain to be learned, Parsons (1987) tended to focus on the depth of thinking involved in learning about art. The two approaches seem to need each other.

THE DOMAIN OF ART

If the aim is to characterize learners' theory of a domain, it is helpful to start with an account of the domain. This is especially true when the domain is as complex as is art.

The concept of art applies to diverse cases. It extends from the cheap end of a working sketch to the expensive end of a fine art masterwork. The diversity creates problems. How do we compare a scribble with a Rembrandt self-portrait? Realistic with abstract works? Are photographs different in an important way from water colors? Is a roadmap a sort of picture? As children grow up they acquire particular ideas for deciding what is art and what is not, categorizing artworks, and evaluating genres and iconographies, and all these are influenced by the particular artistic traditions in which they grow up. They encounter a particular set of pictures within the total possible diversity, and that set influences their particular conceptions of art. If we are to describe their conceptions and the changes in them, we need a more general account of the possibilities—an abstract map of the domain as a whole—in which to locate their particular conceptions.

Our theory of the possibilities takes a functional form. We agree with Schier (1986), who argued that pictures can trigger the recognition of an appearance. Appearances greatly interest children, and much of the literature in philosophical aesthetics concerns what can be said about appearances. With this view, pictures are representations of things that have an appearance. By *appearance*, we mean appearance to someone. In formal terms, our view is that depiction is the representation of things that have a visual appearance by using a medium to display a visual appearance.

If pictures are representations, misunderstandings are always possible because no picture can give a full visual replication of something not itself. A full visual replication of the Duke of Wellington would need that gentleman to step forward in person. The gap between the appearance of the picture and the reality represented is one reason that picturing is always capable of reinterpretation. The same gap makes it difficult for children to develop a satisfactory theory of pictures. They have to think through the structure of appearances that seem at once to match and not to match. The temptation, especially at the beginning, is to forget about the artist and the viewer and to look for a simple match between the appearance of the picture and the appearance of the scene. However, there cannot be a simple match between them. The match must be filtered first through the mind of the artist and then through that of the viewer. To see the importance of that, let us consider one of the most influential discussions of the idea of representation.

Goodman (1976) wrote: "If I tell you I have a photograph of a certain black horse, and then I produce a snapshot in which he has come out a light speck in the distance, you can hardly convict me of lying, but you may well feel that I misled you" (p. 29). Imagine you were a patron commissioning a picture of the horse. What grounds would you have for complaint? You might complain that Goodman's horse was too far away from the camera to make a recognizable picture–world match. Goodman would smile and hand you a close-up in which all you see is a patch of hide. To settle your commission, you would have to negotiate a viewing distance with Goodman in advance that would show you the horse as a horse. That is the traditional, and usually taken for granted, solution to the problem of saying what sort of picture–horse match is being commissioned.

In your negotiations with Goodman, your demands would be prompted by your need to bring your recognitional capacities of real horses into line with your scrutiny of the photo. You may consciously focus on the distance between the camera and the horse, but you also put yourself center stage. You may think you have only a picture–world relation to complain about or perhaps a set of picture–world–camera (i.e., artist) relations, but you must also include yourself, the viewer, and your own interpretation. Your negotiation, fully articulated, cannot be confined to only the picture–world–artist terms, but must include the viewer. What unifies these four terms in this illustration is an expectation that the artist should make it possible for you to manage the relation between your recognitions of the picture and the world. Your disappointment may be traced to a feeling that the artist took liberties with some sort of unspoken artist–viewer communicative contract. So he did, and much of the interest of art comes from the extension of our vision as artists play tricks with our communicative expectations.

This scheme is not peculiar to pictures. It applies to all communicative systems. For instance, Heal (1978) said this about language: "When noises have meaning they do not only have distinctive relations with human beings who use them or respond to them but also distinctive connections with some . . . states of affairs . . . in the world" (p. 367). In short, recognizing a representation requires a viewer to classify a picture as intended by an artist to picture something particular (Harrison, 1997). Our theory of pictures centers on pictorial functions: on what pictures can do for viewers under a variety of conditions. The result is that any satisfactory theory of pictorial display must encompass four terms and their relations: artist, viewer, picture, and world. Figure 4.1 shows that net of relations. There are six relations in it, denoted by lines between the boxes. A picture that is of some subject is directed at a viewer and about (expressive of) the

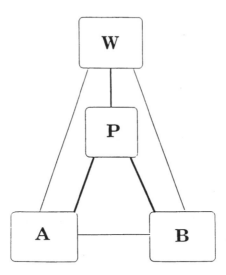

FIG. 4.1. The net of relations that constrains the assumptions of learners about pictures. P is the picture, W is the world, A is the artist, and B is the beholder or viewer.

attitude of the artist toward the subject (Freeman & Sanger, 1995). Because of the complexity of this net, we should expect to find great unevenness in pictorial reasoning as learners try to coordinate their inferences over these relations. No educator need be apologetic about working with learners on such intricate reasoning even in the face of the contemporary hegemony of the sciences.

MESSING WITH THE NET

We have already suggested that part of the creativity of art lies in the efforts of artists to disturb some of the relations of this net. For most of the 20th century, many artists have tried to eliminate one of the terms of this map. Let us briefly look at what happens to pictorial reasoning when intuitive theories are defied in this way. This may shed some light on the difficulties children face when they are not yet able to coordinate one or more of these terms.

The first example is abstract expressionism. The basic idea of abstract expressionism was to strip representation out of painting—to remove the world element of the net. Reactions to such paintings were diverse. Some called them bold and dramatic, or spare and delicate; others found them unintelligible. It is still difficult for many viewers to see why they are artworks. When the Australian National Gallery bought "Blue Poles" by Jackson Pollock, it caused outrage. The general public held that it was the sort of thing that appears when one paints a barn door carelessly. The attempt by the artist to represent nothing rendered the artistry invisible, and viewers had nowhere for their concept of art to grip.

Another kind of case, the *objet trouvé*, omits the artist by starting with the natural world. It is, in principle, possible for a hyperactive ant to leave a pattern on the sand that looks like Winston Churchill (see Putnam, 1981). The pattern on the sand is a natural kind produced by a force of nature. Here the role of the artist is eliminated and the conceptual net collapses. It can be repaired only by someone willing to claim the role of artist and thereby turn the sand pattern into a picture. One could, for instance, take a cast or photo of the sand pattern and put it on display. The display of such objects in art galleries relies on the ambiguity between attributing responsibility to the natural producer and to the eye of the artist. It is no accident that Damien Hirst's shark framed in a tank and Carl Andre's unframed bricks challenge the hard-won reasoning of a vast section of the viewing public. The challenge is to believe that there is a representation at all.

In yet another kind of case, some forms of performance art, in which the artist steps into the place of the artwork, leave the work itself—that is, the medium—invisible to the viewer. Again, the response may be anyone could do that. The general point is that our intuitive theories require all four terms if we are to make sense of representations.

THE EARLY ROOTS OF UNDERSTANDING REPRESENTATION

What is the origin, developmentally, of the notion of representation? Young children obviously do not start already equipped with it. When children in nursery school are given crayons and paper, they experiment with them eagerly, but they are usually more interested in the process of making marks on the paper than in what the marks look like when they have finished. They will try different crayons, different movements, different colors. They enjoy the activity for itself, as they enjoy running. However, they will end it abruptly in favor of other activities and, characteristically, they do not pay much attention to the results. They do not appear to think of the marks they make as representations.

In this situation, an adult may point to some marks on the paper and ask: "What is this?" One way in which young scribblers assign representational significance to their work is enactive. They may use a marker as a pretend rabbit, say, and make it hop across the paper, leaving traces that are a record of the hopping, rather like footprints made by running (see Freeman, 1993; Gardner & Wolf, 1987). This is obviously an early structure, not yet at the level where attention is on the appearance of the marks on the paper and what they might represent pictorially.

When the idea of picturing is secure—a developmental achievement—children can often say in advance what they are going to draw. In an intermediate case, children will offer interpretations of the marks after the fact. Even when an independent observer cannot tell what the scribbles represent, children may be ready to do this. It is interesting that, when the child has not expressed a representational intent in advance and is questioned about the whole drawing (What is this?), interpretations are not so common. Sometimes, of course, a child will go along with the question, inventing answers as they come to mind: This is a house. And this is Mom. But often enough no answer is forthcoming. Adi-Japha, Levin, and Solomon (1997) elicited many interpretations when they pointed to a part of the scribble and asked what that part was. Not all parts elicited interpretations to an equal extent: Smooth lines were mostly ineffectual, but inflected and broken lines were powerful stimuli. One conclusion is that the act of making an inflection in a line involves some investment of attention, and this primed a (short-lived) willingness to make an act of representational interpretation. There was no inflection advantage when the children were asked about other people's scribbles or about their own scribbles after a long delay.

Once, before the cognitive revolution of the 1960s, it was common to disapprove of the adult "What is it?" question because it might impose adult conceptions on the natural creative activity of the child. Nowadays, we would approve it because it helps the child construct some basic ideas that are fundamental to understanding art. One such idea is that the child has produced something that is finished—a product that is meant to be looked at or perhaps put on display. This is a root of the idea of a *work of art*. Another idea is that the marks on the paper represent something. This is the beginning of the idea that artworks are meaningful—that they are more than pieces of paper with marks on them. They are about something; they are representations. They must be understood and require interpretation, intuitive or reflective. Of course, they do not have to picture something to be about it. They do not, as sentences do, carry propositions about the world that can be judged true or false. However, they do have meaning as artworks, using their own medium and requiring to be understood in their own terms. This is quite compatible with having an emotional content. Indeed pictures can be vehicles for the expression of emotion just because they are meaningful. The emotional content may be (part of) what they are about.

All of this has its beginning in the "What is this?" question—a question that puts the emphasis on the picture–world relation. We have already said that interpretations of children generally are shaped by an awareness of the picture in relation to, sequentially, the world, the artist, and the viewer. This is where the picture–world relation begins. In our culture, we have several ways of speaking and thinking about art that reflect the three emphases (world, artist, and viewer) or sets of relations within the net. These ways of speaking overlap variously but can be distinguished from each other. Children learn to use these ways of speaking and thinking, and this learning promotes their growing awareness of the relations within the net. In other words, intuitive theories of art by children are spurred by their encounters with various ways of speaking about art. "What is this?" is usually the first such encounter.

We focus on the acquisition of three basic ways of speaking about art in our culture—three ways that capture the picture's relation with the world, the artist, and the viewer. In sequence, these are talk about (a) picturing and the beauty of the pictured, (b) expression and the intentions of the artist, and (c) judgment and the interpretation by the viewer. These ways of speaking are central in understanding art, and virtually everyone in our culture learns them at some level.

Moreover, they have to do with more than art. They play a part in our understanding of self and society as well as art. Understanding art is always about understanding more than art because art is about the fundamental themes just suggested—about beauty, identity, and states of mind. Understanding art is especially important today because of the increasingly important role of visual materials in our society. Visual images, usually presented in the context of words, surround us in quantities and forms that never existed before—in books, photographs, advertisements, movies, televisions, on the computer screen, and through the Internet. Reality comes to us increasingly mediated through visual forms. We learn who we are and how we relate to each other increasingly through a combination of visual images and texts. This makes it seem inevitable that art will increasingly become more important in the school curriculum.

THE PICTURE–WORLD RELATION

It is not difficult to gain evidence about the assumptions about pictures by children. Turner (1983) took a group of 14-year-olds to the Tate Gallery. They were unanimous in disliking "Pool of London" by Derain. It is a fauvist work, in which liberal use was made of non-naturalistic colors.

The children judged that Derain was not accurate in his colors. In their eyes, the picture did not respect visual facts about the scene, and they blamed the artist with some vigor.

Consider also the opinions of twelve 11-year-olds, a group of children studied by Freeman and Sanger (1995). The children were asked whether an ugly thing would make a worse picture than a pretty thing. They were almost unanimous: 10 out of 12 said that if you painted something ugly the picture would be bad because it would be an ugly picture. It may be significant that these children were rural islanders and had had little art training. They were some 3 years behind metropolitan children in their views about art (see Freeman, 1995). The general point is that all learners, and particularly young children, have a tendency to focus on the picture–world relation. This results in the preference for realistic works and also the location of the beauty of a picture in its subject matter.

Beauty plays a particularly significant role in the thinking of younger children about art. In the interviews of Freeman and Sanger (1995), the children were asked, not whether the picture would turn out uglier or prettier, but whether it would turn out better or worse. It was the children who conflated quality with beauty. This conflation appears to be characteristic of early developmental views.

Consider the following semistructured interview partly reported in Parsons (1987). Debbie, who was 13 years old, strongly disliked a work by Ivan Albright, entitled "Into the World Came a Soul Called Ida." She thought it very ugly. We do not reproduce the picture here; instead, let us try to glimpse it through Debbie's eyes.

When she was asked to describe the picture, Debbie said:

> There's a lady sitting in a chair, with her legs exposed, they're bare and they're really ugly. They've got bumps all over them and she's sitting there with a powder puff in one hand and a mirror in the other and I guess she's doing her make-up. . . . And she's. . . . I don't know, she's got fabric all over the floor. She's not dressed very nicely. She sort of looks like a witch.
> [What do you think the theme or subject of the painting is?]
> A lady doing her make-up, I don't know.
> [Is she a young woman?]
> No, she's middle-aged—no, a little older.
> [What's the feeling in this painting?]
> I don't like it.
> [Why not?]
> I don't know, it's just the legs are getting on my nerves.
> [What's the feeling in the painting?]
> She looks like she's totally bored with everything. And she's just sitting there, putting on her make-up. You know, "Who cares?"

[Why do you suppose the painter painted it?]

He was angry with his mother-in-law [laughs]. I don't know . . . I don't know, he just felt like it. He saw some lady going down the street and he said: "She looks sickening.". . . . He was angry at her for some reason.

[Is this a subject you'd expect a painter to choose?]

No.

[Why?]

Well, if a painter was going to paint something—most painters paint beautiful women, or they really look nice in beautiful surroundings, and this just—it so contrasts with that.

[It's not a beautiful painting?]

I don't think so. (Parsons, 1987, p. 41)

It seems that Debbie assumes that the subject matter of a work—that part of the world that is represented—determines the character of the work. The Albright is ugly because it represents something that is ugly. She is aware of the artist but sees that role as limited to choosing what to represent. She may have some conception that that choice was determined by the anger of the artist. Even so, the role of the artist is limited only to the choice of sitter: He felt angry and so he chose to depict someone ugly. In short, Debbie channels her response primarily through consideration of the subject matter. She is also in possession of some assumptions about the artist. The rural children of Freeman and Sanger (1995), who were subject dominated too, also had some recognition of the expressivity of an artist. When asked whether the feelings of an artist determine picture quality, 9 out of 12 said that it did.

Like Debbie, they seemed not to be aware of their own role as viewers in shaping their responses. When asked whether the feelings of a viewer determine how they evaluate a picture, 9 out of 12 of the islander children denied it. Debbie articulated some common values—should we call them prejudices?—about beauty and ugliness, especially with respect to women, and she took them as if they were facts. She spoke of beauty and ugliness as if they were facts that she perceived, rather than value judgments that she had constructed. She assumed that what she said was a description and not an interpretation. She had learned these values from the culture in which she grew up, but she had no sense of that. In short, she was not aware of her interpretive role as the viewer.

The concepts that learners use when responding to artworks are fairly difficult ones. The concept of representation is difficult. Debbie and most of the rural children seem to treat it as if it were the same as resemblance—as if ugliness passed from the subject matter to the picture in some unmediated fashion. With respect to the role of the artist, we saw a glimmer of an appeal to it in Debbie's transcript, although she mentioned the artist primarily as relating to the subject matter. With respect to a conception of the viewer, there was no glimmer at all, no sense that ugliness was in the eye of Debbie.

THE FIGURE OF THE ARTIST

We have seen that the 11-year-olds in the study of Freeman and Sanger (1995) tended to search the subject matter (the external world) for an answer. A group of 14-year-olds had a different answer: Nine out of 12 of them assumed that the artist was the responsible agent, beautifying a picture by her skills and enthusiasm regardless of the subject. That view rests on a more complex coordination of elements of the net. In another transcript from an interview, from Parsons (1987), we see how a learner struggles with the figure of the artist. She uses a way of speaking that casts an artwork as an expression of the artist. The assumption is that the artist is intentionally expressing some thought or feeling and that this expression is the key to understanding the work. In this case, the artist (rather than the external world) is responsible for the way the work looks. It follows that many of the details are there for a reason of the artist and are a part of the meaning of the work. This leads one to examine the details in a different way to discover the meaning.

Consider how Wendy (16 years old) talked about the Albright, the same work that Debbie described:

[Would you describe what you see here?]

I see a woman who is way past her prime of life. . . . She looks like she's mourning for her lost beauty. You can tell when she was younger she was probably fairly pretty.

[How can you tell?]

Because I don't think that people that aren't pretty worry much about their looks. Just by her features and stuff you can tell, given that all her wrinkles were gone. . . . She's not admiring herself at all. It's kind of like: harsh reality dawns. It's pathetic, because she's wearing this pink silk thing and the high heel shoes, and she's just disgusting.

[So there's a contrast between the clothes she's wearing and her physical aspect?]

Yeah. But the lingerie and the shoes she's wearing are dumpy too. They're old like she is.

[Anything else that points to her oldness?]

Yeah, things seem run down. The top of the table is nice but things seem run down. . . . Is that a piece of paper burned on the floor? The flowers are dead. . . .

[What is the subject of the painting?]

It tries to put across the thing with beauty and it's all so superficial. You get old and it's putting across the pointlessness of the whole looks thing, the obsession with beauty.

[Is that a good subject for a painting?]

I like it because I think that this painting definitely does have a lesson to it. I mean, I can picture her 30 years earlier sitting in the same chair, doing the same thing and being absolutely beautiful, because she has such a woeful expression. I admire the painter, if that's what he was trying to put across, for seeing through that, because it's hard for people to do. I mean they know it but everyone is as guilty as the next person as being vain or concerned about how people look.

Here we see that interpreting the work in terms of the intentions of the artist encourages Wendy to search the work and its details for their significance, the flowers on the table, and the burnt paper on the floor. That was something that Debbie, who channeled her thinking through the appearance of Ida, did not do. Wendy is also able to imaginatively reconstruct the state of mind of Ida, principally by scrutinizing the facial expression and gestures and simulating how she would feel if she had that expression and those gestures. This enables her to empathize with Ida rather than reject her. The result is that Wendy can find an overall message in the work: "the pointlessness of the whole looks thing, the obsession with beauty."

Another example comes from Henry, an undergraduate, who could not quite make sense of "La Cirque" by Chagall but was sure that the artist intended a meaning. He was not as successful as Wendy in this instance, but he had the same assumptions and strategies:

Well, OK, you've got all the performers and everything else—but I think it has a deeper meaning than simply it being a circus. I get the sense that it isn't quite even close to being a circus. Such as this violin, or bass, with a bird's head and wings, the candelabra, the two-faced figure—that's different—the head on the bottom of the figure with the women's head on top. This doesn't represent anything you can say.

[Why are all those things there, do you think?]

That's—I think he's trying to say something about the circus itself, but I can't pick out exactly what he is saying from it.

[It is complicated.]

OK, there's something in here he's trying to say with the juggler, or whatever, with the head. In fact it looks as if he's juggling his own head there. And the colours, too. The audience in the background is more of a muted, darker blue-purple colour, whereas the performers are in colours that kind of stand out from the rest of the audience and everything else. . . . (Parsons, 1987, pp. 98–99)

Henry here, like Wendy, examines particular passages of the work and asks what the artist intended by them. He talks as if it is the same thing to speak of the intention of the artist and to speak of the work itself. It is worth noticing that this way of speaking suggests that the artist is deliberately expressing something and is therefore aware of what he is trying to express. Henry speaks as if the artist has particular intentions for particular passages. He also speaks as if the artist is ahistorical, not significantly affected by his own history or culture, knowing not only what he wants to say but also freely choosing the means of saying it. In effect, Henry thinks of the artist as being very like himself, so that to decipher the intentions of the artist, Henry imagines what he, Henry, would have meant by a particular passage. In other words, Henry is unaware that what an artist expresses may be shaped by his historical or cultural background, as is, for example, the response by Chagall to the oppression of the Jews huddled in a shtetl. Henry shows, too, no awareness of the possibility that an artist may not be aware of what is expressed in his work.

This ahistorical view is cognitively simpler than a historically informed one. For to think of the artist as significantly shaped by historical and cultural influences implies a difference from oneself. Neither Henry nor Wendy speak as if they are aware of the influences that shape their own attitudes and influence their interpretations. In fact, neither one acknowledges their own activity as a viewer despite the intensity they invest in that activity. They have mastered a way of speaking that acknowledges the role of the artist in constructing the meaning of a work but not that of the viewer.

AWARENESS OF THE RELATIONS OF THE SELF

To become aware of one's own interpretative activity requires one to realize that the character of one's response to a work is partly a function of one's own particular situation. Such a realization amounts to abandoning the belief that one can get the meaning of a picture simply by seeing what there is to be seen or consulting the intentions of the artist.

An example comes from an interview with Donna, an undergraduate. Parts of Donna's reactions to the Albright seem very like the reactions of Wendy. When trying to figure out the state of mind of Ida, she said:

> She looks like she wants to be—it's almost like she's here but wants to be there, where—I don't know how to explain it—where she wants to be beautiful and have the characteristics of beauty, and is kind of forlorn because she realises they've gone. Perhaps one time she had them and can't accept the fact that she no longer does. I don't know why I think that. There is just

almost like a forlorn look on her face and the way she has got the powder
puff. (Parsons, 1987, pp. 133–134)

Unlike Wendy, when asked why she interprets it that way, Donna talked
of her own interpretative bias:

I refuse to think of the fact that I am over twenty. I'm surprised when I
realise I am. But I think it's human nature to want what we don't have.
Maybe it [the Albright] is a general statement that there's always forlorn-
ness.
    [You see that in the painting?]
    That's the way I would interpret it, maybe.
    [You are interpreting it?]
    Yeah, I am. And I'm trying to figure out if I know—if I know somebody
like this or if it's just me. I kind of think it's me. I'm reacting to that very personally, and I think that's because I am where I am in my life, and I resent
the fact that my life is half over and I feel like I'm nine years old, just getting
discovered. I don't want to be there, and maybe that's what I'm seeing in
that. That's my frustration right now. (Parsons, 1987, pp. 133–134)

A related recognition is that different people may make different interpretations depending on their individual character and experiences. For
example, Dorothy, an undergraduate, saw "Head of a Man" by Paul Klee
as being about masculinity and femininity, but she was not sure how others would see it. She said:

Femininity and masculinity just seem to, you know, stand out, but [Paul
Klee] really didn't take a position either way. So, you know, I'm a girl and I
notice the femininity part first. I'm sure if a guy came in he would notice the
masculinity part first.
    [Is there a way to decide whether one interpretation is better than anoth-
er?]
    I think it depends on the person's background. For instance, I play
sports. And while I was in high school I was pressured by—not pressured,
but I was afraid people would think I was, you know, like a boy, so when I
look at this, I see me playing sports, and then I see me being very feminine.
So if some other person would come in here and would look at this picture,
because of their background they would look at it and find something completely different. (Parsons, 1987, p. 135)

Dorothy shows here that she is aware, not only of her own interpretative activity, but also of the way in which she has been shaped by her particular experience. This raises questions about the relationship between
the interpretation made by a viewer and that made by the artist, two more
relations in the net that have to be coordinated. One can see Lewis,

another undergraduate student, working some of the consequences out in the following extract:

[You say he wants other people to get what he is trying to say. Then in a way the success of a painting depends on whether people can get what he is trying to say?]

Well, not necessarily success. But like, the artist, the reason he painted it is he just wanted to. He likes to paint and he wanted to get his thoughts and feelings on paper and, you know, that's the most important thing. And, like, another thing, I would imagine that an artist would like people to look at his picture and see, like, what the artist is trying to say. But they might not. They might see something he didn't think of. But that doesn't necessarily mean it's wrong. Like, that person's view could be just as important as the artist's.

[So even if the artist had something in mind, you couldn't say someone else's view of it was wrong?]

Yeah, the artist knows what he's trying to say and he's painted it out. That's what's important to him. But, like, a person that sees it, he sees something completely different, you know, really meaningful to him. His point of view is going to be just as important as the artist's. (Parsons, 1987, p. 78)

At this point, Lewis realized that the viewer and artist have particular and potentially different interpretations of the artwork, that these are influenced by their cultural backgrounds and particular circumstances, and that this is true of all viewers. These insights raise questions about where the meaning of a work lies. Certainly Lewis understands that when different people have different interpretations of a work, it is not obvious that there is only one correct view of it. Of course, there is more for Lewis to learn, as there is for all of us. However, Lewis appears to be willing to examine his own response for bias, to listen to the interpretations of others, and perhaps to discuss which is most reasonable.

IMPLICATIONS FOR TEACHING ART

The cognitive revolution of the 1960s (Baars, 1986; Gardner, 1985) had the desirable effect of establishing art as a cognitive domain, as requiring thinking and intelligence. The previous view, which can still be found in some of our schools, assigned the arts (along with morality, religion, and values in general) to the affective side of the cognitive–affective divide. They were considered a matter of feeling and intuition, highly subjective, suitable for the development of creativity and self-expression, perhaps also of sensitivity and perception. However, they were not thought of as involving the sort of intelligence fostered by other school subjects. This noncognitive view of the arts was an important reason for their tradition-ally marginal place in the school curriculum. The effect of the cognitive revolution of the 1960s was therefore very welcome because it strongly suggested that the arts deserve more recognition in the curriculum and in any serious consideration of human development.

However, the particular way in which the cognitive revolution was brought to the arts created a particular view of cognition in the arts that is limited and more suited to the modern than to the postmodern artworld. Its outstanding characteristic was that it located cognition only in our deal-ings with the visual aspects of artworks and refused to allow a role to nat-ural language in our understanding. The account we have given obvious-ly finds place for visual thinking and for linguistically shaped thinking in a complex and holistic understanding. It is in this aspect that the major implications for education can be found.

The cognitive revolution was brought to the arts by Arnheim (1969) and Gombrich (1977), and it was further developed by Goodman (1976); all of them focused in an exclusive way on the visual character of cogni-tion in art. Arnheim (1969) taught us to understand visual perception as fundamentally cognitive because it requires processes such as the selec-tion, focusing, and abstraction of aspects of what is available for percep-tion. Arnheim's (1969) famous phrase for this was *visual thinking*. Gom-brich (1977) taught us to understand the making of representations not as simple copying but as the gradual invention of functional equivalents, as a process of matching the visual effect of our efforts with the visual effects of what is to be represented. Goodman (1976) taught us to think of the various media of art as languages, each having its own terms—such as line, tone, shape, and color—with which we can create and recognize meaning.

The works of these giants have resulted in a powerful and dominant par-adigm of cognition in the arts that has produced a fruitful line of research in development and has influenced education significantly. The paradigm focuses on the character of the media of artworks and on the intelligence required to make or read them—a language of art or what Davis (1997) recently called a *symbol-systems* approach. There has been considerable activity in studies of the development of children in the arts that use this paradigm (see Winner, 1982). The research has aimed to uncover the oper-ation of intelligent processes in the artmaking of children (especially in drawing and painting, but also ceramics and other media) and also in their responses to art (e.g., their ability to recognize style). There is a distin-guished history of investigation of the development of children in these two subareas, especially in the subarea of artmaking (see Freeman & Cox, 1985; Golomb, 1992; Thomas & Silk, 1990; Winner, 1982).

There has also been a number of efforts in the last 30 years to develop art curricula based on this dominant paradigm of cognition in the arts—

curricula that have substance and promote visual thinking. This has meant a continuation of the traditional focus on artmaking, regarded as a matter of problem solving and the intelligent manipulation of the medium. It has also meant some attention to response to artworks, usually in the form of style recognition, and to reflection on the artmaking process. An important outcome of this line of thinking, which has had considerable educational influence, is the theory of *Multiple Intelligences* (Gardner, 1985)—a distinctly modular view of mind and intelligence. There can be no doubt that the outcome has been extremely beneficial to the general cause of the arts in education.

In our view, however, the limitations of this exclusive focus on the purely visual have become more obvious as postmodern art emerges from the modern. The account we have given construes thinking in art as an indivisible interactive combination of visual and linguistic elements. Only that combination can account for the fact that children or adults have an intuitive theory of art. Our account also allows us to acknowledge the influence of culture on the developing theories of children. It allows an explanation of how it is that children come to think about art in the way their culture thinks; for example, how they come to think of performances as artworks or of any artwork as an expression of emotions. If we are to explore the more extended understandings of artworks that we have previously discussed, understandings that go far beyond what we could call *perceptions*, they might better be called *interpretations*.

In terms of research, there have been various attempts to enlarge the dominant paradigm of visual thinking (see Kindler, 1997). More interpretive approaches have focused on the development of intuitive theories of children of art and on their abilities to categorize and interpret artworks. However, there is much more to be done along these lines. It seems fair to say that the systematic study of the understanding by children of artworks remains relatively undeveloped (Freeman, 1995; Parsons, 1987).

In terms of educational consequences, the interpretive approach puts as much weight on the study and understanding of adult artworks as on artmaking and that it sees these two activities as an essential combination. The artmaking by children should be basically an exploration of themes and ideas discovered in the artworks of adults, and an understanding of those themes, ideas, and artworks is the fundamental purpose of teaching art in public schools. It encourages teachers to engage students in interpretive talk about artworks and in the study of what has been said by others about them. This may or may not use the formal resources of art criticism and history.

Our account of intuitive theories also suggests that a main consideration of teachers should be the underlying conceptual development of students. Educational tasks and exercises, whether oriented to artmaking or talking about artworks, should be calculated to engage some aspect of those theories at an appropriate conceptual levels. It should neither go over their head, as a lot of talk about art does, nor fail to challenge them conceptually, as artmaking too often does. It should engage their intuitive theories and require them to work with, digest, and stretch those conceptual networks. Fundamentally, this is a consequence of an emphasis on intuitive thinking in any subject matter.

We have already discussed some examples in the foregoing. For example, it is valuable, at the right point, to ask a scribbler what her scribbles represent because it stimulates the child to think about representation—in this case, the picture–world relations. It is valuable to discuss with a student like Wendy a work like the Albright because it provokes her to think through her understanding of the intentions of the artist (i.e., the artist–world–picture relations). It is valuable to engage students like Lewis in puzzles about interpretation and multiple viewpoints and to wrestle with questions of whose interpretations are more valuable and for what reasons. The value of all such cases depends on the sense of the teacher of how her students intuitively understand the artworks in question. Perhaps the most important implication of this approach is that a teacher should talk with her students about a range of artworks, their own and those of adults, and should listen to them carefully, trying to grasp how they understand and how they do not understand. Such a grasp will allow her to respond to and promote the best development of their understanding of art, which, as we have suggested, is always an understanding of something more than art, an understanding of values, of other people, and ultimately of self.

The level of understanding displayed by Lewis previously mentioned suggests why this approach, the interpretative approach to development in art, is of central educational interest. With this view, understanding art requires a grasp of complexity, a tolerance of ambiguity, and a degree of self-awareness that our democratic and increasingly multiply voiced societies demand of citizens. Intellectual functioning of this kind is hard to achieve and is best fostered, we think, through the study of art. We hope that an account of the intuitive theories of learners and the complexities they need to master will be of help to teachers.

REFERENCES

Adi-Japha, E., Levin, I., & Solomon, S. (1997). Emergence of representation in drawing: The relation between kinematic and referential aspects. *Cognitive Development, 13*, 23–49.

Arnheim, R. (1969). *Visual thinking*. Berkeley: University of California Press.

Baars, B. J. (1986). *The cognitive revolution in psychology*. New York: Guilford.

Davis, J. (1997). The "U" and the wheel of "C." In A. M. Kindler (Ed.), *Child development in art* (pp. 10–23). Reston, VA: National Art Education Association.

Freeman, N. H. (1993). Drawing: Public instruments of representation. In C. Pratt & A. F. Garton (Eds.), *Systems of representation in children: Development and use* (pp. 113–132). Chichester, England: Wiley.

Freeman, N. H. (1995). The emergence of a framework theory of pictorial reasoning. In C. Lange-Kuttner & G. V. Thomas (Eds.), *Drawing and looking* (pp. 135–146). Hemel Hempstead, England: Harvester Wheatsheaf.

Freeman, N. H., & Cox, M. V. (1985). *Visual order: The nature and development of pictorial representation*. Cambridge, England: Cambridge University Press.

Freeman, N. H., & Sanger, D. (1995). The commonsense aesthetics of rural children. *Visual Arts Research, 21*, 1–10.

Gardner, H. (1985). *The mind's new science*. New York: Basic Books.

Gardner, H., & Wolf, D. (1987). The symbolic products of early childhood. In D. Gorlitz & J. F. Wohlwill (Eds.), *Curiosity, imagination and play* (pp. 305–325). Hillsdale, NJ: Lawrence Erlbaum Associates.

Golomb, C. (1992). *The child's creation of a pictorial world*. Berkeley: University of California Press.

Gombrich, E. H. (1977). *Art and illusion: A study in the psychology of pictorial representation* (5th ed.). Oxford, England: Phaidon.

Goodman, N. (1976). *The languages of art*. Indianapolis, IN: Hackett.

Harrison, A. (1997). *Philosophy and the arts*. Bristol, England: Thoemmes.

Heal, J. (1978). On the phrase "theory of meaning." *Mind, 87*, 359–375.

Kindler, A. M. (Ed.). (1997). *Child development in art*. Reston, VA: National Art Education Association.

Parsons, M. J. (1987). *How we understand art: A cognitive developmental account of aesthetic experience*. Cambridge, England: Cambridge University Press.

Putnam, H. (1981). *Reason, truth and history*. Cambridge, England: Cambridge University Press.

Schier, F. (1986). *Deeper into pictures*. Cambridge, England: Cambridge University Press.

Thomas, G. V., & Silk, A. M. J. (1990). *An introduction to the psychology of children's drawings*. Hemel Hempstead, England: Harvester Wheatsheaf.

Turner, P. (1983). Children's responses to art: Interpretation and criticism. *Journal of Art and Design Education, 2*, 185–198.

Willats, J. (1997). *Art and representation: New principles in the analysis of pictures*. Princeton, NJ: Princeton University Press.

Wellman, H. M. (1990). *The child's theory of mind*. Cambridge, MA: MIT Press.

Winner, E. (1982). *Invented worlds: The psychology of the arts*. Cambridge, MA: Harvard University Press.

CHAPTER FIVE

The Intuitive Mind and Early Childhood Education: Connections With Chaos Theory, Script Theory, and Theory of Mind

Doris Pronin Fromberg
Hofstra University

In the United States, early childhood education, the education of children from birth to 9 years, grew out of Western European traditions during the 19th century and evolved through the 1950s out of a maturationist, linear child development framework that still predominates. This linear framework, laced with a strong measure of sentiment and caring, meshes with the predominant public elementary school image of learning as discrete additive steps and stages. Within this academic framework, education focuses on the attainment of universal skills and a body of information. In the pursuit of these goals, in the name of developing a citizenry capable of democratic governance and a competent workforce, elementary education policymakers have set a priority on the development of reading, writing, and arithmetic skills. Most schools have shared these goals and made the three Rs the centerpiece of primary education. The primary curriculum has overtaken the kindergartens, which during the past two decades, have begun to look like first grades. At the same time, it is a common occurrence to see teachers of 2-year-olds ritually worshipping the calendar each morning as their children squirm or sit with glazed looks in an attempt to please the teacher.

In my opinion, this sort of linear, world-to-child schooling in early childhood education is a form of sanctioned child abuse. Moreover, it is apparent that the three Rs as the focus of primary education has been tried repeatedly and has failed. This three Rs academic approach to education has particularly added to the disenfranchisement of inner-city, rural, low-income, minority children and children for whom English is a second language.

An intellectual early childhood education, in contrast, is nonlinear and adapts to children who come to school from diverse sociocultural backgrounds with diverse needs. An intellectual orientation focuses on meanings that grow from experiences within the sciences and social sciences. The sciences and social sciences serve as the entry point, purpose, and motivation for acquiring and using skills for representing meanings.

Teachers with an intellectal perspective define skills that both include and extend beyond the three Rs. Multiple ways to integrate representation take such forms as drawing, other arts, writing, reading, measuring, comparing, and calculating. Children within a nonlinear setting also have opportunities to practice problem-solving and critical thinking skills because projects provide more than one form of representation or outcome. Intuitive thought processes characterize problem solving and nonlinear learning focused on diverse meanings.

An Example of an Intellectual Classroom

Thus, intellectual education is education for knowledge, understanding, and self-directed use. It has a distinctive look that you might observe on entering a classroom. Learning in a nonlinear early childhood classroom mainly takes place in small groups or with individuals who work with the teacher. Space follows function when the teacher provisions areas or booths, as in a fair, within each of which different activities take place, such as science exploration, small-muscle construction activities, large-muscle sociodramatic activity, art productions, drawing–writing, reading, and special projects.

The schedule consists of long time blocks in which children in small groups or individually may self-organize the course of events. It is worth noting that the careful seeding by the teacher of an environment that is rich with relevant learning materials and opportunities helps children focus their organization in fertile ways. It is conceivable that different children doing different things at different times may have equivalent experiences. For example, whether you are surveying lost teeth, favorite colors and books, or birthdays each month, children learn the skill of surveying as a way to categorize the physical or social world and a variety of ways to represent their learning; they predict, calculate, count, measure, draw, and write about the events that they survey. Thus, if mathematical, social science, and literacy concepts grow out of creating a survey that children represent on a chart, different children engaged in surveying different phenomena may have equivalent experiences.

An Example of an Academic Classroom

The image of an academic early childhood classroom, in contrast, focuses on linear, analytic, and singular approaches. Children engage mainly in whole-group instruction or work individually on tasks. Teachers may expect children to do similar things at similar times and have similar outcomes. The teacher often demonstrates once and moves on. Paper-and-pencil tasks that require a single correct answer in worksheets and workbooks occupy children who are seated. The worksheet can be a testing or guessing activity for young children. A casual observer of young children engaged in such a uniform activity realizes that some children are fully centered on the task, getting done as quickly as possible, whereas others are spending the entire time rooting around in their book bag or staring out the window. In an attempt to maintain the attention of young children to teacher-determined events, the schedule of the teacher divides the day into many short periods of time, entailing many transitions as each whole-group activity closes down and another begins. Teachers cover curriculum; like the workbook, the strategy is to move on regardless of whether the children get covered.

The teacher in an academic classroom typically does not acknowledge the significance of intuitive-learning processes. For example, when 7-year-olds were discussing the believability of the written work of one child, they were serving as editors for one another and giving the child-author feedback on voice and audience. This is an example of the self-organization of children—an intuitive process. The teacher, however, functioning from a linear perspective, asked them to stop being off task and return quietly to their individual work (Dyson, 1987).

Integration of Intellectual and Academic Knowledge

The teacher in an intellectual early childhood classroom, however, provides many opportunities for children to collaborate and engage in non-linear, intuitive-learning processes and experiences. Some of the experiences in the intellectual classroom also subsume analytical functions. For example, when children play card games, board games, and ball games, they are learning about counting, number relationships, adding, and subtracting as they explore strategies for moving the game forward. Teachers in an intellectual setting encourage children to be active in organizing their work and in collaborating relevantly with other children. Thus, academic information is a byproduct of intellectual processes.

A thumbnail way to distinguish an analytic versus an intuitive approach is to study the preponderance of the types of questions that teachers ask children. Teachers who analyze audiotapes of their questions often find that most of their questions require a yes–no or single correct answer or informational responses. Yes–no and information questions follow a linear path. They are often inauthentic because the teacher already knows the answer. In contrast, for example, kindergarten and primary teachers can ask authentic nonlinear questions that focus on descriptions, opinions, connections, and some explanations for which the teacher communicates an interest in learning about the perceptions of children. The linear questions empower the teacher, whereas the nonlinear questions empower the children to organize ideas. As children organize their ideas, they are utilizing intuitive-thought processes.

A THEORETICAL CONTINUUM: ANALYTIC AND INTUITIVE THINKING

Educators, policymakers, and lay people in Western cultures tend to value linear, analytical, and deterministic thought more than intuitive thought. Their preference, often unexamined, influences how educators interact with young children. Logical thought is linear, and educational institutions typically use linear standardized tests that assess mainly analytical functions. The analytic and intuitive modes of knowing the world are often polarized within this tradition of the mind–body schism in Western European thought. Table 5.1 is a conglomerate continuum that describes this cultural stance.

Most meaningful questions and real situations in life, however, do not lend themselves to linear, single correct answers. Real-life phenomena appear to function with some degree of both regularity and unpredictability, often without the capacity of an observer to explain how the immediate situation functions. Meaningful experiences often tend to proceed in curved, sometimes meandering, pathways; to be best represented in tacit ways; to be generative; and to be subject to transformations rather than accruals. The assessment of learnings resulting from intuitive-thought processes takes place over time and indirectly by seeing how children use their knowledge and manifest attitudes toward learning. (*Intuitive thought*, stated as a noun, does not adequately represent the perspective and treatment in this chapter of intuitive thought as an underlying process. Therefore, it is possible to apprehend intuitive-thought processes only indirectly as they surface in various generative and transformational forms.)

Intuitive thought connotes nonlinear dynamic systems that represent meanings and the real-world experiences of children. The perspective of nonlinear dynamic systems has the potential to embody a paradigm shift in early education that more nearly resembles the real-world experiences of young children.

TABLE 5.1
Analytic and Intuitive Thought: Connotative Perceptions

Analytic	Intuitive
Linear	Nonlinear
Parsimonious	Complex
True	Ambiguous
Absolute	Relative
Cognitive	Affective
Mind	Heart
Logical	Experiential (Holmes, 1881/1923)
Rational	Irrational
Scientific	Artistic
Empirical	Qualitative
Abstract	Paradigmatic imagination (Bruner, 1986)
Realistic	Modeled–imagined
Predictable	Unpredictable
Certain	Uncertain
Fixed	Catastrophic
Stable	Random (Casti, 1994)
Prose	Poetry
Mediated	Immediate
Interpreted	Tacit
Deductive	Inductive
Demonstration	Inference (Westcott, 1968)
Top–down	Bottoms-up (Bruner, 1986)
External verification	Internal validity
Rigorous	Effortless
Factual	Mysterious
Formal	Informal
Verbalization	Visualization–imagery
Efficient	Diffuse
Conscious	Nonconscious
High cognitive control	Low cognitive control (Hammond, Hamm, Grassia, & Pearson, 1997)
Explicit–overt	Implicit–covert
Public	Private
Universal	Particular
Knowledge-by-description	Knowledge-by-acquaintance (Ross & Ginsburg, 1997)
Elements	Network
Secure	Insecure
Standard	Wisdom
Sequential	Immediate
Transmission	Constructivism
Male	Female
Pragmatic	Romantic
Propositional	Narrative (Bruner, 1986)
Coherence	Correspondence (Hammond, 1996)
Left-brain	Right-brain

Rather than either one perspective or the other, there is a body of inter-disciplinary literature that suggests moving beyond an *either–or* to an *and* perspective. Human judgments, decision making, creativity, and problem solving employ a balance between analytic and intuitive-thought process-es (Dorfman et al., 1996; Fromberg, 1995; Goldstein & Hogarth, 1997; Shirley & Langan-Fox, 1996; Udall, 1996; Vogel, 1997).

REALITY: THEORIES AND REPRESENTATIONS

By looking at chaos and complexity theory, the dynamics of script theory and narrative structures in sociodramatic play, and theory of mind research, the confluence of an isomorphic[1] dynamism of meanings emerges in support of a paradigm shift in early education that integrates intuitive-thought process-es. This paradigm shift for early education has profound implications for rethinking the nature and venue of learning, decision making, and empow-erment. It is a conception that can integrate education, teaching, and learn-ing. When students encounter difficulty learning from one perspective, rather than blaming the learner, the effective teacher tries many different approaches (Haberman, 1995; Ladson-Billings, 1995).

Consider the example of a teacher and 5-year-old children discussing a folk tale. The children heard the folk tale about an enormous turnip: It began when one adult tried to pull it out of the ground and could not do it. Another adult, then a child, a dog, a cat, and finally a mouse added to the chain of helpers. At last, the turnip came out. When the teacher and children discussed the story, children offered various explanations that included:

[the mouse] was stronger.
　　If all of them pulled, the enormous turnip would come up.
　　That was only the strength they needed.
　　. . . they needed all to pull.
　　Maybe the mouse lived under there . . . Maybe he pushed it up when it was coming out.
　　Maybe he was stronger than they were.
　　Animals could be stronger than people.
　　. . . when the mouse came he could pull the roots up.
　　If the cat and mouse pulled theirselves it comes up.
　　Maybe someone was inside the dirt and he saw the roots and he pulled it so they couldn't pull the turnip.
　　If the mouse pulled it up by himself it would work.
　　But the mouse has the most power. (Paley, 1981, pp. 1–2)

---

[1]*Isomorphism* here refers to similar underlying relationships that may appear in different surface forms.

If the teacher had stopped the discussion after the correct response, she might never have discovered the variety of other perspectives. If she had stopped the discussion after the correct response, children would figure out that a single correct response generally was expected. By exposing the underlying thinking processes of young children, diagnostic and adaptive teaching had a chance to take place.

CHAOS AND COMPLEXITY THEORY

In a parallel way, chaos–complexity theory offers us an alternative way to look at learning that legitimizes nonlinear experiences and representations. In the example of the turnip, the children were experiencing a nonlinear concept identified within chaos theory as the sensitive dependence on initial conditions (SDIC), which is present throughout human experience. The field of chaos theory studies such underlying regularities in everyday life experiences that humans often experience as nonlinear. An example of SDIC would be a small humiliation early in school life (e.g., a child who the teacher places in a patently less able group may experience a sense of low self-esteem and escalating anger) might become transformed into larger responses, such as vandalism, major violence, or both. A small, kind act by a teacher, such as the appreciation by the teacher of collaborative actions by a child with peers or metaphorical creativity despite technically nonstandard writing, may become a buffer to help cushion against future, larger frustrations.

In contrast, linear thinking typically holds that a small input yields a small output and a large input yields a large output. If somebody misses a train by 5 seconds, however, there is likely not to be merely a 5-second delay in getting to the city; there may be a much longer delay. Thus, the 5-second lateness, a small input, may result in a large ouput, lateness by an hour. Current research on the early development of the brain suggests that small inputs or small neglects during the first few years have massive potential for influencing development (Shore, 1997). In a related way, nonlinear experiences in the real world, such as the weather, may be specifically unpredictable but generally predictable. People in northern climates, for example, generally do not expect snow in the summer but specifically cannot reliably predict the weather across the span of a few days. The butterfly effect (Lorenz, 1960; cited in Peitgen, 1993), a hypothetical flapping of the wings of a butterfly in one hemisphere, may be the sensitive initial condition on which a tornado in another hemisphere depends. With a longer range perspective, therefore, there are underlying regularities that may become apparent.

It is possible in the case of the children in the classroom discussing an enormous turnip, as well as other times in classrooms, that different children doing the same thing at the same time may have different experiences. The reverse may also be true—that different children doing different things at the same time may have equivalent experiences. It is possible to imagine that both of these statements are generally predictably unpredictable but not altogether random, sensitively dependent as they are on initial conditions and contexts.

Self-organization is another concept that is nonlinear and reflects the real world (see Holte, 1993; Robertson & Combs, 1995). Self-organization is a fundamental process that is the antithesis of equilibrium. Tornados, double pendulums, and mobs all reflect self-organizing systems. Despite how-to books, people do not solve problems one step at a time, and young children in a classroom organize themselves to focus productively when they are engaged in a meaningful pastime. For example, 2-year-olds predictably tend to herd at unpredictable times. Self-organization, therefore, is generally predictable and specifically unpredictable. It is possible to observe the generative ways in which young children organize themselves, beginning in toddlerhood, in emploting sociodramatic play constructions and themes, although the enactment varies broadly. It is in the multiple surface forms of enactment, however, that adults can infer the regularity of underlying emplotment processes.

Fractal geometry (Mandelbroit, 1993) is a field that studies the irregular shapes and patterns in nature, such as a fir tree, broccoli, or an irregular coastline. A sufficiently distant perspective reveals that each branch resembles the others in a pattern of scales of different size, similar to nested dolls. Human relationships, as well as irregular shapes, may reflect self-similar fractal relationships. For example, there is often a self-similar relationship between the self-esteem of a child and the teacher. One researcher has found that elementary-age children are more comfortable with mathematics and show stronger mathematical achievements when their teachers feel comfortable with mathematics (Karp, 1988). Although clouds are not Euclidian circles and branches not perfect triangles, schools have typically dealt with the abstract idealized relationships in mathematics and social life without touching on the real, messy realities. Although young children may focus more comfortably on direct perspectives, they are more open than in later years to directly experiencing the underlying processes when idealized forms are set in contexts that are more complex. Brain research suggests that wholistic communication in the brain follows networking patterns that are self-similar across different areas of the brain—comparable to musical reverberations (Calvin, 1996).

The Case for Phase Transitions

From a chaos theory perspective, the real world is filled with good chaos; complexity theory is a subset of chaos theory that refers to the phase transitions between systems, states of matter, or experience. The phase transition imagery of complexity theory (Waldrop, 1992) offers a helpful lens for viewing the processes of balancing, shifting, and oscillating between systems or states; a phase transition is the threshold from one system or state to another, a transformation of matter, energy, or experience. Consider such examples as the instant that a light switch switches the condition of the lamp, that corn pops, that wakefulness crosses over into sleep, the precise moment when a liquid transforms into gas, and a child perceives a fresh meaning. These phase transitions reflect a point of balance between freedom and control, between order and chaos; and in personal terms, the balance between duty versus desire or conformity versus self-expression.

Complexity theory can help explain the qualitative change that takes place during learning; the image of phase transitions defines the process of transforming meaning. Meaning is both the essence and product of thought and educational enterprises.

Conditions for Learning in Early Childhood

A significant condition for learning, for example, is cognitive dissonance (Festinger, 1957) or cognitive conflict–contradiction (Piaget, 1947/1959). Cognitive dissonance is a sequence of predict–experience–contrast. The moment of contrast between the prediction and the actual experience is a phase transition—a kind of surprise and the point at which learning occurs. Contrast is particularly important in creating the conditions for inductive processes and intuitive thought to function. Without contrast, a static situation exists. With contrast, it is possible to perceive movement between the figure (the new) and ground (the known).

Consider the instance when a small group of 4-year-olds both participated and observed as they took turns placing one marble at a time into a short, wide container and into a tall, thin container. The teacher continuously asked if they were placing the same, more, or fewer marbles in either container. When they finished moving all of the marbles, the children agreed that there were more marbles in the tall container. They then repeated the same activity with the containers covered by boxes. The teacher kept asking them to imagine the level of the contents as children placed one marble at a time into the covered containers. When she asked them to predict whether there were the same, more, or fewer marbles in the covered containers, they predicted that there would be the same amount in each container. Some of the children seemed surprised when the teacher uncovered the containers and their predictions contradicted the appearance of the tall, thin container. They repeated the activity a few times to satisfy the children who disbelieved the equality of the marble distribution. This sort of activity empowered the children and created a degree of imbalance to stimulate a phase transition from nonconservation toward conservation of quantity.

Integrated conditions for learning in early childhood education, such as induction and cognitive dissonance as well as social activity, physical manipulatives, play, revisiting, and competence (Fromberg, 1995), reflect the dynamism of learning as phase transitions. In a learning-focused child-to-world classroom, there is a match between the motives and meanings of young children and the supportive provisions that teachers can make to accommodate the children.

A PARADIGM SHIFT IN EARLY EDUCATION

The significance of chaos–complexity theory for early education is that it illuminates a paradigm shift that approaches a realistic image of the dynamics, content, products, mode of communication, roles of teacher and student, ways of organizing time and groups, and assessment that may occur within the ongoing learning process. Table 5.2 outlines the implications of chaos–complexity theory as a paradigm shift in early education. Looking at a continuum of philosophy that defines interrelated facets of the educational process, it is possible to outline educational functions.

The paradigm shift outlined in Table 5.2 supports the purposes of education that include a democratic, nonlinear, and participatory political image. It suggests that ethical and caring relationships both enrich and inform learning. It suggests that teachers have a responsibility to keep trying to match their plans with the possibilities for perceiving meanings by the students. It replaces demands with influence and external rewards–punishments with personal motives of students for the social construction of knowledge. It replaces a focus on single correct answers to inauthentic questions with multiple interpretations of authentic questions. It replaces the recognition by the teacher of a limited range of static representational forms with appreciation for multiple forms of representation. It empowers the learners to learn as the teacher more truly teaches than controls. The motives of students and teachers can become joined.

To further communicate the multiple perspectives within which these assumptions reside, it is helpful to consider script theory (Schank & Abelson, 1977), which is observable in sociodramatic play and its narrative structures as well as theory of mind. Both script theory and theory of mind stud-

TABLE 5.2
Implications of Chaos/Complexity Theory: A Paradigm Shift in Early Education

Philosophy	
Behaviorism	Social construction/transaction
Deterministic	Emergent
Academic	Intellectual
Predictable behavior	Unpredictable patterns
Small input : small output	Sensitive dependence on initial conditions

Content	
Focus on information	Focus on meanings & connections
Facts and memory	Vivid imagery & meanings
Focus on content teaching	Focus on student learning
Knowledge as transmitted (closed loop)	Knowledge as self-organizing (dynamic systems)
Separate parts	Interrelated–fluid connections
Single correct method & answer	Multiple models
Workbooks	Active projects–experiences

Product	
Information	Isomorphic imagery
Uniform representations	Multiple representations

Communication	
Linear	Transactional[a]

Teacher's Roles	
Major planner	Negotiated, flexible
Teacher control	Shared responsibility
Culturally transparent pedagogy	Culturally relevant pedagogy
Technical–interpretive reflection[b]	Interpretive–ethical reflection[b]
External rewards–punishments	Social construction of knowledge

Student's Roles	
Information gleaner	Connection maker
Respondent	Problem setter and solver
Individual competition	Collaborative community member

Time	
Mostly short blocks	Short and long blocks

Grouping	
Mostly whole-group, individual tasks	Mostly smaller groupings, cooperative and individual

Assessment	
Uniform, standardized	Multiple forms
For closure	For ongoing planning

[a]Rosenblatt, 1969.
[b]Van Manen, 1977.

ies illuminate the generative character of the intuitive thought processes of the young child.

SCRIPT THEORY IN SOCIODRAMATIC PLAY

When young children engage in sociodramatic play, it is possible to observe them balancing reality and fantasy, cognition and metacognition, and scaffolding narrative structures. During sociodramatic play, a child usually engages in activity with one or more other children and sometimes an adult. As the children engage in sociodramatic play, they use their knowledge of past events as a starting point and elaborate it imaginatively by the mutual planning and execution of an oral playwriting process; the children acquire their event knowledge within their particular cultural contexts. The oral scripts that they develop collaboratively represent a full range of their experiences and their mutual imaginative embellishments.

During the intermittent planning episodes of sociodramatic play, preschool-age children engage in metacommunication about what roles they will play—for example, a 4-year-old child says, "You be the doctor. I'll be the baby," and they then become those roles. The interaction then follows a script narrative that they negotiate and renegotiate within as well as outside of the playframe. During the negotiation and playing out of the script, it is possible to see how they have been thinking about events and to observe their intuitive-thought processes. The confluence of intuitive (imagery) and analytical (metacommunication) thought results in mutual problem solving and joint oral authorship. Observers of the sociodramatic play of young children have witnessed a kind of narrative syntax that incorporates this capacity for collaborative problem solving (Ariel, 1992; Eckler & Weininger, 1989; Harris & Kavanaugh, 1993).

Script theory embodies a kind of syntactic structure and multicultural context for sociodramatic play. Scripts contain a finite set of figurative structures that can generate an infinite set of combinations—a grammar for play (for an extended discussion, see Fromberg, 1999). Reflecting the underlying kinetic regularities of chaos–complexity theory, and supporting the learning of meanings through the representations of dynamic themes, sociodramatic play represents the generative, intuitive-thought processes in which young children collaboratively engage as they represent meanings. Although children understand the signals of play such as voice change, posture, gestures, or facial expression, they seem to follow certain organizational rules. Their play explicitly represents their implicit understanding of the script. The script represents a combination of the event knowledge that they contribute to the play and the shared event knowledge that extends their event knowledge during the play.

Phase transitions are observable as children move between negotiating their development of the script through metacommunication and then embody their narrative imagery in direct action and dialogue. This problem-solving process in sociodramatic play integrates the analytical and the intuitive, demonstrating the *and* of the phase transition rather than the either–or polarity depicted in Table 5.2.

Observations of phase transitions during sociodramatic play reflect the growing metacognition of children—an interest of theory of mind researchers.

THEORY OF MIND

Theory of mind research focuses on how and when young children become aware of their own thoughts, motives, and feelings as well as the beliefs, motives, and feelings of others. Researchers have studied young children at play as one way to access these insights.

It is apparent that young children engaged in sociodramatic play are aware that they are playing and that their playmates have thoughts, motives, and emotions they can assemble and dissemble; they continuously move outside of the playframe to communicate about their communication (reality) and then promptly reenter the playframe to continue the play (model–fantasy). In doing so, the mutual feedback helps children to increasingly develop an awareness of their own thoughts and those of others, and they become empowered to anticipate and influence others.

Sociodramatic play offers an opportunity to observe children as they engage in the process of collaborative oral playwriting and acting. This recursive process of narrative construction demonstrates the development of the theory of mind of young children. Theory of mind researchers have noted that there is an isomorphic relationship between theory of mind of children and their pretend play (Astington, 1993; Bartsch & Wellman, 1995; Garvey, 1993; Leslie, 1995). The theory of mind researchers vary in their interpretation of when, from the ages of 2 to 4 years, children have explicit awareness of themselves or others as thinkers or players. Nevertheless, the value of theory of mind research lies in its recognition of, and quest for, a clearer view and understanding of the nonlinear dynamics of the beliefs, thoughts, and meanings of young children.

As is the case with script theory, theories of young children about their thoughts, beliefs, motives, and feelings as well as those of others develop through the processes of phase transitions. It is helpful to think of the development of theory of mind phenomena, along with script theory, as an early childhood syntax of experience that is wholistic and intuitive. Consider the analogy of an alphabet composed of wooden building blocks. The alphabetic letters and the separate wooden blocks alone take their meaningful value from the contrasting patterns, the relationships among them, that generate the infinite representations in the form of words. In similar generative ways, theory of mind develops as a transformational phenomenon. Such inductive processes depend on intuitive thinking.

The role of the teacher, therefore, is to create exposures to experiences in which children may apprehend phase transitions. Teachers do this by engaging in discussions when children can share their feelings and experiences with one another, and to create opportunities during which children might learn through many exposures that other people have feelings, motives, and thoughts that may be similar and different from their own. When a 3-year-old hurt another intentionally, for example, the teacher first gave comfort to the hurt child, describing sympathetically that it hurts when somebody pinches you; the teacher then engaged observer children in comforting the victim and only then invited the aggressor to offer comfort. By observing the response of the teacher and the hugs of the other children, the aggressor had an opportunity to perceive another viewpoint, part of building toward a theory of mind.

Theory of mind researchers highlight the intuitive-thinking processes with which children interpret the world and try to distinguish between the tacit understandings of children and their capacity to act or verbalize their understandings. Just as it is helpful to consider a long-range perspective in considering chaos theory concepts, it is necessary to look at underlying regularities through indirect means to appreciate the power of intuitive-thinking processes and imagination in construction by children of their theory of mind and oral playwriting scripts.

IMPLICATIONS FOR EARLY EDUCATION

Within the context of a confluence of isomorphic processes that include chaos theory, script theory, and theory of mind, it is possible to speculate that formal schooling today offers legitimacy to only a limited and fixed part of the spectrum of human knowledge and has had only a limited impact on the possibilities for learning. Schooling tends to empower teachers and students to address a limited range of facts and ideas that fit most neatly into a linear, Western European conception best suited to the industrial model from which it draws its genetic roots. Children often enter into a conspiracy with teachers to find the single, expected answer to many issues for which there is no single and easy correct answer.

Issues of human interaction, existential issues, and all of the things that human beings wonder about with commitment and a significant investment of feelings often defy simplistic and linear explanations. The huge range of nonlinear understanding and multiple forms of possible representations, therefore, tend to languish in such schooling (see Eisner, 1982/1994; Gardner, 1983).

INTUITIVE THOUGHT PROCESSES AS CONNECTIVE LEARNING

A scholar in the field of artifical intelligence made the point that analogy is significant in creative processes and he values fluid concepts as central to understanding fluid forms of representation (Hofstadter & the Fluid Analogies Research Group, 1995). For example, when we look at a profile rather than a full frontal view of another person, we are always representing the totality of the person by analogy. As is the case with complexity theory and nonlinear dynamics, fluid forms of representation have distinctive underlying patterns, although we may imagine them in continuous motion.

A focus on the fluidity of learning is not easy to integrate after teachers have been schooled in the definitive, static models of the past–present. From the chaos–complexity perspective, it is the connections that count. Intuitive-thought processes, imagery, imagination, and analogy are significant ways of knowing, solving problems, and being creative in general, but frequently are marginal to the work of formal education.

Consider, therefore, the unit-planning tradition in early education that verbalizes a Deweyan approach to experiential education while focusing on particular sociobiological views of the developmental capacities of children. This view often translates into relatively content-sparse benevolent pastimes that involve units consisting of sensory labeling, singing, reading about, drawing, dancing, uniform crafts, and exploring objects that represent static concepts such as popcorn, hats, bears, or winter. Static unit studies in early childhood education, such as winter, senses, bears, buses, or ritual-defined holidays, often rely mainly on the predigested pile of information given by the teacher for the students to parrot back. Static units limit opportunities for intuitive connection making, imagination, analogy building, and creativity; teachers often expect children to produce sometimes trivial and uniform representations. These units often begin on Monday and end on Friday of the same week and depend on verbalisms.

Dewey (1938/1959) bewailed such fragmentation of his views. In contrast, dynamic themes are part of the paradigm shift in early education that is consistent with teaching that accounts for the dynamic nature of early learning that is content rich. Most meanings worth learning about have connections that are fluid.

In a futurist context, it is worth highlighting the difference between intuitive thoughts and intuitive-thought processes. It is worth noting that intuitive thoughts may impede some forms of scientific thinking and serve as a deficit to teachers who approach their preparation with unreflective thought. Logical thought, however, may be a reciprocal impediment to acquiring new thinking and ways of knowing the world by closing down possibilities. Intuitive-thought processes, however, are pivotal to creative problem solving and connection making.

The 21st century will be transformed by escalating change in the ubiquitousness and miniaturization of computers (like scrap paper today), biotechnology, and space travel that we can barely imagine (Kaku, 1997). Now and in the future, the world needs people who can see the bigger picture, who can collaborate with others, consider multiple consequences, imagine alternative solutions, and solve problems in creative ways. Therefore, the preponderance of linear educational practice does not effectively serve early education or the directions of society toward the next century. A changing world needs thinkers who can both utilize intuitive-thought processes flexibly and reflect on their intuitive thoughts, moving beyond either–or to and.

DYNAMIC THEMES CURRICULUM

Within the current context, however, a curriculum that focuses on dynamic themes reflects a paradigm shift in early education that recognizes the value of intuitive-thought processes. It is possible to imagine the dynamic nature of the intuitive-thought processes of the young child as a river that transports meanings. Teachers who employ the approach of a dynamic themes curriculum attempt to triangulate with the development of children, the dynamic ways in which young children learn, and the nature of knowledge that the culture values. Teachers, after all, continue to make decisions concerning the experiences from which children can acquire knowledge and expand their understandings.

Teachers who plan a dynamic themes curriculum with children recognize that, although the acquisition of meaning is central to human communication and learning, the dynamics of meaning remain ineffable because there is a transformational relationship between underlying regularities and the variety of surface representations. At the same time, there is considerable evidence that the fluid systems that generate meanings across many perspectives of human experience—including linguistics (Chomsky, 1972), psychology (Jung, 1968/1970), anthropology (Levi-Strauss, 1949/1969, 1964/1969), communications theory (McLuhan,

1963), computer technology (Minsky, 1967), games theory (Moore & Anderson, 1968), script theory (Nelson et al., 1986; Schank & Abelson, 1977), genetic research (Pfeiffer, 1962), and topology (Steiner, 1970)—appear to be isomorphic: They reflect similar dynamics of underlying regularities that become transformed into infinite forms of representation.

For example, dynamic themes such as cyclical change or indirect progress or conflict–contrast (differences are important) or synergy (the sum exceeds the parts) are meanings that cut across the spectrum of separate disciplines (Fromberg, 1995). The perceptual regularities that underlie the spectrum generate multiple forms of representation. They reflect fluid forms that underlie physical, social, aesthetic, cognitive, and representational experiences. Dynamic themes follow the contours of the syntax of experience of young children and their inductive and intuitive ways of learning. At the same time, dynamic themes can represent the broad range of human knowledge.

The Example of Cyclical Change

The dynamic theme of cyclical change, for example, is present in the physical, natural, and social worlds, and the arts. Therefore, different children doing different things at different times may have equivalent experiences. In effect, if children have experiences with some aspects of cyclical change in either the life cycle of frogs or land snails; whether they survey the food cycle or adopt a tree for study throughout the year, the underlying imagery of cyclical change is equivalent. Whether children study the electrical circuitry of a lightbulb or a buzzer on their playhouse; whether they create a photographic timeline of class pets or a school trip, they would be having equivalent experiences in cyclical change. Within these experiences, they would have many opportunities to represent their experiences by integrating the three Rs and the arts.

The Example of Synergy

It is possible to learn about the dynamic theme of synergy (the whole is more than the sum of its parts) when a teacher juxtaposes experiences that reflect the underlying imagery of synergy in sociological experience (adopting a construction site and documenting events and the roles of construction participants by interviewing the workers, creating a timeline, drawing, writing, and reading about collaboration), historical and geographical experience (creating an immigration map, timeline, and museum of family artifacts as well as engaging in multicultural festivals), political experience (role-playing presidential elections, charting the predictions and findings in class and in the nation), chemical experience (cooking transformative foods such as popcorn, eggs, or whipping cream; measuring changes in volume and shape after cooking or decomposing), movement education (collaborative dance development or creative dramatics), music (group creation of melodies, poetic song development, exposure to orchestras, or engaging in rhythm band activity), experiences representing collaboration (role-playing, dancing, drawing, writing, or graphing), and arts (quilt or mural creations to commemorate events throughout the year and color mixing).

The teacher, in providing resources, considers the underlying regularities in a dynamic theme because they reflect the underlying intuitive-thought processes by which young children make connections and learn. To coordinate effective early education, it would be worthwhile for teachers of young children to follow the contours of the systems of children for constructing meaning; teachers need to increase their familiarity with the phase transitions that help children illuminate change.

INTUITIVE-THOUGHT PROCESSES
AS CONNECTION MAKING

It is essential to recognize that the paradigm shift in early education that intentionally integrates intuitive-thought processes is not a simple phase-transitions pill that will cure the ills of current educational practice. It is a complex constellation of multiple processes that interact within particular multicultural contexts of individual children, both societal and personal.

The case for valuing complexity within early education is an attempt to apprehend meaning in ways that match the processes by which young children might construct and construe experience. The confluence of dynamic models suggests that teachers would integrate the nonlinear nature of the phase transition process into their work with children to build on the nonlinear syntax of experience in early childhood. At the same time, however, the folkloric tradition in the practice of many schools limits instruction to linear ways of working. Those children who come from middle-class homes tend to survive the linear approach (Heath, 1983), which schools measure in linear ways and then use the results for competitive purposes.

As educators, therefore, it is possible to continuously redefine what we mean by teaching and learning. If learning is the center of the educational enterprise, then integrated meaning needs to be the center of teaching. Multiple meanings, in turn, mean multiple forms of representation for dynamic themes.

There are decisions for teachers to make that may begin, for example, by identifying a single next step as small as providing students with one additional choice or reducing one transition during the school day. Such small inputs, a sensitive dependence on initial conditions, can become much bigger outputs that touch on the basic issues of intuitive thought, power, control, and self-directed learning—self-organization—when you consider this sort of trajectory. A paradigm shift in early education that incorporates nonlinear dynamic systems and celebrates intuitive-thinking processes, therefore, promises relevance for an uncertain future that can benefit from creative problem solvers.

REFERENCES

Ariel, S. (1992). Semiotic analysis of children's play: A method for investigating social development. *Merrill-Palmer Quarterly, 38*(1), 119–138.

Astington, J. W. (1993). *The child's discovery of the mind*. Cambridge, MA: Harvard University Press.

Bartsch, K., & Wellman, H. M. (1995). *Children talk about the mind*. New York: Oxford University Press.

Bruner, J. S. (1986). *Actual minds, possible worlds*. Cambridge, MA: Harvard University Press.

Calvin, S. H. (1996). *How brains think*. New York: Basic Books.

Casti, J. L. (1994). *Complexification: Explaining a paradoxical world through the science of surprise*. New York: HarperCollins.

Chomsky, N. (1972). *Language and mind*. New York: Harcourt Brace.

Dewey, J. (1959). *Experience and education*. New York: Macmillan. (Original work published 1938)

Dorfman, J., et al. (1996). Intuition, incubation and insight: Implicit cognition in problem solving. In G. Underwood (Ed.), *Implicit cognition* (pp. 257–296). Oxford, England: Oxford University Press.

Dyson, A. H. (1987). The value of "time off task": Young children's spontaneous talk and deliberate text. *Harvard Educational Review, 57*, 396–420.

Eckler, J. A., & Weininger, O. (1989). Structural parallels between pretend play and narratives. *Developmental Psychology, 25*(5), 736–743.

Eisner, E. (1982/1994). *Cognition and curriculum reconsidered* (2nd ed.). New York: Teachers College Press.

Festinger, L. (1957). *A theory of cognitive dissonance*. New York: Harper & Row.

Fromberg, D. P. (1995). *The full-day kindergarten: Planning and practicing a dynamic themes curriculum* (2nd ed.). New York: Teachers College Press.

Fromberg, D. P. (1999). A review of research on play. In C. Seefeldt (Ed.), *Current findings in theory and practice* (3rd ed., pp. 27–53). New York: Teachers College Press.

Gardner, H. (1983). *Frames of mind*. New York: Basic Books.

Garvey, C. (1993). Diversity in the conversational repertoire: The case of conflicts and social pretending. *Cognition and Instruction, 11*(3&4), 251–264.

Goldstein, W. M., & Hogarth, R. M. (Eds.). (1997). *Research judgement and decision-making*. New York: Cambridge University Press.

Haberman, M. (1995). *Star teachers of children in poverty*. West Lafayette, IN: Kappa Delta Pi.

Hammond, K. R. (1996). *Human judgment and social policy*. New York: Oxford University Press.

Hammond, K. R., Hamm, R. M., Grassia, J., & Pearson, T. (1997). Direct comparison of the efficacy of intuitive and analytical cognition in expert judgment. In S. M. Goldstein & R. M. Hogarth (Eds.), *Research on judgment and decision making: Currents, connections, and controversies* (pp. 144–180). New York: Cambridge University Press.

Harris, P. L., & Kavanaugh, R. D. (1993). Young children's understanding of pretense. *Monographs of the Society for Research in Child Development, 58*(1, Serial No. 231).

Heath, S. B. (1983). *Ways with words*. New York: Cambridge University Press.

Hofstadter, D., & the Fluid Analogies Research Group. (1995). *Fluid concepts and creative analogies: Computer models of the fundamental mechanisms of thought*. New York: Basic Books.

Holmes, O. W. (1881/1923). *The common law*. Boston: Little, Brown.

Holte, J. (Ed.). (1993). *Chaos: The new science*. Lanham, MD: University Press of America.

Jung, C. G. (1970). *Analytical psychology*. New York: Vintage. (Original work published 1968)

Kaku, M. (1997). *Visions: Science revolution for the twenty-first century*. New York: Basic Books.

Karp, K. (1988). *The teaching of elementary school mathematics: The relationship between how math is taught and teachers' attitudes*. Unpublished doctoral dissertation, Hofstra University, Hempstead, NY.

Ladson-Billings, G. (1995). *The dreamkeepers: Successful teachers of African American children*. San Francisco: Jossey-Bass.

Leslie, A. M. (1995). Pretending and believing: Issues in the theory of ToMM. In J. Mehler & S. Franck (Eds.), *COGNITION on cognition* (pp. 193–220). Cambridge, MA: MIT Press.

Levi-Strauss, C. (1969). *The elementary structures of kinship* (J. H. Bell & J. R. von Sturmer, Trans., R. Needham, Ed.). Boston: Beacon. (Original work published 1949)

Levi-Strauss, C. (1969). *The raw and the cooked* (J. Weightman & D. Weightman, Trans.). New York: Harper Torchbooks. (Original work published 1964)

Mandelbroit, B. (1993). Fractals. In J. Holte (Ed.), *Chaos: The new science* (pp. 1–33). Lanham, MD: University Press of America.

McLuhan, M. (1963). We need a new picture of knowledge. In A. Frazier (Ed.), *New insights and the curriculum* (pp. 57–70). Washington, DC: Association for Supervision & Curriculum Development.

Minsky, M. (1967). *Computation: Finite and infinite machines*. Englewood Cliffs, NJ: Prentice-Hall.

Moore, O. K., & Anderson, A. R. (1968). The responsive environment project. In R. D. Hess & R. M. Bear (Eds.), *Early education* (pp. 171–189). Chicago: Aldine.

Nelson, K., et al. (1986). *Event knowledge: Structure and function in development*. Hillsdale, NJ: Lawrence Erlbaum Associates.

Paley, V. G. (1981). *Wally's stories*. Chicago: University of Chicago Press.

Peitgen, H.-O. (1993). The causality principle, deterministic laws, and chaos. In J. Holte (Ed.), *Chaos: The new science* (pp. 35–43). Lanham, MD: University Press of America.

Pfeiffer, J. (1962). *The thinking machine*. Philadelphia: Lippincott.

Piaget, J. (1947/1959). *The psychology of intelligence*. London, England: Routledge & Kegan Paul.

Robertson R., & Combs, A. (Eds.). (1995). *Chaos theory in psychology and the life sciences*. Hillsdale, NJ: Lawrence Erlbaum Associates.

Rosenblatt, R. (1969). Towards a transactional theory of reading. *Journal of Reading Behavior, 10*(1), 31–43.

Ross, B., & Ginsburg, B. (1997). Communicative genes and the evolution of empathy. In W. Ickes (Ed.), *Empathic accuracy* (pp. 17–43). New York: Guilford.

Schank, R., & Abelson, R. (1977). *Scripts, plans, goals and understanding: An inquiry into human knowledge*. Hillsdale, NJ: Lawrence Erlbaum Associates.

Shirley, D. A., & Langan-Fox, J. (1996). Intuition: A review of the literature. *Psychological Reports, 79*(2), 563–584.

Shore, R. (1997). *Rethinking the brain: New insights into early development*. New York: Families and Work Institute.

Steiner, G. (1970). *Language and silence*. New York: Atheneum.

Udall, N. (1996). Creative transformations: A design perspective. *Journal of Creative Behavior, 30*(1), 39–51.

Van Manen, M. (1977). Linking ways of knowing with ways of being practical. *Curriculum Inquiry, 6*(3), 205–228.

Vogel, G. (1997). Untitled. *Science, 275*(5304), 1269.

Waldrop, M. M. (1992). *Complexity: The emerging science at the edge of order and chaos*. New York: Simon & Schuster.

Westcott, M. (1968). *Toward a contemporary psychology of intuition: A historical, theoretical, and empirical inquiry*. New York: Holt, Rinehart & Winston.

PART III

INTUITIVE CONCEPTIONS
AND TEACHER LEARNING

Conceptual Change in Teachers' Intuitive Conceptions of Learning, Motivation, and Instruction: The Role of Motivational and Epistemological Beliefs

Helen Patrick
Northern Illinois University

Paul R. Pintrich
University of Michigan

Current cognitive theory and research stress the centrality of knowledge representations of an individual for learning and behavior. As in all cognitive theories, these knowledge representations are assumed to influence perception, attention, thinking, learning, problem solving, and behavior in a variety of ways. In some ways, understanding the acquisition and change in the knowledge base of an individual is the central question in cognitive development. Of course, there are many different models of knowledge acquisition and change (cf. Keil, 1998; Wellman & Gelman, 1998), but in teaching and learning contexts general models of conceptual change have been fruitful and useful (e.g., Chi, Slotta, & de Leeuw, 1994; Dole & Sinatra, 1998; Gardner, 1991; Pintrich, Marx, & Boyle, 1993; Strike & Posner, 1992).

These models of conceptual change have been applied to student learning in a host of domains, especially in the natural sciences such as biology, physics, chemistry, astronomy, and geology (e.g., Carey, 1985; Keil, 1998; Osborne & Freyburg, 1985), but they have been used in mathematics and the social sciences as well (e.g., Bruer, 1993; Carretero & Voss, 1994; Gardner, 1991). Although these models differ in their assumptions about what changes in conceptual change, from postulating smaller knowledge units like p-prims (Smith, diSessa, & Roschelle, 1993), ontological shifts in categorization (Chi et al., 1994), or revisions of theories (e.g., Vosniadou, 1994), most of the models do agree on a number of central features of conceptual change.

First, in line with a general cognitive approach, student conceptions can influence thinking and learning by directing perception and attention to certain features of information as well as guiding the processing, understanding, and use of information. Second, these processing influences may be implicit as students may not be aware of their own conceptions or the influence their conceptions can have on their own thinking and learning. Third, the conceptions may be intuitive in that they make sense, are useful, or are supported in some contexts, especially in everyday life. Fourth, students can have naive, simplistic, or inappropriate conceptions that can impede or interfere with learning of more veridical or useful conceptions. Fifth, these naive or intuitive conceptions can be difficult to dislodge, revise, restructure, or change through instruction. Finally, given the resistance in changing these conceptions, the process of conceptual change is assumed to be difficult, time-consuming, and long term and to require a high level of student cognitive and metacognitive engagement as well as persistence.

The application of general models of conceptual change to conceptions and beliefs of teachers has not been as systematic or pervasive as in the research on student conceptions and learning. Nevertheless, research on the role of conceptions and beliefs of teachers in learning to teach has suggested many of the same characterizations for intuitive conceptions of teachers as for students (Pajares, 1992; Richardson, 1996; Richardson & Placier, in press; Wideen, Mayer-Smith, & Moon, 1998). Teacher beliefs and conceptions are assumed to influence their cognition and behavior; in particular, it has been suggested that beliefs and implicit theories about learning, motivation, and instruction (by teachers) influence their actual instructional behavior in the classroom. In addition, these beliefs are assumed to be implicit or tacit because teachers may not be aware of how they influence their behavior. As with student conceptions, teacher conceptions may be useful and supported in some contexts, and this makes them difficult to change. Teacher conceptions and beliefs may be simplistic, inappropriate, or misleading and may need to be revised and restructured as part of any program of teacher education (Borko & Putnam, 1996). Finally, the process of change and restructuring of teacher beliefs is also time-consuming, difficult, and long term and requires cognitive and metacognitive engagement (often labeled *self-reflection* in the teacher education literature) and persistence (Pajares, 1992; Richardson, 1996; Wideen et al., 1998).

At the same time, most of this research on student or teacher conceptions has not examined the role of motivational or epistemological factors in the process of conceptual change. As Pintrich et al. (1993) pointed out, most models of student conceptual change have focused on the cognitive factors involved and have not examined the role of motivational factors.

The same point seems to be relevant in the teacher beliefs literature. Given the parallels between the student and teacher beliefs literature, an analysis of the role of motivational and epistemological factors that might facilitate or constrain conceptual change in teachers seems warranted. Accordingly, the purpose of this chapter is to discuss conceptual change of teachers, particularly the role of various motivational and epistemological factors in facilitating such change. We begin with an overview of the findings on intuitive conceptions of teachers about central aspects of teaching—beliefs about learning and motivation of students, and about student instruction. The following section outlines how the motivational and epistemological factors of teachers may influence their conceptual change about these teaching-related beliefs. Finally, in the last section, we discuss the implications of our analysis for teacher education, specifically the teaching of educational psychology.

PRESERVICE AND NOVICE TEACHERS' INTUITIVE CONCEPTIONS OF LEARNING, MOTIVATION, AND INSTRUCTION

Teachers have conceptions and beliefs about a number of different aspects of education that can influence their behavior in the classroom. In this chapter, we focus on conceptions about learning, motivation, and instruction (by teachers) because these constructs are central to teaching and are usually core-content areas in most educational psychology courses for teachers. We take a developmental perspective and discuss these beliefs in terms of three phases: (a) preservice teachers' conceptions on entering teacher education, (b) preservice teachers' conceptions during their teacher education program, and (c) novice or beginning teachers' beliefs in their first few years of actual teaching. At the same time, the literature on conceptions and beliefs of teachers is large, fragmented, and not easily summarized. Accordingly, our review is not intended to be comprehensive, but illustrative of the kinds of conceptions about learning, motivation, and instruction that teachers hold during their progression to becoming a teacher. In addition, it must be noted that many of the studies we draw on have small samples, and it is not at all clear how generalizable the patterns are for all teachers (cf. Wideen et al., 1998).

Preservice Teachers' Conceptions on Entering Teacher-Education Programs

The conceptions that beginning preservice teachers hold about student learning are, for the most part, formed on the basis of their own experience as primary- and secondary-school students (Borko & Putnam, 1996;

Calderhead, 1996). Those beliefs, also held by many practicing teachers, are consistent with traditional theories of learning as the successful transmission of intact and well-defined bodies of knowledge (Holt-Reynolds, 1992; Nespor, 1987). Accordingly, learning is seen as being a relatively mechanical reception of information, and is indicated by following procedures correctly, mastering skills through direct instruction and independent practice, and remembering (Borko & Putnam, 1996; Calderhead, 1996).

Prospective teachers generally believe that learning by students is highly dependent on relatively stable characteristics that are, for the most part, outside the control of teachers. The most salient of these characteristics is student intelligence or ability, viewed typically as a relatively fixed capacity that places limits on learning by students (Dweck & Leggett, 1988; Nespor, 1987). Therefore, preservice teachers tend to believe that the ability of students affects their learning to a large extent.

In addition to ability, entering preservice teachers tend to view learning as being strongly dependent on the motivation of students (Holt-Reynolds, 1992). In conceptualizing motivation, they seem to mean a relatively traitlike characteristic of students. Accordingly, they speak about students as being motivated or unmotivated. Failure of students to learn, if not due to low ability, tends to be perceived as being due to insufficient motivation. Incidentally, these beliefs are shared by many experienced teachers (Nespor, 1987). Although prospective teachers tend to see student motivation as being largely outside the control of teachers, they believe that teachers should try to motivate their students. In describing the most important characteristics of a really good teacher, entering preservice teachers rated the ability to motivate students as one of the most important features (Weinstein, 1989).

Entering prospective teachers' conceptions of instruction tend to be formed from their observations of their own school teachers and parallel the traditional transmission views they hold about learning (Borko & Putnam, 1996). They tend to think of teaching as telling information to students, particularly through lectures or recitations (Blumenfeld, Hicks, & Krajcik, 1996; Calderhead, 1996; Holt-Reynolds, 1992). Furthermore, many preservice teachers assume that in teaching they need only to follow set sequences of tasks laid out in prescribed and packaged curricula and textbooks (Blumenfeld et al., 1996)—a belief that is shared by many experienced teachers (Battista, 1994).

Prospective teachers' beliefs about really good teaching appear to be focused almost exclusively on the social and emotional dimensions of the classroom (Weinstein, 1989). Beginning preservice teachers typically mention characteristics such as caring, patience, enthusiasm, and the ability to relate to students when asked what is most important about good teaching. For example, one preservice teacher noted, "If they don't like me, I just can't teach them" (Hollingsworth, 1989, p. 173). In contrast, preservice teachers appear to pay less attention to their role in facilitating the learning and understanding of students. For example, Weinstein (1989) found that when prospective teachers were asked about good teachers, they did not mention helping students to understand subject matter, developing strategies for learning, facilitating the motivation of students, or fostering a love of learning.

Interestingly, prospective teachers entering teacher-education programs also seem to hold similarly simplistic views of their own learning in becoming teachers (Book, Byers, & Freeman, 1983; Calderhead, 1991). They appear to expect that either the knowledge necessary for teaching will be passed onto them by their college instructors or cooperating teachers (Calderhead, 1991; Hollingsworth, 1989) or that formal learning is not especially relevant—teaching is "a matter of personality" that "grows out of oneself" (Calderhead, 1991, p. 533) or is something that anyone can do and "about which there is little to learn other than through instincts and one's own experiences" (Book et al., 1983, p. 10).

Preservice Teachers' Conceptions During Teacher-Education

Teacher-education programs typically promote beliefs and practices that are consistent with constructivist models of teaching and learning and inconsistent with the direct transmission models that entering preservice teachers endorse. As a result of their educational psychology and other teacher-education courses, many preservice teachers undergo some change in their conceptions of learning. They tend to move from their intuitive-transmission views of learning to articulate perspectives that are consistent with the constructivist theories being emphasized (Hicks & Blumenfeld, 1995; Hollingsworth, 1989; Rust, 1990). For example, at the end of their teacher-education program, all 14 preservice teachers in the study by Hollingsworth stated a belief that students should actively construct their own knowledge. Hicks and Blumenfeld (1995) noted, too, that the language and terms used by preservice teachers were often quite sophisticated and impressive with respect to indicating a change in their view of learning.

The extent of preservice teachers' conceptual change tends to be influenced by the beliefs they held on entering the teacher-education program (Hollingsworth, 1989; Tillema, 1994). It also appears that the constructivist conceptions of learning that they develop do not replace their previously held transmission beliefs about learning, but coexist with them to some extent. That is, it seems that facilitating conceptual change within teacher-education programs is very difficult. For example, after participating in a 9-month course, only 5 of the 14 preservice teachers Hollingsworth (1989) followed had developed what was considered a satisfactory view of the learning of students. From analyzing preservice teachers' discussions during lesson planning, Blumenfeld and Hicks (Blumenfeld et al., 1996; Hicks & Blumenfeld, 1995) also identified that the changes in preservice teacher beliefs are typically incomplete. They found that the teachers at times still saw student learning in terms of the students being able to follow procedures. In addition, the preservice teachers often evaluated the developmental appropriateness of tasks according to whether the students could do them easily, rather than considering whether students would be cognitively challenged or actually learn from the tasks.

Preservice teachers often believe that factors outside their control influence the ability of students to learn at school. These factors include the maturity of students, their home environment, and society in general (Calderhead, 1996). For example, one preservice teacher, after speaking with her cooperating teacher, concluded that the difficulties in concentrating and learning the students were having "stem from a social problem of watching too much television. Their brains have a lot of trouble thinking after thriving on constant entertainment and action" (Pultorak, 1996, p. 288).

Although extremely little research attention has been directed at identifying preservice teachers' beliefs about motivation, it appears they do not change markedly from those held on entry to their teacher-education programs. They typically continue to see motivation as a relatively traitlike characteristic of students, and one that is crucial to classroom engagement and learning of students. For example, Holt-Reynolds (1992) found that the prospective teachers in her study "talked about learning as if it were exclusively an issue of motivation" (p. 341). Although they tend to believe that student motivation is affected by many factors outside teachers' control, preservice teachers believe they should try to motivate their students, invariably through invoking interest or fun (Blumenfeld et al., 1996; Calderhead, 1996; Holt-Reynolds, 1992). In fact, the preservice teachers in the study by Holt-Reynolds (1992) made decisions about their lessons on the basis of interest rather than other factors such as the development and use of cognitive skills.

During the course of their teacher education, it appears that many preservice teachers do change their views about instruction to incorporate the constructivist principles presented in their educational psychology and other teacher-education classes. However, it appears that this conceptual change is difficult to promote and is only partially successful (Blumenfeld et al., 1996; Holt-Reynolds, 1992). Preservice teachers' new beliefs often do not appear to replace their older preconceptions about teaching. Instead they seem to adopt new beliefs without giving up their previous conceptions. Such incomplete conceptual change often results in misconceptions of important constructs. For example, Holt-Reynolds (1992) noted preservice teachers' misconceptions about active and passive learning. Whereas both preservice teachers and their instructor advocated teaching methods that involve the active learning of students, the preservice teachers viewed sitting and listening as an active process. Consequently, they saw lecturing as an instructional method that enabled students to be active learners and argued that listening to a lecture requires thinking, which is an active process. Other justifications for using lecturing extensively were congruent with a transmission model of learning. They made comments such as: "[Lecturing] can be very helpful to pass out a lot of information in a short time" (Holt-Reynolds, 1992, p. 337), and "In history, I'm sorry. It's just not going to come out of them. I'm going to have to lecture" (Holt-Reynolds, 1992, p. 333).

Another misconception that affects preservice teachers' beliefs about instruction involves the prior knowledge of students. Blumenfeld and Hicks (Blumenfeld et al., 1996; Hicks & Blumenfeld, 1995) found that while planning lessons, the preservice teachers in their study often considered only information that had been formally presented in previous lessons when they thought about the prior knowledge of students, and did not take their learning from outside of the classroom into consideration.

Although preservice teachers tend to believe that individual differences regarding students and their environment affect the ability of students to learn, they tend to underestimate the impact that individual differences can have on instructional decision making. They also seem to have difficulty in relating conceptions of individual differences of students to beliefs about instruction. For example, while planning lessons, preservice teachers demonstrated they had difficulty recognizing that students bring diverse background experiences and knowledge to the classroom, and in appreciating how this diverse range and level of prior knowledge could influence new learning (Blumenfeld et al., 1996; Hicks & Blumenfeld, 1995).

As previously discussed, preservice teachers see good teaching as motivating students through providing interest and fun. Although the preservice teachers in the study by Holt-Reynolds (1992) favored lecturing as the most efficient way to teach their students, they did endorse other formats. Their reasoning was that they believed different formats would provide interest. The focus on appealing to student interest, however, appears to be channeled toward providing embellishments, rather than necessarily being intrinsically related to the learning objectives. For example, the preservice teachers in Blumenfeld et al. (1996) tried to facilitate motivation through planning complex procedures or introducing social elements to the task, regardless of the extent to which they were linked to the desired cognitive outcomes. The limited association that many preservice teachers seem to make between motivational and cognitive aspects of academic tasks has also been identified with experienced teachers (e.g., Blumenfeld, Puro, & Mergendoller, 1992).

Novice Teachers' Conceptions After Teacher Education

Novice teachers typically begin their professional teaching careers with conceptions of student learning that have changed to some degree during their teacher education. However, these new beliefs are fragile. As they experience the complex and difficult demands of being a professional teacher with sole responsibility for their own classroom and students, many novice teachers come to revert to their earlier conceptions of learning. They appear less likely to speak about learning in terms of students actively constructing their own understandings and are more likely to articulate views about learning similar to those expressed on entering teacher-education programs. In addition, attention to student learning by novice teachers is typically overshadowed by their concerns with management issues.

Novice teachers continue to see learning by students as being influenced strongly by factors outside their control, such as personal characteristics or their home environment (Kilgore & Ross, 1993; Phelan & McLaughlin, 1995). For example, one beginning teacher began questioning her previous belief that children are natural learners and commented to researchers that some children do not want to learn (Phelan & McLaughlin, 1995). Another novice teacher in the same study spoke about how important maturity is for students and that they have the self-control necessary for learning. She also expressed her belief that this maturity has to come from within the child and could not be learned from teachers or parents (Phelan & McLaughlin, 1995). In another case study, a first-year teacher who found her class to be more challenging than she had anticipated explained her difficulties in terms of the limited ability of her students: She said "her 4th graders knew that they were dumb and that she couldn't change the way that they were" (Kilgore & Ross, 1993, p. 280).

Interestingly, it appears that lesser focus on student learning by novice teachers, in preference to concern with classroom management, changes after the initial years of teaching. Longitudinal studies of graduate teachers, into and past their beginning years, suggest that once they feel comfortable with managing their classes and have established routines, many teachers come to focus on the learning of their students (Condon, Clyde, Kyle, & Hovda, 1993; Kilgore & Ross, 1993). For example, the first-year teacher who commented that her students were dumb had, by her fifth year, changed her teaching to be consistent with a notion of active learning and construction of knowledge. She commented that, in her fifth year, she was teaching "the way she was taught to teach" (Kilgore & Ross, 1993, p. 280) and that her beliefs "were just dormant for a little while that first year" (p. 284). The return for some teachers to a focus on learning was noted also by the graduates followed up by Condon et al. (1993). They noted that over time concerns about the learning by students, such as getting students to think and attending to different learning styles, replaced an earlier focus on right answers, discipline, tests, and grading.

There is little research that investigates the conceptions of motivation of novice teachers. However, comments reported within case studies give glimpses of how novice teachers view motivation. It appears that novice teachers continue to think of motivation as being important for learning, a relatively stable student characteristic, and one that can be increased by providing fun and interest (Calderhead, 1996). Interestingly, however, given the centrality of motivation in their beliefs about learning, novice teachers generally do not focus on student motivation. Instead, as previously noted, issues of management and discipline are paramount (Condon et al., 1993; Kilgore & Ross, 1993; Regan & Hannah, 1993).

As with their tendency to relinquish their newly developed views of learning during the novice stage of teaching, the beliefs of beginning teachers about instruction appear also to revert to those held early in their teacher education (Rust, 1994). The apparent reversion by many novice teachers to the traditional views of teaching as largely transmission of information appears to be related to the initial struggles that many experience on taking responsibility for managing their own class (Rust, 1994; Veenman, 1984). Common difficulties often experienced by novice teachers, and that appear to make it difficult for them to teach in ways they had initially visualized, include: issues concerning classroom organization; unruly, disruptive student behavior; inadequate teaching materials; communicating with parents; developing collegial and supportive relationships with other teachers; and negotiating the political realities of schools (Rust, 1994; Veenman, 1984).

In contrast to their underestimation of individual differences during the preservice stage, beginning teachers become much more aware of student differences. It seems, however, that many find the tremendous variation in student characteristics overwhelming and come to believe that more traditional means of teaching are necessary for catering to the range of students. For example, one teacher, in discussing a whole language program that she had been previously excited about, said, "That [whole language instruction] sounds great, but you have to have all kids that are the same" (Phelan & McLaughlin, 1995, p. 169). This teacher expressed the belief that such teaching approaches were fine for classes that were relatively homogenous, such as those in the two nearby private schools, but were not realistic for classes containing students with a wide range of abilities.

The increased saliency of individual differences, apparent once teacher graduates began teaching, also appears to strengthen their belief that student motivation is affected by many factors outside the control of the teacher. For example, perceived student motivation also influenced the novice teacher who revisited her preservice plans to use whole language instruction and collaborative groups previously mentioned. She expressed the belief that students have to be sufficiently motivated before the teacher can use holistic and child-centered approaches, and she questioned how realistic those instructional methods were for her diverse students. She said, "It's great with kids that are really motivated. But there are kids who aren't like that" (Phelan & McLaughlin, 1995, p. 169).

Consistent with their preservice stage, novice teachers continue to try to elicit student motivation through interest and fun. For example, the apparent star of the case studies by Regan and Hannah (1993) of novice teachers made her decisions about instruction based on her own interests and those of her students. Another novice teacher in the same study created special occasions to increase general student interest, such as "black day" when all the students had to wear black and received rewards for dressing that way. As with preservice teachers, the attempts by novice teachers to elicit or enhance the motivation of students seem to be focused on embellishments rather than addressing the learning objectives of classroom lessons.

However, not all the novice teachers appear to revert to their intuitive views of teaching. When the novice teachers in the study by Condon et al. (1993) talked about their best teaching experiences, they spoke about actively involving students in the lesson, building on the interests of students, providing opportunities for choice and responsibility, and being a facilitator. Their apparent beliefs sound consistent with those supported by their teacher-education program. It is unclear, however, of the degree to which social desirability pressures influenced the comments by the teachers because they were interviewed by representatives of their teacher-education program.

As with beliefs about learning, some teachers appear to reframe their views about teaching after their first few years (Condon et al., 1993; Regan & Hannah, 1993). As their initial concerns with management and discipline subside, teachers often focus on aspects such as providing relevant learning experiences or attending to individual learning styles. For example, a teacher in her second year of teaching said, "This year I feel very confident in my management so I can spend more time in the academics and teaching and doing the kinds of things I want to do" (Regan & Hannah, 1993, p. 310). It seems clear that there is a developmental progression in teacher beliefs as they gain more experience in their classroom.

PRESERVICE AND NOVICE TEACHERS'
CONCEPTUAL CHANGE

Given this brief review of the intuitive conceptions of the teachers and their change through the preservice and novice teaching periods, it is apparent that some degree of conceptual change typically occurs. However, it is not clear how to best characterize what changes in terms of conceptual change. For example, are there specific p-prims or diverse pieces of knowledge (e.g., Smith et al., 1993) that teachers seem to use to describe learning, motivation, and instruction? For example, the idea that "more motivation leads to better achievement" (Smith et al., 1993) may be an abstraction from daily life that has explanatory power for teachers. This abstraction may be useful in some contexts, but also may not represent motivation adequately because it seems to imply a quantitative drive conception of motivation, rather than a more qualitative view of motivation that assumes how one is motivated is just as important as how much one is motivated. Nevertheless, these types of basic abstractions may be used by teachers as they think about learning, motivation, and instruction.

Beyond these basic units, are there certain types of ontological commitments (e.g., Chi, 1992; Chi et al., 1994) that teachers seem to make that need to be changed as they develop more useful conceptions of learning, motivation, and instruction? In this case, it may be that teachers see learning and motivation as entities, something that individuals have or do not have, instead of dynamic, developing, and evolving processes. This type of categorization system would result in different ways of viewing learning and motivation, and the commitment to these categories may be difficult to change. Or can teachers' conceptions be characterized as models or implicit theories of learning, motivation, and instruction? For example, it may be that teachers hold general transmission or constructivist models or implicit theories, and these general theories constrain their thinking about learning, motivation, and instruction. There is a clear need for future research on this issue that formally and explicitly addresses the nature of representations and conceptual change by teachers.

Toward a Model of Conceptual Change
for Teachers' Conceptions

Although the exact nature of the representations of teachers needs to be explored more fully both theoretically and empirically, models of student conceptual change that propose that students hold theories or models of the phenomena (Carey, 1985; Vosniadou, 1994) and that conceptual change involves the modification and restructuring of these theories may be useful in describing teacher conceptions. At the same time, in terms of applying this conceptualization to teacher beliefs, it is not clear if their beliefs fit all the criteria of a theory, at least in terms of the theory–theory research (e.g., Wellman, 1990; Wellman & Gelman, 1998). Wellman (1990) suggested three criteria for evaluating conceptions in terms of representing them as a theory. They include coherence, ontological distinctions, and a causal-explanatory framework.

In this case, coherence would involve the interrelations and interconnections among the different ideas about learning, motivation, and instruction (Wellman, 1990). At one end of the coherence continuum, the conceptions would be unconnected discrete ideas and bits of knowledge and beliefs; at the other end, the ideas would be organized in more formal ways, as in scientific theories with theorems and principles providing explicit descriptions of the relations among the ideas. It seems obvious that teacher beliefs are not organized in formal scientific ways, but they do seem to show some coherence. For example, as previously noted, the idea that learning and cognition are mainly the mastery of facts and skills as well as simple memory for content knowledge is compatible with a transmission model of instruction where the teacher tells the students these facts and expects them to recall them at some later time. In addition, an entitylike view of motivation as something that students either have or do not have parallels the general idea regarding learning and cognition that students can either have (recall) or not have (forget) facts and ideas that were taught to them. It does appear that there is some coherence here in terms of the relations among learning, motivation, and instruction even if teachers are not explicitly aware of these relations.

The second criterion, ontological distinctions, refers to the idea that a theory makes some ontological distinctions or category decisions between different entities and processes in the domain (Wellman, 1990). In the research of Chi et al. (1994), an important ontological distinction in science is noted between objects and processes. For example, they find that students often have an ontological commitment to view heat and temperature as objects instead of processes. Moreover, this categorization of them as objects automatically assigns certain category features of objects to them that are not compatible with their true nature as processes. Conceptual change in this case occurs when students do not assign them to the object category any longer, but instead view them as processes.

In the case of teacher beliefs, it does appear that teachers assign student motivation to an object category and see students as either having it (motivated) or not having it (unmotivated), as discussed in the previous section. In contrast, most current social cognitive models of motivation attempt to describe student motivation in more qualitative and multidimensional terms (Ames, 1992; Pintrich & Schunk, 1996), not just in terms of a simple dichotomous category. In addition, many current models of motivation would describe student motivation as more of an ongoing dynamic process of interactions between the student and the context, rather than as an object that students either have or do not have (Pintrich & Schunk, 1996).

In terms of learning and cognition, the object–process ontological distinction may not be as sharply delineated as with motivation, but some of the research reviewed earlier does suggest that teachers may see cognition as more of an object than as a dynamic, constructed process. Finally, most teachers, and most psychological theories for that matter, do make a clear categorical distinction between the person and the context and discuss how the features of the instructional context can influence the individual person and vice versa. In contrast, sociocultural models such as Vygotskian and neo-Vygotskian models of learning and instruction (e.g., Rogoff, 1998) suggest that the boundaries between the person and context may be too sharply drawn. Teaching prospective teachers about these sociocultural models may be difficult because these models attempt to break down the ontological distinction between persons and contexts and change the unit of analysis to a larger unit involving not just the individual but the dyad, group, or person in context. This may require a change in ontological commitment on the part of teachers, which is not easy because the person–context distinction is so intuitively appealing and useful in many contexts (even for researchers in this area).

The third criterion involves the provision of a causal-explanatory framework by the theory or model (Wellman, 1990). This may be the most difficult criterion for teacher beliefs and conceptions to satisfy in terms of an implicit theory. Given our earlier description of teacher beliefs about learning, motivation, and instruction, there are some glimmers of a causal-explanatory framework, albeit the framework may not be consistent. For example, teachers seem to conceptualize student motivation as a stable entity and, given this belief, seem to be consistent in their view that they may not be able to influence student motivation much in the classroom. However, they seem to allow for a multitude of external nonclassroom factors that can influence student motivation (i.e., media, peers, parents, etc.). In this case, it appears that student motivation can be caused or determined by external factors outside the classroom, and the teacher can do little to influence motivation except, perhaps, to make the classroom interesting to motivate the students. This inconsistency in assumptions about the potency of various external factors, including classroom factors, that could facilitate or constrain motivation suggests that teachers may not have a consistent causal-explanatory framework for motivation.

In summary, it may be useful to conceptualize teacher beliefs about learning, motivation, and instruction as aspects of an implicit theory or model, albeit not all the formal criteria may be satisfied in terms of the theory–theory research (Wellman, 1990; Wellman & Gelman, 1998). Nevertheless, the beliefs of teachers do seem to have some coherence in terms of their different conceptions and the relations among them. The analysis of the ontological distinctions and commitments that are inherent in the beliefs of teachers seems to be a useful way to discuss some aspects of the theories of teachers. Finally, there seems to be some aspects of a causal-explanatory framework in place, although it may not be completely internally consistent. Given this analysis, it may be useful to think of conceptual change in teacher conceptions in terms of theory revision and change in ontological distinctions.

It is important to understand the content of teacher conceptions and how they might be represented or structured in terms of describing teacher conceptual change. Accordingly, the general idea that teacher conceptual change might involve theory revision and ontological change is an important bridge to the cognitive literature on conceptual change and learning. However, teachers, just like students, are also motivated in different ways in terms of their own learning and changing the content of their own beliefs. Accordingly, the focus of this chapter now shifts to a discussion of the role of teacher motivation as a facilitator or constraint on conceptual change in the content of teacher beliefs. Up to this point, we have discussed student motivation as one aspect of the content of teacher beliefs. In contrast, we now turn to a consideration of how teacher motivation may influence teacher conceptual change, including the content of their beliefs about student motivation as well as learning and instruction. We also discuss the role of epistemological beliefs as a factor in teacher conceptual change. The basic approach is to suggest how conceptual change is related to three general cognitive factors and then to discuss how these cognitive factors are related to motivational and epistemological beliefs. The linkage of these different cognitive and motivational factors sketches an argument for how motivation and epistemological beliefs might then facilitate or constrain teacher conceptual change.

The Role of Motivational and Epistemological Factors in Teacher Conceptual Change

Pintrich et al. (1993) suggested that many of the cognitive factors that seem to be important for conceptual change are also related to motivational and epistemological factors. An important cognitive factor in most models of conceptual change is that some level of metacognitive awareness, also called metaconceptual awareness, reflection, or monitoring and regulating cognition, seems to be necessary for theory or ontological change. In other words, individuals have to become aware that their theory may not be adequate in some ways and through reflection become dissatisfied enough with their theory to change it. This process of meta-conceptual awareness and the resulting dissatisfaction and attempts to self-regulate thinking should be tied to motivational constructs (Pintrich et al., 1993).

In addition, much of the work on conceptual change suggests that an important second cognitive factor is that students must engage the material at some deeper level of processing, not just approach the material in terms of memorizing the content to pass an examination. Students must engage the material using deeper processing strategies such as elaboration or organizational strategies, as well as selectively attend to important cues in the environment that might signal discrepancies between their conceptions and other more veridical conceptions. This type of deeper cognitive processing should result in deeper understanding of the content and should be related to conceptual change (see Pintrich et al., 1993). Moreover, this type of deeper processing has been related to several adaptive motivational beliefs (Pintrich & Schrauben, 1992).

Finally, a third general set of cognitive processes includes engaging in general scientific thinking and problem solving such as questioning ideas and theories, hypothesizing new ideas, collecting and analyzing data, and revising causal-explanatory theories on the basis of new evidence. This type of scientific thinking should result in conceptual change and theory revision. In addition, all of these cognitive processes may be linked to motivational beliefs and epistemological factors, at least theoretically (Hofer & Pintrich, 1997; Pintrich et al., 1993). That is, the willingness of students to engage in the cognitive processes related to conceptual change processes can be facilitated or constrained by motivational and epistemological factors. The remainder of this section outlines how teachers' own motivation and their epistemological beliefs may be related to the three general cognitive processes and how they may facilitate or constrain teacher conceptual change.

The Role of Goals.   One of the most important motivational beliefs that is directly related to the nature and quality of cognition and metacognition is the goals that students adopt toward their learning. There are multiple models of goals (Pintrich & Schunk, 1996), but in academic learning contexts, one of the most relevant models concerns the adoption of mastery or performance goals (see Ames, 1992; Dweck & Leggett, 1988). Mastery goals orient the learner to focus on learning, understanding, and mastery of the task, whereas performance goals orient the learner to focus on outperforming others and a concern for grades and performance. In general, research has shown consistently that mastery goals are associated with more cognitive engagement, increased use of deeper processing and metacognitive strategies, and self-regulated and self-reflective learning (Pintrich, 2000; Pintrich & Schrauben, 1992). In addition, this research has shown that mastery-oriented students are more likely to persist at difficult tasks and, given their goal of learning and mastery, should be more likely to persist at the difficult task of building coherent models and theories. Accordingly, as Pintrich et al. (1993) suggested, students who adopt a mastery goal are more likely to demonstrate conceptual change.

Applying this to the case of teacher conceptions, it would be expected that preservice teachers who adopt a mastery orientation to their learning in educational psychology and other teacher-education courses might engage the material at a deeper level with concomitant conceptual change. That is, if preservice teachers truly have a goal of learning and understanding, then when they are confronted with different and difficult ideas about student learning and motivation and the implications for instruction, they might be more likely to think deeply about these new ideas, attempt to reconcile them with their own prior conceptions, and attempt to develop more coherent models of learning, motivation, and instruction. For example, the idea that student cognition and motivation are not static entities, but more similar to developing processes, may be a difficult ontological shift for preservice teachers to make given their prior conceptions. However, if these teachers were oriented to a goal of mastery and learning, they may be likely to engage the process conception more deeply, reflect on the meaning and implications of this ontological shift, and develop a more coherent view of student learning and motivation. Of course, this type of ontological shift would have to be supported not just by a mastery orientation of the students, but also by accompanying classroom instruction that scaffolds and supports this type of conceptual change (e.g., Anderson et al., 1995; Renninger, 1996; Strauss, 1996).

At the same time, it is not clear that many undergraduates in general, or preservice teachers specifically, adopt a mastery goal orientation to their learning in college (Pintrich, 1990). Many undergraduates may be more likely to adopt a performance orientation or are more extrinsically motivated by grades, although in the absence of a mastery goal, extrinsic goals can have some beneficial effects (Pintrich & Garcia, 1991). In addition, there is some recent work (Elliot & Church, 1997; Harackiewicz, Barron, & Elliot, 1998) that suggests that performance goals that orient the student toward approaching good grades and high levels of performance are positively related to actual achievement on multiple-choice tests in traditional college courses. Of course, this effect may be moderated by contextual factors such as the nature of assessment (multiple-choice tests) and grading practices (e.g., grading on a curve), but it does suggest that approach performance goals are not necessarily detrimental to learning. It remains to be seen whether this positive effect for performance goals will generalize to the types of academic content and tasks that are often used in educational psychology classes or teacher-education courses that require more reflection and thought (papers, portfolios, etc.) than multiple-choice tests. Nevertheless, most models of mastery and performance goals do propose that individuals' goals can be influenced by the classroom context and are more amenable to change than some other motivational constructs. In this case, it may be more productive to attempt to develop a mastery-oriented classroom structure than to be concerned about the role of performance goals.

The Role of Interest and Value. Pintrich et al. (1993) also suggested that personal interest and task value beliefs are related to the three general cognitive factors previously discussed and should then be linked to conceptual change. For example, high levels of personal interest seem to be related to learning, comprehension, and understanding as well as deeper cognitive engagement and metacognition (Pintrich & Schrauben, 1992; Schiefele, 1991). *Personal interest* is generally defined as a fairly stable, individual difference variable that reflects the positive affect by the individual and liking of the task or content area (Pintrich & Schunk, 1996).

In terms of teacher learning and development, it is not clear what their personal interest is in the topics of student learning, motivation, and instruction. At one level, it seems that they should be interested in these topics because teachers deal with these issues every day in classrooms. On the other hand, it seems that teachers are often not particularly interested in these topics, at least as typically represented in our psychological theories and models and presented in our educational psychology classes (e.g., Anderson et al., 1995). Preservice teachers may be more interested in issues of classroom management and the practical aspects of classrooms than more general issues of learning, development, and motivation. As previously noted, there is some evidence that teachers become less interested in classroom management as they come to master it after several years of actual teaching experience, and at this point become more interested in student learning and development. It may be that if personal interest is more stable or at least developmentally sensitive to differential experience, it may not be a construct that is that amenable to change and not a viable pathway for teacher conceptual change in teacher-education programs.

In contrast, task value beliefs can refer to beliefs of students about the utility of the task or material as well as the general importance of the task and material (Eccles, 1983). Paralleling the findings for interest, it also appears that students who think the task is important and useful to them in some way are more likely to be cognitively engaged and use more cognitive and metacognitive strategies (Pintrich & Schrauben, 1992). Applying this to teachers, those individuals who see some utility or importance to psychological content may be more likely to consider how they can revise their own beliefs about learning, motivation, and instruction in light of this new information. At the same time, it is not clear that teachers see much utility to this information because it is typically represented in our theories and models (Anderson et al., 1995; Doyle & Carter, 1996). For example, teacher educators have argued that teachers may represent their knowledge of teaching in terms of stories or narratives that do not easily map onto general and decontextualized psychological principles and theories as commonly presented in educational psychology courses (Carter, 1993; Doyle & Carter, 1996). If this is the case, it may be difficult to increase the perception of the utility of educational psychological material unless it is conveyed in a more contextualized manner in our courses and teacher-education programs.

The Role of Efficacy and Control Beliefs.   Pintrich et al. (1993) noted that goals, interest, and value represent the reasons that students might engage in the cognitive processes related to conceptual change, but another important component of motivation concerns students beliefs about their capabilities to accomplish different tasks (self-efficacy) and control their own learning (control beliefs). Adaptive efficacy and control beliefs are positively related to the use of deeper processing strategies and self-regulatory processes that should lead to more conceptual change (Pintrich et al., 1993; Pintrich & Schrauben, 1992). Accordingly, teachers who are confident in their capabilities to learn and feel that they have some control over their own learning may be more open to learning about new ideas and theories that might contradict their beliefs. As Tschannen-Moran, Hoy, and Hoy (1998) suggested, teacher efficacy can play an important mediating role in learning to teach, in the potential for teacher growth and learning, as well as actual teacher classroom behavior.

This perspective on the role of efficacy in teacher beliefs and learning reflects confidence by the teachers in their capability to learn as well as to use various cognitive and self-regulatory strategies or tools for thinking. However, as Pintrich et al. (1993) suggested, efficacy could also refer to confidence by the students in their own beliefs. If students are confident that their own beliefs and implicit theories are the most useful and productive models of learning, motivation, and instruction, then conceptual change would be impeded or constrained by high-efficacy beliefs. Most of the conceptual change models suggest that an important aspect of instruction is the destabilization of the confidence of students in their own beliefs through the use of conflicting data, ideas, or theories (Pintrich et al., 1993). Dole and Sinatra (1998) made a similar argument for conceptual change by integrating models of persuasion and communication from social psychology with the conceptual change literature. Accordingly, attempts to engage students in conceptual change must balance two conflicting aspects of efficacy: attempting to maintain student efficacy for learning new ideas while also trying to weaken their efficacy or confidence in their own ideas. This is not an easy task; it is easy to imagine students either reacting to change efforts by hardening their confidence in their own beliefs or feeling completely inefficacious and lost by the presentation of new models and ideas. In fact, it is a common refrain for students in teacher-education courses to note that they used to know what to think, but now they are completely confused and lost. The important issue here is that, although students may feel confused, which may be a first step in conceptual change (dissatisfaction with own ideas), they need to maintain their self-efficacy so that they can eventually come to learn and integrate the new ideas.

The Role of Epistemological Beliefs. Besides these motivational factors, students' own personal epistemology might be related to their learning and conceptual change (Hofer & Pintrich, 1997) as well as teacher learning and change (Pintrich, 1990). There are many different models of personal epistemology, but four dimensions seem important in most of the different models (Hofer & Pintrich, 1997): beliefs about the certainty of knowledge, simplicity of knowledge, source of knowledge, and ways of justifying knowledge. Most of the models assume that individuals vary on these dimensions from less sophisticated or early developing positions to more sophisticated or later developing positions on these dimensions.

Personal beliefs about the certainty of knowledge reflect the conception by the individual of how fixed or fluid knowledge is over time. Most models of epistemological beliefs and thinking propose that the belief that knowledge is fixed and immutable to be at a lower level of development or sophistication in comparison to the other end of the continuum, where knowledge is viewed as changing on the basis of new information, developments, research, and theories (Hofer & Pintrich, 1997). Individuals who believe that knowledge is fixed and does not change are probably less likely to engage in conceptual change activities in contrast to those who are more open to the possibilities that knowledge can change with time and new developments. In terms of teacher thinking and beliefs, if teachers hold this epistemological belief, they may be less receptive to new developments in teaching and learning and this position will constrain conceptual change. In fact, much of the research on teacher change with experienced teachers suggests that these more experienced teachers are often resistant to new ideas and models of teaching and learning (Richardson &

Placier, in press). Although the resistance may be due to the comforts of practice, if these experienced teachers also believe that knowledge is fixed and immutable, this epistemological belief will certainly support their propensity to reject new ideas and models.

The second dimension of epistemological thinking concerns the belief about the simplicity of knowledge. Simplicity of knowledge refers to belief by an individual that knowledge is simple and made up of discrete facts anchoring one end of the continuum, and the belief that knowledge is more complex, relative, situational, and contextual, marking the other end of the continuum (Hofer & Pintrich, 1997). Students who view knowledge as simple seem to approach learning with this view and attempt to memorize or draw out simple facts and conclusions from the materials (e.g., Schommer, 1990). In the same manner, teachers who want the one right or correct answer to questions about student learning, motivation, and instruction may be operating from the "knowledge is simple" end of the continuum of epistemological thinking. If this is the case, this personal epistemological belief would seem to constrain teacher-education efforts to have teachers think about models and theories of learning, motivation, and instruction in more contextualized and situational ways (Pintrich, 1990).

The third dimension of epistemological thinking concerns beliefs about the source of knowledge or where knowledge originates. Most models propose a developmental progression from believing that knowledge originates outside the self and comes from external authorities telling the individual the truth, as in students wanting professors to tell them the correct answer. At the other end of the continuum is the belief that knowledge can be constructed by the individual in interaction with others and in relation to different theories, models, and evidence (Hofer & Pintrich, 1997). In contrast to the other two dimensions, teachers may not be at the lowest end of this continuum because they often seem to reject the ideas presented by external authorities in their teacher-education courses. In terms of the developmental progression of epistemological thinking, they may be more likely to use a relativistic way of thinking, where all knowledge is relative and personal and any individual's opinion is as valid and useful as any other individual's view. In this case, they would be likely to reject alternative views of learning, motivation, and instruction when presented in formal educational psychology or other teacher-education courses.

Related to the source of knowledge, the fourth dimension concerns how individuals evaluate knowledge claims including their use of evidence and their reliance on authority and experts. Following the general developmental progression, there seems to be a shift away from dualistic beliefs about knowledge to a more multiplistic view of knowledge that includes a careful consideration of evidence, including what counts as evidence, and a willingness to consider alternative viewpoints with a more reasoned and rational perspective (Hofer & Pintrich, 1997). Again, teachers may not be at the lowest level of epistemological thinking on this dimension, but more likely in the middle of the developmental progression where there is much more reliance on personal experience and knowledge than other sources of evidence. This reliance on personal knowledge leads to more relativistic reasoning (all individuals' opinions or views are equally valid) given that it is difficult to adjudicate between or make decisions about the validity of varying personal experiences. Certainly, as novice teachers gain more experience in the actual classroom, their personal knowledge and experiences can be a useful resource for them in thinking about learning, motivation, and instruction. However, as previously noted, preservice teachers may not have much relevant personal knowledge or experience to draw on except for their own life experience as students, not as teachers (Richardson, 1996; Richardson & Placier, in press). Attempts to help preservice teachers revise their beliefs and thinking need to help them reframe and revise their own personal experiences in light of their new role as teachers. Besides the difficulty of changing these beliefs, prospective teachers' general epistemological beliefs about the role of evidence and justification for knowledge might constrain the opportunities for conceptual change.

In summary, we have suggested that teacher conceptual change is related to three general cognitive factors including: (a) metaconceptual awareness and reflection; (b) deeper cognitive processing and use of cognitive strategies; and (c) general scientific thinking and processing. In turn, we have developed the argument that these general cognitive factors can be facilitated by three adaptive motivational beliefs including: (a) adoption of mastery goals for learning and understanding; (b) higher levels of personal interest, utility, and value in the educational psychological content regarding student cognition and motivation as well as instruction; and (c) high levels of personal self-efficacy and control for learning and understanding educational psychological content.

We also suggested that there are four dimensions of epistemological beliefs whereby, depending on the position of the teacher on the continuum, conceptual change may be facilitated or constrained. The four most facilitative positions seem to be: (a) a belief that knowledge is always developing based on new evidence, research, models, and theories; (b) a belief that knowledge is not simple, but complex, situational, relative, and contextual; (c) a belief that knowledge can be constructed by the individual but in relation to warranted claims about evidence, models, and theories developed by others; and (d) a belief that knowledge should be justified by the use of evidence and a rational, reasoned, and careful consideration of alternative viewpoints. Of course, much of this argument awaits actual empirical data, but it does offer suggestions for future research as well as implications for teaching educational psychology.

IMPLICATIONS FOR TEACHING
EDUCATIONAL PSYCHOLOGY

Our overview of intuitive conceptions of teachers about student learning, motivation, and instruction has shown that their conceptions do undergo change during the preservice and novice teacher periods. In addition, change appears to be achieved more effectively during the preservice and novice teaching periods than after teachers have gained years of teaching experience (Cronin-Jones & Shaw, 1992). This review, the need for conceptual change, and our discussion of how motivational and epistemological factors might facilitate or constrain such change show that teacher educators need to work consciously at facilitating preservice teachers' conceptual change. There are a number of implications for the teaching of educational psychology that result from the material we have presented. We offer the following suggestions, not as directives that should always be followed in the teaching of educational psychology, but more in the spirit of design principles (cf. Brown, 1997) that can be used to design instructional contexts that fit with local and situational needs. Accordingly, we would expect that some of these suggestions would prove useful in some contexts but not in others depending on the constraints operating in the educational psychology class and the larger teacher-education program in which it is situated.

Teachers of Educational Psychology Should Be Aware of Their Students' Entering Beliefs About Learning, Motivation, and Instruction. Because preservice teachers' conceptual change depends on their entering beliefs (e.g., Tillema, 1994), instructors need to have an accurate awareness of their students' beliefs. Holt-Reynolds (1992) noted that preservice teachers and instructors often discuss important constructs without being aware that each views the same constructs in markedly different ways. This was illustrated by the previously discussed incongruence between preservice teachers' conceptualization of active learning and that of their instructor (Holt-Reynolds, 1992). Therefore, instructors may wish to ask students to define and illustrate central constructs rather than assume a shared understanding of terms. Instructors might also want to assess the entering beliefs of their students every semester to understand the individual variation in their current classroom.

In addition to investigating specific beliefs of students, there is a need for teacher educators to systematically identify commonly held belief systems characteristic of preservice teachers. This should help improve instruction, just as the literature in science that has documented various naive and alternative conceptions about natural phenomena has helped organize science curriculum and instructional efforts. In particular, there is a paucity of research addressing conceptions of teachers about student motivation. This is unfortunate given the tremendous importance that teachers ascribe to student motivation as affecting both the learning of students and their own instructional approaches.

There Should Be Multiple Opportunities for Students to Become Aware of Their Own Beliefs and to Challenge and Confront Them. As previously noted, if preservice teachers are unaware of their own implicit theories and beliefs, they will be unlikely to engage in activities that will lead to conceptual change. Accordingly, instructors should create multiple opportunities to help preservice teachers identify their implicit beliefs and articulate them more explicitly and formally. Activities such as concept maps or the creation of other physical representations of their beliefs and models can help students objectify their beliefs. Because they result in some tangible representation, they allow for self-examination and enable others (the educational psychology instructor, peers, and cooperating teachers) to confront and challenge these beliefs and theories.

An example of such an activity was given by Renninger (1996), who asked the preservice teachers in her educational psychology class to consider whether they viewed snorkeling or carpentry as the better metaphor for the learning process. She then had students, in small groups, draw a model of learning that relates to the metaphor they chose. The class then shared and discussed the different models, and she encouraged students to identify characteristics of learning that are repeated across different models (e.g., exploration, personal investment, and hands-on learning). Finally, Renninger explained the purpose of the activity, including how it served as a foundation for the rest of the course. She repeated this activity at the end of their educational psychology course and asked students to make comparisons between their new and initial models.

Another format that provokes student teachers into making their conceptions explicit and linking their beliefs with practices is the lesson planning in which Blumenfeld et al. (1996) engaged prospective teachers. This process of planning and writing rationales enables explicitly stated beliefs and assumptions to be confronted and reexamined. Additionally, tasks such as planning lessons may facilitate conceptual revision because they involve students in integrating, synthesizing, and applying learning across different areas (Blumenfeld & Anderson, 1996).

The Encouragement of a Community of Learners Focused on Mastery and Understanding Should Help Students Engage in Conceptual Change. The revision of intuitive conceptions and the conceptual change process is difficult and challenging. Students need to be supported in their attempts to revise their own beliefs. As we have suggested, the willingness of students to grapple with their existing beliefs and revise them is undoubtedly important to the conceptual change process. A learning environment that emphasizes students' relative performance or besting others (i.e., a performance orientation) is likely to impede conceptual change. In contrast, a learning environment that emphasizes learning and understanding (i.e., a mastery orientation) should encourage students to engage with the material in a deeper, more reflective manner with greater potential for conceptual change. This type of mastery-focused context usually increases student interest, value, and self-efficacy (Pintrich & Schunk, 1996). There are a number of suggestions for how to structure learning environments to encourage a mastery orientation (e.g., Maehr & Midgley, 1996), but some include the use of authentic, interesting tasks; a grading system focused on mastery, not normative grading on a curve; and the use of evaluation criteria that highlight conceptual change and learning, not memorization of facts.

Explicit Discussion of the Various Epistemological Beliefs and Stances That Might Underlie Students' Implicit Theories and Beliefs.

The four dimensions of epistemological beliefs may facilitate or constrain preservice teachers' conceptual change, as previously noted. Most teacher-education programs, and certainly educational psychology courses, present to prospective teachers not only different models and theories of learning, motivation, and instruction, but also a different epistemology for thinking about these issues. The epistemology involves a move away from a reliance on simple and certain knowledge, including personal experience, and a relativistic manner of thinking to a more complex, situational, and reasoned perspective that is warranted by various sources of evidence. However, preservice teachers may be inclined to seek general rules and overinterpret research implications as prescriptive. Therefore, Phelan and McLaughlin (1995) suggested that teacher educators should illustrate the implicit tensions and uncertainty of teaching. This may include instructors metacognitively reflecting on their decisions and discourse as they conduct classes and verbalizing those reflections so that students witness the complexity of instructional decision making (cf. Lampert, 1985). The revision of epistemological beliefs is not an easy developmental progression; students will need support and scaffolding as they confront these issues in the classroom.

In summary, the process of conceptual change in teacher beliefs and thinking is not a trivial task. There are a host of cognitive, motivational, and epistemological factors that can facilitate or constrain teacher conceptual change. Educational psychology instructors can help facilitate conceptual change by assisting preservice teachers to identify and articulate their beliefs about learning, motivation, and instruction and by highlighting inconsistencies in their thinking and language. Additionally, designing their courses to motivate students to engage with the material deeply, and making explicit the epistemological beliefs that support preservice teachers' implicit theories, can further facilitate their conceptual change. Of course educational psychology courses are just one aspect of a teacher-education program. However, if we are able to make some of these changes in our courses, we may well contribute to the conceptual change process in areas that are at the heart of teacher-education programs and teaching in general.

REFERENCES

Ames, C. (1992). Classrooms: Goals, structures, and student motivation. *Journal of Educational Psychology, 84*, 261–271.

Anderson, L. M., Blumenfeld, P., Pintrich, P. R., Clark, C. M., Marx, R. W., & Peterson, P. (1995). Educational psychology for teachers: Reforming our courses, rethinking our roles. *Educational Psychologist, 30*, 143–157.

Battista, M. T. (1994). Teacher beliefs and the reform movement in mathematics education. *Phi Delta Kappan*, pp. 462–470.

Blumenfeld, P. C., & Anderson, L. (1996). Editors' comments. *Educational Psychologist, 31*, 1–4.

Blumenfeld, P. C., Hicks, L., & Krajcik, J. S. (1996). Teaching educational psychology through instructional planning. *Educational Psychologist, 31*, 51–61.

Blumenfeld, P. C., Puro, P., & Mergendoller, J. (1992). Translating motivation into thoughtfulness. In H. Marshall (Ed.), *Redefining student learning* (pp. 207–240). Norwood, NJ: Ablex.

Book, C., Byers, J., & Freeman, D. (1983). Student expectations and teacher education traditions with which we can and cannot live. *Journal of Teacher Education, 34*, 9–13.

Borko, H., & Putnam, R. T. (1996). Learning to teach. In D. C. Berliner & R. C. Calfee (Eds.), *Handbook of educational psychology* (pp. 673–708). New York: Macmillan.

Brown, A. (1997). Transforming schools into communities of thinking and learning about serious matters. *American Psychologist, 52*, 399–413.

Bruer, J. (1993). *Schools for thought: A science of learning in the classroom.* Cambridge, MA: MIT Press.

Calderhead, J. (1991). The nature and growth of knowledge in student teaching. *Teaching and Teacher Education, 7*, 531–535.

Calderhead, J. (1996). Teachers: Beliefs and knowledge. In D. C. Berliner & R. C. Calfee (Eds.), *Handbook of educational psychology* (pp. 709–725). New York: Macmillan.

Carey, S. (1985). *Conceptual change in childhood.* Cambridge, MA: MIT Press.

Carretero, M., & Voss, J. (1994). *Cognitive and instructional processes in history and social science.* Hillsdale, NJ: Lawrence Erlbaum Associates.

Carter, K. (1993). The place of story in the study of teaching and teacher education. *Educational Researcher, 22*(1), 5–12, 18.

Chi, M. (1992). Conceptual change within and across ontological categories: Examples from learning and discovery in science. In R. Giere (Ed.), *Cognitive models of science: Minnesota studies in the philosophy of science* (pp. 129–186). Minneapolis: University of Minnesota Press.

Chi, M., Slotta, J., & de Leeuw, N. (1994). From things to processes: A theory of conceptual change for learning science concepts. *Learning and Instruction, 4*, 27–43.

Condon, M. W. G., Clyde, J. A., Kyle, D. W., & Hovda, R. A. (1993). A constructivist basis for teaching and teacher education: A framework for program development and research on graduates. *Journal of Teacher Education, 44*, 273–278.

Cronin-Jones, L., & Shaw, E. L. (1992). The influence of methods instruction on the beliefs of preservice elementary and secondary science teachers: Preliminary comparative analyses. *School Science and Mathematics, 92*, 14–22.

Dole, J., & Sinatra, G. (1998). Reconceptualizing change in the cognitive construction of knowledge. *Educational Psychologist, 33*, 109–128.

Doyle, W., & Carter, K. (1996). Educational psychology and the education of teachers: A reaction. *Educational Psychologist, 31*, 23–28.

Dweck, C. S., & Leggett, E. L. (1988). A social-cognitive approach to motivation and personality. *Psychological Review, 95*, 256–273.

Eccles, J. (1983). Expectations, values, and academic behaviors. In J. T. Spence (Ed.), *Achievement and achievement motives* (pp. 75–146). San Francisco: Freeman.

Elliot, A., & Church, M. (1997). A hierarchical model of approach and avoidance achievement motivation. *Journal of Personality and Social Psychology, 72*, 218–232.

Gardner, H. (1991). *The unschooled mind.* New York: Basic Books.

Harackiewicz, J., Barron, K. E., & Elliot, A. J. (1998). Rethinking achievement goals: When are they adaptive for college students and why? *Educational Psychologist, 33*, 1–21.

Hicks, L., & Blumenfeld, P. C. (1995, April). *Planning: A vehicle for understanding student thinking.* Paper presented at the annual meeting of the American Educational Research Association, San Francisco, CA.

Hofer, B. K., & Pintrich, P. R. (1997). The development of epistemological theories: Beliefs about knowledge and knowing and their relation to learning. *Review of Educational Research, 67*, 88–140.

Hollingsworth, S. (1989). Prior beliefs and cognitive change in learning to teach. *American Educational Research Journal, 26*, 160–189.

Holt-Reynolds, D. (1992). Personal history-based beliefs as relevant prior knowledge in course work. *American Educational Research Journal, 29*, 325–349.

Keil, F. (1998). Cognitive science and the origins of thought and knowledge. In W. Damon (Series Ed.) & R. M. Lerner (Vol. Ed.), *Handbook of child psychology: Vol. 1. Theoretical models of human development* (5th ed., pp. 341–413). New York: Wiley.

Kilgore, K., & Ross, D. (1993). Following PROTEACH graduates: The fifth year of practice. *Journal of Teacher Education, 44*, 279–287.

Lampert, M. (1985). How do teachers manage to teach? Perspectives on problems on practice. *Harvard Educational Review, 55*, 178–194.

Maehr, M., & Midgley, C. (1996). *Transforming school cultures.* Boulder, CO: Westview.

Nespor, J. (1987). The role of beliefs in the practice of teaching. *Journal of Curriculum Studies, 19*, 317–328.

Osborne, R., & Freyburg, P. (1985). *Learning in science: The implications of children's science.* Portsmouth, NH: Heinemann.

Pajares, F. (1992). Teachers' beliefs and educational research: Cleaning up a messy construct. *Review of Educational Research, 62*, 307–332.

Phelan, A. M., & McLaughlin, H. J. (1995). Educational discourses, the nature of the child, and the practice of new teachers. *Journal of Teacher Education, 46*, 165–174.

Pintrich, P. R. (1990). Implications of psychological research on student learning and college teaching for teacher education. In W. R. Houston (Ed.), *Handbook of research on teacher education* (pp. 826–857). New York: Macmillan.

Pintrich, P. R. (2000). The role of goal orientation in self-regulated learning. In M. Boekaerts, P. R. Pintrich, & M. Zeidner (Eds.), *Handbook of self-regulation: Theory, research, and applications* (pp. 451–502). New York: Academic Press.

Pintrich, P. R., & Garcia, T. (1991). Student goal orientation and self-regulation in the college classroom. In M. L. Maehr & P. R. Pintrich (Eds.), *Advances in motivation and achievement* (Vol. 7, pp. 371–402). Greenwich, CT: JAI.

Pintrich, P. R., Marx, R., & Boyle, R. (1993). Beyond cold conceptual change: The role of motivational beliefs and classroom contextual factors in the process of conceptual change. *Review of Educational Research, 63,* 167–199.

Pintrich, P. R., & Schrauben, B. (1992). Students' motivational beliefs and their cognitive engagement in the classroom academic tasks. In D. Schunk & J. Meece (Eds.), *Student perceptions in the classroom* (pp. 149–183). Hillsdale, NJ: Lawrence Erlbaum Associates.

Pintrich, P. R., & Schunk, D. H. (1996). *Motivation in education: Theory, research and applications.* Englewood Cliffs, NJ: Prentice-Hall.

Pultorak, E. G. (1996). Following the developmental process of reflection in novice teachers: Three years of investigation. *Journal of Teacher Education, 47,* 283–291.

Regan, H. B., & Hannah, B. H. (1993). Ten teachers teaching: The interplay of individuals, their preparation and their schools. *Journal of Teacher Education, 44,* 305–311.

Renninger, K. A. (1996). Learning as the focus of the educational psychology course. *Educational Psychologist, 31,* 63–76.

Richardson, V. (1996). The role of attitudes and beliefs in learning to teach. In J. Sikula (Ed.), *Handbook of research on teacher education* (pp. 102–119). New York: Macmillan.

Richardson, V., & Placier, P. (in press). Teacher change. In V. Richardson (Ed.), *Handbook of research on teaching.* Washington, DC: American Educational Research Association.

Rogoff, B. (1998). Cognition as a collaborative process. In W. Damon (Series Ed.) & D. Kuhn & R. S. Siegler (Vol. Eds.), *Handbook of child psychology: Vol. 2. Cognition, perception, and language* (5th ed., pp. 679–744). New York: Wiley.

Rust, F. O. (1994). The first year of teaching: It's not what they expected. *Teaching and Teacher Education, 10,* 205–217.

Schiefele, U. (1991). Interest, learning, and motivation. *Educational Psychologist, 26,* 299–323.

Schommer, M. (1990). Effects of beliefs about the nature of knowledge on comprehension. *Journal of Educational Psychology, 82,* 498–504.

Smith, J., diSessa, A., & Roschelle, J. (1993). Misconceptions reconceived: A constructivist analysis of knowledge in transition. *The Journal of the Learning Sciences, 3,* 115–163.

Strauss, S. (1996). Confessions of a born-again constructivist. *Educational Psychologist, 31,* 15–21.

Strike, K. A., & Posner, G. J. (1992). A revisionist theory of conceptual change. In R. Duschl & R. Hamilton (Eds.), *Philosophy of science, cognitive psychology, and educational theory and practice* (pp. 147–176). Albany, NY: State University of New York Press.

Tillema, H. H. (1994). Training and professional expertise: Bridging the gap between new information and pre-existing beliefs of teachers. *Teaching and Teacher Education, 10,* 601–615.

Tschannen-Moran, M., Hoy, A. W., & Hoy, W. K. (1998). Teacher efficacy: Its meaning and measure. *Review of Educational Research, 68,* 202–248.

Veenman, S. (1984). Perceived problems of beginning teachers. *Review of Educational Research, 54,* 143–178.

Vosniadou, S. (1994). Capturing and modeling the process of conceptual change. *Learning and Instruction, 4,* 45–69.

Weinstein, C. S. (1989). Teacher education students' perceptions of teaching. *Journal of Teacher Education, 40,* 53–60.

Wellman, H. (1990). *The child's theory of mind.* Cambridge, MA: MIT Press.

Wellman, H., & Gelman, S. (1998). Knowledge acquisition in foundational domains. In W. Damon (Series Ed.) & D. Kuhn & R. S. Siegler (Vol. Eds.), *Handbook of child psychology: Vol. 2. Cognition, perception, and language* (5th ed., pp. 523–573). New York: Wiley.

Wideen, M., Mayer-Smith, J., & Moon, B. (1998). A critical analysis of the research on learning to teach: Making the case for an ecological perspective on inquiry. *Review of Educational Research, 68,* 130–178.

CHAPTER SEVEN

Teaching Educational Psychology to the Implicit Mind

Anita Woolfolk Hoy
P. Karen Murphy
Ohio State University

With the dominance of cognitive perspectives in education and psychology has come an interest in the thinking of teachers. Since the 1980s, research has burgeoned on teachers' knowledge and beliefs; reviews are plentiful (e.g., Borko & Putnam, 1996; Calderhead, 1996; Clark & Peterson, 1986; Fenstermacher, 1994; Kagan, 1990, 1992; Nespor, 1987; Pajares, 1992; Rentel, 1994; Richardson, 1994, 1996). Researchers have investigated both explicit and implicit beliefs of preservice, novice, and experienced teachers. Although some investigators have sought to identify beliefs (cf. Weinstein, 1988, 1989), others have examined how knowledge and beliefs affect learning to teach (cf. Hollingworth, 1989) or instruction in particular subjects (Richardson, 1994).

This interest in the knowledge and beliefs of teachers is fueled by several sources. In research on effective teaching, dissatisfaction with findings about teacher behaviors led to a concern with teachers' thinking, planning, and intentions (Clark & Peterson, 1986; Fenstermacher, 1979). Several current perspectives on learning—from information processing to constructivist views—highlight the influence of knowledge on attention, understanding, and memory. What we already know, our knowledge base, "is a scaffold that supports the construction of all future learning" (Alexander, 1996, p. 89). Thus, researchers focused on the knowledge, implicit and explicit, that scaffolds learning to teach. Finally, teacher educators recognized the power of prospective teachers' entering beliefs in shaping their responses to preparation programs (Pajares, 1992; Richardson, 1996).

As noted by Borko and Putnam (1996), ". . . the knowledge and beliefs that prospective and experienced teachers hold serve as filters through which their learning takes place. It is through these existing conceptions that teachers come to understand recommended new practices" (p. 675).

The purpose of this chapter is to examine the implications for educational psychologists and teacher educators of prospective teachers' implicit knowledge and beliefs about students, teaching, learning, and learning to teach. We begin by exploring the nature and origin of teachers' knowledge and beliefs, then consider how prospective teachers' conceptions affect their own learning in a teacher-preparation program and what might be done to enhance learning in light of these influences. Finally, we examine the implications of prospective teachers' knowledge and beliefs for teaching educational psychology.

DEFINING KNOWLEDGE AND BELIEFS

Understandings of the term *knowledge* can be traced back to the time of Socrates circa 400 B.C. For example, in *Meno and Theaetetus*, Plato suggests that human knowledge has three components (i.e., belief, truth, and justification). Based on this understanding, philosophers have traditionally defined *knowledge* as a justified true belief (e.g., Moser & vander Nat, 1987). Specifically, knowledge is a belief that satisfies two conditions: (a) the truth of what is believed, and (b) the justification someone has for believing it. To embrace such a definition, however, one must accept that knowledge requires belief, but belief does not require knowledge, and the notion that individuals could agree on the nuances of justification (e.g., Goldman, 1986; Hussey, 1990).

A perusal of the learning literatures suggests a quite different definition. In fact, researchers in these areas generally define *knowledge* as one's idiosyncratic reserve of skills, information, experiences, beliefs, and memories. For example, in a review of research about how students learn, acquire, and use language, Alexander, Schallert, and Hare (1991) asserted that knowledge "encompasses all that a person knows or believes to be true, whether or not it is verified as true in some sort of objective or external way" (p. 317). In contrast to the more philosophical definition of knowledge, the Alexander et al. (1991) definition assumes that beliefs are a category of knowledge. It is this latter definition that has been widely accepted in the literature on teaching and learning (e.g., Alexander & Murphy, 1998; Murphy & Woods, 1996).

According to Richardson (1996), anthropologists, social psychologists, and philosophers—three groups that have studied the nature of beliefs and their connection to actions—generally agree on a definition of *beliefs* as "psychologically held understandings, premises, or propositions about the world that are felt to be true" (p. 103). As such, beliefs have much in common with concepts such as attitudes, values, judgments, opinions, dispositions, implicit theories, preconceptions, personal theories, and perspectives and often are used interchangeably with these terms (Pajares, 1992). Years ago, Rokeach (1968) suggested that beliefs are organized in ways that are not logical but psychological, with some beliefs being more central and more connected to other beliefs, and thus more difficult to change. Further, beliefs may be organized in clusters, allowing incompatible beliefs to be held in separate clusters and thus protected from each other (Green, 1971).

Knowledge and Beliefs

As the preceding paragraphs suggest, conceptions of knowledge and beliefs have been widely debated. A major distinction cited is that knowledge must have some truth condition or some evidence to back up the claim, whereas beliefs can be held—felt to be true—without necessarily having a base in evidence (Richardson, 1996). Nisbett and Ross (1980) considered beliefs to be a type of knowledge. They described two components of generic knowledge. The first is a cognitive component organized schematically. An example of this aspect of knowledge is a teacher's knowledge of the school rules. The second aspect of knowledge is a belief component that involves evaluation and judgment, such as the teacher's knowledge that some of the rules are unrealistic or unfair (Pajares, 1992). Rokeach (1968) subsumed knowledge as a kind of belief. He suggested that all beliefs have a cognitive component (knowledge), an affective component (judgment, evaluation, and emotion), and a behavioral component when action is necessary (Pajares, 1992).

Nespor (1987) suggested that knowledge and beliefs can be distinguished along four dimensions: presumption of existence, ideal or alternative state, affective or evaluative loading, and episodic structure. Beliefs assert that things (such as intelligence or personality traits) exist or do not exist. A part of a belief is an image of the ideal or alternative that contrasts with current reality. Beliefs also are associated with evaluations—feelings about what is and what should be, as in the previous example about the fairness of school rules. Finally, beliefs often are connected with well-remembered episodes or events. A belief about the unfairness of school rules might be traced to an unfortunate personal encounter with a rule.

For much of the research on teachers' cognition, however, no clear distinctions are made between knowledge and beliefs. As Garner and Alexander (1994) noted, this lack of distinction is attributable, in part, to the fact that few studies have investigated teachers' conceptualizations of these terms. One notable exception is a series of studies conducted by Alexander and colleagues (e.g., Alexander & Dochy, 1995; Alexander, Murphy, & Woods, 1996; Alexander, Murphy, Guan, & Murphy, 1998) investigating how teachers and students of varying educational levels conceptualize knowledge and beliefs. Specifically, the respondents in these studies consistently conceptualized knowledge as factual, externally verified, or widely accepted content, whereas beliefs referred to ideas or thoughts that individuals perceived as true or wanted to be true. Unlike knowledge, beliefs also included subjective claims for which truth or validity was unimportant. Despite these conceptual differences between knowledge and beliefs, the majority of respondents perceived knowledge and beliefs as overlapping constructs. Simply put, respondents posited that, although some knowledge and beliefs remain independent, many ideas fall in the realm of what is both known and believed. Given that teachers often seem to define knowledge and beliefs as overlapping constructs, a precedent set by other researchers of teacher cognition (e.g., Borko & Putnam, 1996; Fenstermacher, 1994; Kagan, 1992), within this review we discuss knowledge and beliefs as overlapping and somewhat interchangeable constructs.

Implicit Knowledge and Beliefs

Teachers' practical knowledge, first studied by Elbaz (1983), is "an account of how a teacher knows or understands a classroom situation" (Richardson, 1996, p. 104). A related concept is craft knowledge, or the knowledge that teachers acquire within their own practice. This is "the professional knowledge which teachers use in their day-to-day classroom teaching, knowledge which is not generally made explicit by teachers and which teachers are not likely always to be conscious of using" (Brown & McIntyre, 1993, p. 19). As such, this knowledge is similar to Schon's (1983) conception of knowledge in action. The knowledge is contextual, situated, and often tacit. Yinger (1987) suggested that this knowledge cannot be separated from the actions taken by the teacher. It is through this practical knowledge that teachers can improvise to participate in changing classroom situations. Researchers in this tradition have examined connections between teachers' personal constructs and their teaching practices (e.g., Bussis, Chittenden, & Amarel, 1976; Clandinin, 1986; Cochran-Smith & Lytle, 1990) and have emphasized reciprocal relationships between personal theories and practice. Practical knowledge is a forerunner of action, but also is changed by reflection on actions. This often tacit knowledge may be embodied in images, routines, procedures, and rhythms of classroom life (Richardson, 1996).

Prospective teachers also have a store of tacit knowledge about students, learning, and teaching. Pajares (1993) noted that many college students begin their preparation for careers as strangers to the professional world they hope to join. Architects, physicians, and lawyers have ways of behaving that are unfamiliar to the novice and thus students of those professions expect to learn new knowledge, behaviors, and beliefs. The learning process "involves minimal conflict or threat, for [the students] have slight allegiance to prior expectations or ties to former practices and habits" (Pajares, 1993, p. 46). Students of teaching, however, are "insiders." They need not discover the classroom or see it with new eyes because they are completely familiar with the territory—having spent the last dozen or so years of their lives in similar places. In learning to be teachers, they "simply return to places of their past, complete with memories and preconceptions of days gone by, preconceptions that often remain largely unaffected by higher education . . ." (Pajares, 1993, p. 46). These preconceptions, being so familiar and accessible, are powerful influences because in learning to teach, as in all learning, what prospective teachers already know determines to a great extent what they will pay attention to, perceive, learn, remember, and forget (Greeno, Collins, & Resnick, 1996; Resnick, 1981; Shuell, 1986, 1990, 1996).

> By the time prospective teachers come to our educational psychology courses, they almost surely have constructed deep and powerful implicit models of learning based on many thousands of hours of being taught. And why is this important? Because research in cognition and education shows time and again that mental models organize how students learn what is taught in a domain and are quite resistant to change via instruction. . . . (Strauss, 1996, p. 18)

As Strauss indicated, implicit knowledge and beliefs about teaching are firmly in place when prospective teachers enter preparation programs. As such, the question becomes, what are the sources of these beliefs?

The Origins of Implicit Knowledge and Beliefs

Richardson (1996) listed three categories of experiences that influence knowledge and beliefs about teaching: personal experience, experiences with schooling, and experience with formal knowledge. Personal experience includes a wide range of influences such as beliefs about self and others; perspectives on the relationship of schooling to society; personal, family, and cultural values and attitudes; and the impact of gender, ethnicity, socioeconomic status (SES), religion, geography, and life events. Research has shed light on some of these personal influences by examining how life experiences are encoded in images or metaphors. Two examples are case studies of a principal whose image of community, formed growing up in a tightly knit Toronto Island town, strongly influenced his work (Clandinin & Connelly, 1987) and a teacher whose metaphor of teaching as nurturing could be traced to her years of experience as a parent (Bullough & Knowles, 1991).

Much has been written about the influence of being a student on beliefs about learning and teaching (Calderhead & Robson, 1991; Lortie 1975). A number of case studies document the role of experiences with particular teachers in shaping individuals' images and beliefs about good and bad teaching (Britzman, 1991; Crow, 1988; Grant, 1992; Knowles, 1992). Lortie (1975) described the extensive apprenticeship of observation that fosters deeply held beliefs about teaching. Strauss (1996) noted that, during their precollege education, prospective teachers are in school learning situations for at least 12,000 hours. Some researchers studying the development of expertise assert that it takes about 10,000 hours to become an expert in a particular field (Simon, 1995). Thus, at the very least, prospective teachers come to college experts on being schooled; implicit models of what it means to teach and learn are inferred from these thousands of hours of schooling.

Experiences with formal knowledge include both knowledge of academic subjects such as mathematics or history and pedagogical knowledge, as usually encountered in formal teacher preparation programs. Beliefs about the nature and value of school subjects can be shaped by such factors as family and community norms or personal experiences learning the subject. Many beginning teachers lack connected conceptual understandings of the subjects they will teach (Bennett & Carre, 1993; McDiarmid, 1993) and this can influence their beliefs about how to teach the subject (Eisenhart et al., 1993). The impact of formal teacher education courses generally is seen as the least powerful influence on teachers' beliefs (Richardson, 1996), but some research has shown that these courses may have effects years later as experienced teachers rehear the words of their former professors with new ears (Crow, 1988; Featherstone, 1993).

Because the origins of beliefs about teaching are tied to personal experiences, the beliefs can be expected to vary. Yet some consistencies have been identified in the beliefs of teachers. The following sections explore these findings.

TEACHERS' KNOWLEDGE AND BELIEFS

Initially, prospective teachers' knowledge about teaching may be limited to what they have learned by being students—an apprenticeship of observation (Lortie, 1975). As teachers gain experience, their beliefs are shaped by their own encounters with fellow educators, students, and parents.

Based on these experiences as students and teachers, what do prospective and practicing teachers know? What is tacit and intuitive for them about teaching?

Before exploring what teachers know and believe, it is important that we conceptually define certain terms central to this discussion. First, when we use the term *implicit* or *tacit knowledge*, we are referring to the knowledge of teachers that they either have not reflected on or knowledge that they are generally unaware they possess (Alexander et al., 1991). For example, beginning teachers may have never had the opportunity to analyze what they know or believe about student assessment. However, due to the enormous amount of time that students spend being assessed, it is likely that new teachers have some implicit or tacit knowledge regarding the subject. In contrast, knowledge that is in use, being analyzed, or currently guiding action is referred to as *explicit knowledge* (Alexander et al., 1991). An example of explicit knowledge would be when teachers actually put their implicit understandings of assessment practice to use in designing an ongoing assessment program in science. It is important to note that implicit knowledge becomes explicit the minute it becomes the object of thought.

Our conceptions and use of the terms *implicit* and *explicit knowledge* should not be confused, however, with implicit and explicit theories of intelligence. Indeed, the line of demarcation between implicit and explicit theories of intelligence is the source of the theory. Specifically, implicit theories of intelligence come from the knower or believer (e.g., teacher) and are somewhat a priori, whereas explicit theories are derived from the mind of the researcher or scientist observing the behavior of a particular individual. As such, explicit theories of intelligence are a posteriori or reasoned explanations for behavior.

Knowledge and Beliefs About Intelligence

Dweck and Bempechat (1983) suggested that teachers' goals are related to their implicit theories of intelligence. Implicit theories of intelligence have been contrasted with explicit theories; the latter are invented by psychologists and others to explain data collected from people performing cognitive tasks. Implicit theories, in contrast, are "constructions of people . . . that reside in the minds of these individuals. Such theories need to be discovered rather than invented because they already exist, in some form, in people's heads" (Sternberg, Conway, Ketron, & Bernstein, 1981, p. 37). Dweck and Bempechat (1983) identified two implicit theories of intelligence: (a) an incremental perspective that sees intelligence as a malleable, dynamic quality; and (b) an entity orientation that views intelligence as fixed and stable. They suggested that these theories of intelligence may guide teaching practices such as selecting tasks, providing feedback, and setting goals. Teachers who hold an entity view of intelligence are likely to emphasize performance goals or looking smart, whereas teachers favoring the incremental perspective stress learning or becoming smart.

Teachers' theories about the nature of abilities also may give rise to distinct instructional practices. Evidence from laboratory simulations conducted by Swann and Snyder (1980) suggested a correlation between teachers' beliefs about the nature of ability and their teaching approaches. In this study, teachers who were led to believe that intelligence is a fixed trait gave students more autonomy in solving problems, setting as a goal that the students find their own solutions to the problems presented. Subjects led to believe that intelligence is modifiable, however, were more directive in their teaching, setting as a goal that they help students develop problem-solving skills. Thus, it appears that teachers' implicit theories of intelligence may be significant influences on teaching and learning in classrooms.

Knowledge and Beliefs About Learning

Much of the research on teachers' knowledge and beliefs about learning focuses on active versus passive views of learning. For example, Brown and Rose (1995)—referencing research on practicing teachers' knowledge of how children learn—concluded that most educators "believe that students learn in a passive manner by reacting to forces external to them, rather than in an active manner as producers of their own knowledge" (p. 21). In contrast, other researchers have found that teachers hold eclectic and commonsense views of learning that highlight the importance of active involvement, the need for an emotionally secure learning environment, and the value of trial and error (Anning, 1988).

Active Versus Passive Learning and Preservice Teachers.   More recent research on prospective teachers' beliefs about learning suggests that many entering students also have a passive or transmissive view of learning. Holt-Reynolds (1992) found that the prospective teachers in a content-area reading course rejected their professor's student-centered view of learning because it conflicted with their beliefs about good teaching and good subject-matter classrooms. Research by Strauss and his colleagues (Strauss, 1993; Strauss & Shilony, 1994) indicated that preservice teachers' implicit mental models of learning resembled information-processing models from the late 1960s (Atkinson & Shiffrin, 1968).

> A basic assumption of their mental models holds that knowledge exists outside the minds of children. It is in the teacher's mind, books, and so forth. Children usually have knowledge, but it is often incomplete or incorrect.

Sometimes they have no knowledge about the domain being taught. This stance leads to viewing teaching (and children's subsequent learning) as having two main parts. First, the teacher must find a way to get knowledge into the children's minds. Second, once it enters the mind, the teacher must teach in ways that children will move the new material from the place where it entered to the place it will be stored, thus adding it to the current store of already-learned concepts, skills, and so on. (Strauss, 1996, p. 19)

Hollingworth (1989), however, found that only half of the 14 fifth-year teacher-education students she studied held passive, teacher-directed views of learning. In addition, several researchers including Hollingworth (1989), Bird (1991), and Richardson and Kile (1992) concluded that prospective teachers can move toward a more constructivist, student-centered view of learning as a consequence of their preparation programs. The depth of these changes varies, however, depending on the strength of entering beliefs about learning and whether the students confronted their entering beliefs.

The Impact of Beliefs About Learning. Anning (1988) found not only that teachers held different commonsense notions of learning, but that teachers with different beliefs about how children learn tended to teach in different ways, providing different kinds of activities for their student and encouraging different kinds of classroom interaction patterns. Richardson, Anders, Tidwell, and Lloyd (1991) found that they could predict how the teachers in their study taught reading comprehension based on the teachers' beliefs about teaching and learning as revealed in extensive interviews. Compared to teachers with a less cognitive perspective, mathematics teachers with a more cognitive perspective on learning taught differently, using more word problems (Peterson, Fennema, Carpenter, & Loef, 1989). Wilson and Wineburg (1988) found that beliefs about the nature and knowledge of history influenced how four different teachers taught their subject.

Attributions and Expectations About Students

The body of work on teacher attributions and expectations documents how student characteristics are related to teachers' beliefs about learning and their actions toward students. For example, when teachers assume that student failure is attributable to forces beyond the students' control, they tend to respond with sympathy and avoid giving punishments. However, if the failures are attributed to a controllable factor such as lack of effort, the teacher's response is more likely to be anger and punishments may follow (Stipek, 1996). These tendencies seem to be consistent across time and cultures (Weiner, 1986).

Since the influential study by Rosenthal and Jacobson (1968), psychologists have debated the meaning, origins, and impacts of teacher expectation effects (Babad, 1995; Brophy, 1982; Cooper & Good, 1983; Good, 1988; Rosenthal, 1987, 1994; 1995; Snow, 1995). Actually, two kinds of expectation effects can occur in classrooms. The first is the self-fulfilling prophecy in which the teacher's beliefs about a student's abilities have no basis in fact, but student behavior comes to match the initially inaccurate expectation. The second kind of expectation effect occurs when teachers are fairly accurate in their initial reading of the abilities of students and respond to students appropriately. The problems arise when students show some improvement but teachers do not alter their expectations to take account of the improvement. This is called a *sustaining expectation effect* because the teacher's unchanging expectation sustains the student's achievement at the expected level. The chance to raise expectations, provide more appropriate teaching, and, encourage greater student achievement is lost. In practice, sustaining effects are more common than self-fulfilling prophecy effects (Cooper & Good, 1983).

Sources of Expectations. There are many possible sources of teachers' expectations (Braun, 1976; Good & Brophy, 1997). Intelligence test scores are an obvious source especially if teachers do not interpret the scores appropriately. Gender also influences teachers; most teachers expect more behavior problems from boys than from girls. The notes from previous teachers and the medical or psychological reports found in cumulative folders (permanent record files) are another obvious source of expectations. Knowledge of ethnic background also seems to have an influence, as does knowledge of older brothers and sisters. The influence of students' physical characteristics is shown in several studies, indicating that teachers hold higher expectations for attractive students. Previous achievement, socioeconomic class, and the actual behaviors of the student are also often used as sources of information. As others have suggested (e.g., Graham & Weiner, 1996; Stipek, 1996), we have found that prospective teachers often assume that when learning does not happen, differences are due in large part to the students' lack of effort or an unsupportive home environment. A sometimes competing explanation offered by preservice teachers is their own failure to be clear and interesting—two characteristics that occur frequently in prospective teachers' beliefs about teaching, as is seen in an upcoming section.

The Effects of Teacher Expectations. Expectations and beliefs focus attention and organize memory so teachers pay attention to and remember the information that fits the initial expectations (Fiske, 1993; Hewstone, 1989). Even when student performance does not fit expectations, the teacher may rationalize and attribute the performance to external causes beyond the control of the student. For example, a teacher may assume that the low-ability student who did well on a test must have cheated and that the high-ability student who failed must have been upset that day. In both cases, behavior that seems out of character is dismissed. It may take many instances of supposedly uncharacteristic behavior to change the teacher's beliefs about a particular student's abilities. Thus, expectations often remain in the face of contradictory evidence (Brophy, 1982).

Teachers often group students for instruction based on expectations about student ability. Some teachers leave little to the imagination; they make their expectations all too clear. For example, Alloway (1984) recorded comments similar to these directed to low-achieving groups:

I'll be over to help you slow ones in a minute.

The blue group will find this hard.

In these remarks, the teacher not only tells the students that they lack ability, but also communicates that finishing the work, not understanding, is the goal.

Once teachers assign students to ability groups, they usually assign different learning activities. To the extent that teachers choose activities that challenge students and increase achievement, these differences are probably necessary. Activities become inappropriate, however, when students who are ready for more challenging work are not given the opportunity to try it because teachers believe they cannot handle it—an example of a sustaining expectation effect.

However the class is grouped and whatever the assignments, the quantity and the quality of student–teacher interactions are likely to affect the students. Students who are expected to achieve tend to be asked more and harder questions, given more chances and a longer time to respond, and interrupted less often than students who are expected to do poorly. Teachers also give these high-expectation students cues and prompts, communicating their belief that the students can answer the question (Allington, 1980; Good & Brophy, 1997; Rosenthal, 1994). Teachers tend to be more encouraging in general toward those students for whom they have high expectations. They smile at these students more often and show greater warmth through such nonverbal responses as leaning toward the students and nodding their heads as the students speak (Woolfolk & Brooks, 1983, 1985). In contrast, with students for whom expectations are low, teachers ask easier questions, allow less time for answering, and are much less likely to give prompts.

It appears that feedback and reinforcement are also somewhat dependent on teacher expectations. Good and Brophy (1997) noted that teachers demand better performance from high-achieving students, are less likely to accept a poor answer from them, and praise them more for good answers. Teachers are more likely to respond with sympathetic acceptance or even praise to inadequate answers from low-achieving students, but to criticize these same students for wrong answers. Even more disturbing, low-achieving students receive less praise than high-achieving students for similar correct answers. On tests when an answer is almost right, the teacher is more likely to give the benefit of the doubt (and thus the better grade) to high-achieving students (Finn, 1972). This inconsistent feedback can be very confusing for low-ability students (Good 1983).

In general, students who are young, dependent, and conforming, or who really like the teacher, are most likely to have their self-esteem affected by the teacher's views (Brophy, 1982). If youngsters see the inevitable mistakes that accompany learning as a consequence of their own lack of ability, they are likely to lower their level of aspiration. Decreased motivation follows lowered expectations. The student and the teacher set lower standards, persistence is discouraged, and poorer performance results. Students start saying, "I don't know" or nothing at all rather than risk failure again. Here the teacher's attributions enter the picture: The teacher accepts the poor performance and attributes it to lack of ability. The lower expectation for the student thus seems to be confirmed, and the cycle continues.

Knowledge and Beliefs About Teaching and Learning to Teach

The work of Anderson (1994), Blumenfeld (1994), Blumenfeld, Hicks, and Krajcik (1996), Brookhart and Freeman (1992), Calderhead (1996), Hollingworth (1989), Kagan (1992), Kagan and Tippins (1991), McLaughlin (1991), Morine-Dershimer (1993), Strauss (1993), Weinstein (1989), Weinstein, Woolfolk, Dittmeier, and Shanker (1994), Zeichner and Gore (1990), and our experience suggested that the following beliefs are characteristic of many prospective teachers:

- Teaching is telling—in clear and interesting ways.
- Teaching is covering the material.
- Teaching is performing—the students are an audience that must be engaged.
- Teaching is directing—leading activities. The best activities for learning are interesting and fun for students.
- Teaching is engaging students—getting their attention, arousing curiosity, connecting with the interests of students, being creative.

- Teaching young children is nurturing—helping students feel good about themselves as they develop social skills.

- Teaching is an interpersonal skill that involves being fair, kind, flexible, and loving.

- Teachers will be effective if they are knowledgeable (so they can tell clearly), interesting (funny or witty helps here), creative, organized, and caring.

- Learning to teach is learning to do—strategies, activities, events that are interesting and fun.

- Learning to teach young children is learning to be—a good, kind, caring, and nurturing person (but most prospective teachers feel they already possess these qualities).

- Learning to teach is best accomplished through trial and error; experience is the best teacher.

In seeming opposition to the first four beliefs—but often held by the same prospective teachers who affirm them—are the notions that learning should be hands-on, that making lessons relevant to students' interests is the key to good teaching, and that caring about and respecting your students will virtually eliminate discipline problems. Good teaching is fun for students. Creative, real-life activities that involve important content will lead directly and almost automatically to learning that content (Kagan & Tippins, 1991; Putnam & Borko, 1997). In their study of prospective teachers' planning, Blumenfeld, Hicks, and Krajcik (1996) found that prospective teachers confound activity form with level of learning. They design learning activities that require complex procedures or social interactions to make the activities interesting, but have little sense of how these complicated procedures are related to learning. Like many in-service teachers (Prawat, 1992), these prospective teachers held a theory of naive constructivism that tends to confound physical and cognitive engagement. They create assessments filled with essay questions or projects, assuming that these methods of evaluation always require higher order thinking. In fact, the essay questions may require only memory and the projects only neatness and superficial completion of each step.

Related to these beliefs and perhaps the most common assumption that we have encountered in perspective teachers is that traditional teaching is bad, whereas good teaching requires being different or surprising. As a case in point, students in our educational psychology courses often cite the example of Robin Williams standing on a desk or tearing the pages from a literature book in the film "Dead Poets' Society." It may be the case, they believe, that there is no one best way to teach, but there is a worst way, and it is the way of the traditional teacher.

Prospective students tend to value public service and the chance to help children (Brookhart & Freeman, 1992). In general, they are very confident in their own abilities as teachers perhaps because they believe they have the qualities necessary to be helpful to children. In fact, Weinstein (1988, 1989) found that many prospective teachers are unrealistically optimistic about their abilities and expect to be above average in all aspects of teaching. They look to experience as their best teacher and do not expect to learn much from their formal teacher training courses (Book, Byers, & Freeman, 1983; Richardson-Koehler, 1988). Trial and error combined with the right personality is their assumed path to teaching expertise (Calderhead, 1988).

Knowledge and Beliefs About Self

One important self-referenced belief for teaching is a sense of efficacy. *Teacher efficacy* has been defined as "the extent to which the teacher believes he or she has the capacity to affect student performance" (Berman, McLaughlin, Bass, Pauly, & Zellman, 1977, p. 137), or as "teachers' belief or conviction that they can influence how well students learn, even those who may be difficult or unmotivated" (Guskey & Passaro, 1994, p. 628). Research has focused on two aspects of teacher efficacy, sometimes called general and personal. General teaching efficacy is the belief that teachers in general can impact the learning of even difficult, unmotivated students from unsupportive home backgrounds. Personal teaching efficacy is a belief on the part of an individual teacher that he or she can reach such students (for a complete discussion of teacher efficacy, see Tschannen-Moran, Woolfolk Hoy, & Hoy, 1998).

Origins of Efficacy Beliefs. The development of teacher efficacy beliefs among prospective teachers has generated a great deal of research interest because once efficacy beliefs are established, they appear to be somewhat resistant to change. There is some evidence that coursework and practice have differential impacts on personal and general teaching efficacy. It seems that general teaching efficacy beliefs are more likely to change when students are exposed to vicarious learning experiences or social persuasion, such as college coursework (Watters & Ginns, 1995), whereas actual teaching experiences during student teaching practica have a greater impact on personal teaching efficacy (Housego, 1992; Hoy & Woolfolk, 1990). General teaching efficacy has also shown a decline during student teaching (Hoy & Woolfolk, 1990; Spector, 1990) suggesting that the optimism of young teachers may be somewhat tarnished when confronted with the realities and complexities of the teaching task.

Effects of Efficacy Beliefs.   Efficacy beliefs of preservice teachers have been linked to attitudes toward children and control as measured by the Pupil Control Ideology Form (Willower, Eidell, & Hoy, 1967). Prospective teachers with a low sense of teacher efficacy tended to have an orientation toward custodial control, taking a pessimistic view of students' motivation, relying on strict classroom regulations, extrinsic rewards, and punishments to make students study. Those prospective teachers who scored high in both general teaching and personal teaching efficacy were more humanistic in their control orientation than students who were high in general but low in personal efficacy, or students who scored low in both (Woolfolk & Hoy, 1990). Once engaged in student teaching, efficacy beliefs also have an impact on behavior. Student interns with higher personal teaching efficacy were rated more positively on lesson-presenting behavior, classroom management, and questioning behavior by their supervising teacher on their practicum evaluation (Saklofske, Michaluk, & Randhawa, 1988).

Although few studies have looked at the development of efficacy beliefs among novices, it seems that efficacy beliefs of first-year teachers are related to stress, commitment, and satisfaction with support and preparation. Novice teachers completing their first year of teaching who had a high sense of teacher efficacy found greater satisfaction in teaching, had a more positive reaction to teaching, and experienced less stress. Confident new teachers gave higher ratings to the adequacy of support they had received than those who ended their year with a shakier sense of their own competence and a less optimistic view of what teachers could accomplish. Efficacious beginning teachers rated the quality of their preparation higher and the difficulty of teaching lower than less efficacious novices. Efficacious novices indicated greater optimism that they would remain in the field of teaching (Burley, Hall, Villeme, & Brockmeier, 1991; Hall, Burley, Villeme, & Brockmeier, 1992).

Among practicing teachers, efficacy is one of the few teacher characteristics consistently related to student achievement (Armor et al., 1976; Ashton, 1985; Ashton & Webb, 1986; Berman et al., 1977). Efficacy also has been related to the willingness of teachers to implement innovations (Berman et al., 1977; Guskey, 1984; Smylie, 1988), teacher stress (Greenwood, Olejnik, & Parkay, 1990; Parkay, Greenwood, Olejnik, & Proller, 1988), less negative affect in teaching (Ashton, Olejnik, Crocker, & McAuliffe, 1982), and willingness of teachers to stay in the field (Glickman & Tamashiro, 1982).

Efficacy beliefs of experienced teachers appear to be quite stable, even when the teachers are exposed to workshops and new teaching methods (Ross, 1994). Teachers who attended an efficacy seminar designed specifically to increase their sense of efficacy had higher efficacy scores immediately following the seminar; however, when the scores were measured again 6 weeks later, the increases had disappeared (Ohmart, 1992). Bandura (1997) suggested that when people gain new skills and have experiences that challenge their low estimate of their capabilities, they "hold their efficacy beliefs in a provisional status, testing their newly acquired knowledge and skills before raising their judgments of what they are able to do" (p. 83).

Once established, efficacy beliefs seem resistant to change. A strong sense of efficacy can support higher motivation, greater effort, persistence, and resilience across the span of a teaching career.

Knowledge and Beliefs About Student Assessment

It is estimated that from the time students begin school through the 12th grade they will spend close to 1,000 hours or 40 solid 24-hour days being formally assessed (Oosterhof, 1999). This rather large figure does not even include the incalculable time that students are informally assessed during their school years. As a result, we have found that our preservice teachers enter their teacher training programs with a host of implicit and explicit notions about assessment. First and foremost is the belief that traditional assessments are remnants of the days of the traditional teacher. Thus, in throwing out the ways of the traditional teacher, preservice teachers often believe that they must also throw out traditional forms of assessment. Instead, prospective teachers believe that they must employ authentic tasks and concomitant, authentic assessments.

In addition, many of our students subscribe to the notion that traditional and standardized assessments are gender and culture biased. As examples, preservice teachers often cite the low test scores of women and minorities on the SAT. Although there are data to support this particular example, we have found that preservice teachers tend to generalize from this one example to all forms of traditional and standardized assessments. Moreover, they do not seem to be aware that poorly constructed performance assessments and portfolios can also be biased assessment measures. Finally, prospective teachers often believe that they should provide only positive feedback to students on assessments (e.g., Pajares & Bengston, 1995; Pajares & Graham, 1998). Moreover, this belief is robust even among more seasoned teachers. In essence, teachers believe that positive feedback will increase students' motivation, whereas specific, negative feedback will decrease motivation. To the contrary, motivation research suggests that specific, constructive (i.e., positive and negative) feedback is the most motivating form of feedback (Stipek, 1996).

Why Are Teacher Beliefs Important in Learning to Teach?

Pajares (1992) synthesized the research on teachers' beliefs and identified a number of assumptions that can reasonably be made in studying these conceptions. Included in these assumptions are: "Beliefs are formed early and tend to self-perpetuate, persevering even against contradictions caused by reason, time, schooling, or experience" (p. 324). "The earlier a belief is incorporated into the belief structure, the more difficult it is to alter. Newly acquired beliefs are most vulnerable to change" (p. 325). "Beliefs are instrumental in defining tasks and selecting the cognitive tools with which to interpret, plan, and make decisions regarding such tasks; hence they play a critical role in defining behavior and organizing knowledge and information" (p. 325). "Individuals' beliefs strongly affect their behavior" (p. 326). In fact, an assumption underlying the study of teachers' beliefs is that "teachers' characteristic beliefs about children and learning have pervasive effects on their behavior, influencing the learning environment that they create for children and for themselves" (Bussis, Chittenden, & Amarel, 1976, p. 16).

Richardson (1996) described two functions of beliefs in learning to teach. First, "existing knowledge and beliefs play a strong role in shaping what student learn and how they learn it" (p. 105). Beliefs about teaching and students serve as filters and scaffolds for learning, focusing attention, shaping meaning, promoting organization, and supporting memory in learning to teach. Second, if knowledge and beliefs affect teachers' decisions and actions, their interactions with students, and their satisfaction with their profession, then beliefs should be a focus for instruction and a target for change during teacher education. Richardson (1996) described the view of Fenstermacher (1979) that one goal of teacher education "is to help teachers transform tacit or unexamined beliefs about teaching, learning, and the curriculum into objectively reasonable or evidentiary beliefs" (p. 105). However, prospective teachers' beliefs about teaching and learning are built over years of school experiences and can be highly resistant to change (Korthagen, 1993). Pajares (1992) cited a consistent body of research indicating that beliefs about teaching are well established by the time students enter college. Thus, teaching the implicit mind is a challenge.

TEACHING THE IMPLICIT MIND

Thus far, we have attempted to make the case that—based on personal experiences, schooling, and formal education—prospective teachers enter their preparation programs with firmly held beliefs and extensive

knowledge about teaching, learning, and schooling. These understandings and beliefs, although individual, often share some consistencies. The
prototypical prospective teacher is likely to believe the following: Teaching is explaining, leading, and directing, but also planning and implementing engaging activities. Motivating is connecting activities with students' interests and making the activities fun. If students are physically
engaged and socially involved, they will learn cognitively. If teachers really care about their students and are kind and respectful, then the teachers will have few discipline problems. All students can learn, but the family backgrounds of many students make learning very difficult. Student
characteristics provide information about who will and will not learn.
Learning to teach is a combination of having the right personality, not
being like the bad traditional teachers, and improving through trial and
error. Thus, the typical prospective teacher would assert, "I have the qualities to be a good teacher and I am optimistic that I will be an above average teacher—better than my peers."

   We also have cited evidence to suggest that teachers' beliefs influence
their planning, instruction, and interactions with their students. If beliefs
are important and if the previous assertions capture some common
beliefs, what is our stance as we attempt to educate these implicit minds?
What do we as teacher educators believe about these beliefs?

Beliefs About Their Beliefs

A number of goals are stated or implied in the literature on taking beliefs
into account in educating prospective teachers. We are encouraged to confront, challenge, transform, provoke, change, extend, and elaborate these
beliefs (e.g., Anderson et al., 1995; Hollingworth, 1989; Pajares, 1993;
Strauss, 1996). These goals are based, in part, on the assumption that
change is needed. In much of the writing on beliefs, there is an implied or
expressed belief on the part of teacher educators that the prospective
teachers' implicit notions of teaching and learning are dysfunctional and
insidious (Wilson, 1990), unrealistic (Weinstein, 1988), or, at the very least,
incompatible with the educational goals of teacher preparation programs
(Florio-Ruane & Lensmire, 1990). However, Pajares (1992) raised an
important issue. It would be useful to have some empirical and trustwor-
thy evidence that particular beliefs continue to be dysfunctional beyond
the preservice experience. We have research indicating that teachers' positive expectations and sense of efficacy are related to student learning, but
what about beliefs that teaching involves engaging students in interesting
activities? In what ways are these beliefs dysfunctional?

   It may be useful to ask not what is wrong, but what is right or at least
part right about entering teachers' beliefs. Although teaching is not sim-

ply being clear and interesting, being vague and boring is not good teaching. Although teaching is more than getting students' attention by being entertaining, losing their attention is not functional. When prospective teachers value telling in clear and interesting ways, their values are consistent with much of the research on effective teaching that identified aspects of explicit instructions related to student learning (Brophy & Good, 1986; Rosenshine & Stevens, 1996). When novice teachers value student activity and engagement, they acknowledge that students have to do something to learn.

What prospective teachers may lack is a deep understanding of the connections among explanation, activity, and learning. How can explanation or activity support, provoke, scaffold, or encourage learning? What makes an explanation or an activity mathemagenic? With some sense of what makes an explanation or activity valuable for learning (beyond it being interesting or fun), prospective teachers might expand and elaborate their beliefs about good teaching to include how to enact those beliefs. Rather than trying to convince prospective teachers that explanation is wrong, we might help them give better explanations. This approach would begin where the prospective teachers are in their beliefs, and thus could be more developmentally appropriate.

Berliner's (1994) notion of five stages of learning to teach (i.e., novice, advanced beginner, competent, proficient, and expert) provides some guidance here. Students in educational psychology classes are moving toward *novices*, which Berliner defined as student teachers and many first-year teachers. Novices need to learn the objective facts and features of the situation. Common places of an environment need to be discriminated, the parts of required tasks must be labeled and practiced, and some rules for action should be learned. Berliner referred to these first rules as context-free, but it might be better to consider them as enabling rules (Adler & Borys, 1996) that provide a basis for initial action. For example, in driving, novices must learn the kinds of meanings and rules tested by most states in written examinations—the meaning of a blinking yellow light or what to do when a school bus stops. Novice teachers need to know what a higher order question is—that it is not defined by form (multiple-choice vs. essay question), but by the kind of thinking required. They should learn some rules, such as wait at least 3 seconds after asking a higher order question. Perhaps with experience, novices can learn to contextualize rules, but the rules provide a beginning—a basis for gaining expertise and efficacy with experience (Barone, Berliner, Blanchard, Casanova, & McGowan, 1996).

If a decision is made to confront or challenge beliefs and thus transform implicit understandings into reasoned explicit beliefs (Fenstermacher, 1979), how might this be accomplished?

Confronting Beliefs

Studies of teacher-education programs and classes that intentionally attempt to confront and change prospective teachers' beliefs about teaching and learning reveal both the problems and possibilities of this endeavor. It appears that successful programs encourage students to discuss the beliefs that guide their thinking and actions, pinpoint the differences between those beliefs and the perspectives that their professors want them to consider, and analyze the advantages and limitations of thinking with and acting on their current beliefs. In addition, professors in successful programs respect their students' beliefs and use them to evaluate research-based principles (Borko & Putnam, 1996; Holt-Reynolds, 1992; Hollingworth, 1989; Ross, Johnson, & Smith, 1991). In essence, it would seem that preservice teachers must make their beliefs explicit before they can ever hope to reflect on them, much less change or modify them (Murphy, 1998).

Pajares (1993) suggested several approaches to challenging beliefs. Some class activities should be designed to create cognitive conflict. Using this conflict, teacher educators can help students identify their own beliefs and explore why certain beliefs resist change. All beliefs should be examined and challenged, not just those that conflict with the beliefs of the teacher educator or the education curriculum. Concept maps, metaphor analysis, debates, and dialogue journals are possible ways to help students become aware of their own beliefs and those of their peers. We have found that asking students to analyze teaching and learning in popular films such as "Dead Poets' Society," "Dangerous Minds," or "Stand and Deliver" helps to surface underlying beliefs and can spark challenges and productive conflict about good teaching. Analyzing these films raises many basic questions about whether teaching is explaining, entertaining, befriending, motivating, challenging, or supporting learning. As students analyze the view of teaching and learning in the films, they are more able to identify (and reconsider) their own implicit beliefs. Johnson and Johnson's (1988) structured controversy process could be used to explore these conflicts and model cooperative learning as well.

Prospective teachers can be encouraged to try on ways of interacting or teaching that conflict with their beliefs as long as the outcomes are likely to be positive and not simply confirming of the beliefs. Often change in behavior precedes change in belief (Guskey, 1989; Rokeach, 1968). Existing beliefs can be challenged by credible sources such as recent graduates of the program or expert teachers. Here videotaped interviews with practicing teachers about the value and uses of educational psychology in teaching might be helpful. Teacher educators, even those who have extensive teaching experience, are not always credible sources. Certainly one caveat is that teachers' knowledge and beliefs are multifaceted constructs that reciprocally influence one another (Murphy, 1998). As such, it is difficult to determine possible outcomes of knowledge and belief confrontation.

Robustness of Knowledge and Beliefs

One reason that knowledge and beliefs are so important in learning to teach is that they are robust in the face of contradictory evidence. No matter what the approach, the conceptual change (e.g., Chinn & Brewer, 1993; Vosniadou, 1994) and persuasion (e.g., Alexander, Murphy, Buehl, & Sperl, 1998; Murphy, 1998) research suggests that knowledge and beliefs resist change—a useful quality for many purposes and life situations. Even researchers who report some success in affecting prospective teachers' beliefs about teaching and learning also express skepticism that these changes will persist or actually influence actions (Ball, 1989; Bird, Anderson, Sullivan, & Swindler, 1992; Civil, 1992).

It is possible that prospective teachers learn a new vocabulary for describing existing beliefs without actually making fundamental changes (Chinn & Brewer, 1993). Feinman-Nemser and Buchmann (1989) described a student teacher who "combined past experiences with ideas she encountered in formal preparation in a way that reinforced earlier beliefs and reversed the intended message of her assigned readings . . ." (p. 371). In the persuasion literature, such behavior is referred to as *case building* (e.g., Chambliss, 1995; Garner & Alexander, 1991). In essence, learners abstract pieces of knowledge from newly presented information that supports their existing beliefs and disregard information that conflicts with those beliefs. Case building most often occurs when two or more stances are provided on a particular topic and none is refuted. As such, any topic for which preservice teachers are presented with multiple perspectives, and no refutational arguments regarding the given perspectives, could encourage case building.

Clearly, asking people to make changes in their fundamental beliefs about teaching and learning is difficult, bold, and perhaps a bit arrogant. The tension between challenge and support—between assimilation and accommodation, between program elements that are consistent with students' current understanding of teaching and elements that question those conceptions—is a tension that must be tolerated and cultivated.

TEACHING EDUCATIONAL PSYCHOLOGY: SOME ASSUMPTIONS

Before discussing how students' existing knowledge and beliefs might influence teaching in an educational psychology class, we make explicit our own biases and preconceptions. What follows are our beliefs about the educational psychology course and the processes of teaching and learning.

The Course

The main goal of an educational psychology course in a teacher preparation program is to help prospective teachers understand, value, and use the knowledge and processes of educational psychology, both in their lives and to support the learning of their future students. In doing so, we might also hope that the course content would help students gain more sophisticated epistemological beliefs, deepen their social and ethical understandings, or strengthen their capacity to be planful and reflective.

Most prospective teachers still encounter educational psychology as a course in a college or university program. Given this situation, certain tensions are likely. The first tension involves the evaluative climate of educational psychology courses. Often students are asked to take risks by reflecting on and changing their beliefs about teaching. It is not enough that they understand the material; they must also base action on their understanding. Initial performances of novices generally are halting and imperfect. Yet given the context of the college course, these beginners typically are graded on their beliefs, changes, actions, and reflections—not the best environment for experimentation and learning.

A second tension that comes with teaching educational psychology as a college course relates to time. There is limited time to study educational psychology and even less time to tie study to practice in field experiences or student teaching. Too many courses and experiences compete for the attention of the prospective teacher. There is no good time to teach the course. If taught early in the college program, the course seems too theoretical to prospective teachers with limited life and classroom experiences. If taught later, the prospective teacher often is in the midst of completing a major or engrossed in student teaching and overwhelmed by the demands of practice.

Finally, other coursework within the teacher preparation program and across the university curriculum is seldom well integrated with the educational psychology course and vice versa. Because courses are not integrated, content is often redundant. Students ask, for example, in how many different courses will they have to define zone of proximal development or prior knowledge before someone helps them understand how to use these ideas in teaching.

The Students

Here we rely more on our combined experiences as teachers than on published work. We have found that students expect that a course with *psychology* in the title will help them cope with their future students' psychological problems—the child with no friends, the student who steals, the adolescent on drugs, or the youngster with emotional problems. Instead, educational psychology courses and texts give students assimilation and accommodation, schema theory, knowledge construction and negotiation, expectancy X value theories, validity, or correlation. In turn, students ask, "Why do we have to study this? My cooperating teacher says I'll never use this information—it's too theoretical." Or we hear, "I already had that." Of course, we believe that students come to understand, value, and use educational psychology, but not without great effort on our part and theirs.

Given the timing of most educational psychology courses early in the prospective teachers' college program, we believe that the most valuable applications of knowledge from the course often are to the students' current lives. Educational psychology should help prospective teachers become expert learners. Thus, we tend to emphasize personal experiences for students such as examining the factors that influenced their identity, improving their study and test-taking strategies, and understanding their learning abilities and limitation. In essence, we espouse the belief that teachers must be expert learners so that they can help their students become the same. In addition, they must become self-aware experts who have a sense of how they developed expertise and how they might make the process visible to others.

Even this use of the course is not an easy sell. The first author was reminded of this one semester when she enthusiastically shared with her class an article from the newspaper, *USA Today*, about study skills. The gist of the article was that students should continually revise and rewrite their notes from a course so that by the end all their understanding could be captured in one or two pages. Of course, the majority of the knowledge at that point would be learned—reorganized and connected well with other knowledge. "See," she told her class, "these ideas are real—not just trapped in texts. They can help you study smarter in college." After a heated discussion, one of the best students said in exasperation, "I'm carrying 18 hours—I don't have time to *learn* this stuff!" Again, our students' beliefs (and the pressures of their lives) make real change a challenge— even change that would seem to benefit the students immediately.

Faced with this reaction, the first author decided to help the students experience the value of integrating their understanding by allowing them to bring one page of notes to the next test. To capture the ideas from four chapters, related readings, and class activities, students had to transform information, organize specifics into more general and generative concepts, and make decisions about what is important. The process seemed to require a different kind of thinking than many students had experienced in preparing for tests. Most students found that the thinking that went into organizing their understanding was the important element. The actual notes were not that useful, in part, because the test questions asked students to apply principles.

Teaching

We have described some educational psychology students' beliefs about teaching. Of course, the perceptions we shared are colored by our own knowledge and beliefs. Although the authors have varying levels of teaching and research experience, we do share some beliefs in common. Teaching is complex and unpredictable, with hundreds of decisions and exchanges occurring every day. In the midst of this uncertainty and high-speed pace, teachers must take warranted and deliberate actions, moving toward ethical and valuable goals and drawing on technical and principled knowledge in the process (Doyle, 1986; Kennedy, 1988; Rentel, 1994). Understanding educational psychology will help teachers in these efforts, but much more is needed—particularly a deep understanding of the academic subjects being taught and a well-developed ethical sense.

Finally, there is no one best way to teach. Different goals and students require different approaches, but in all things, let the students' learning be the guide. As we analyze a case, watch a videotape, or discuss a particular teaching strategy, both authors tend to ask their class, "What do you think the students (in this case, video, etc.) are learning? How do you know? How does this fit with your understanding of the different theories of learning (motivation, development, etc.) we have been examining?" As we focus the attention of our students on the learning of the individuals in the case or video, we get a glimpse of their learning—of the ways that they are understanding educational psychology in action. In turn, we hope that our students also gain a better understanding of their beliefs about teaching and learning.

Learning

Prospective teachers' prior beliefs, expectations, and knowledge influence what they will come to understand, value, and use from any experience, including the study of educational psychology, because knowledge is personal and constructed (Alexander & Murphy, 1998). Knowledge is also situated and difficult to transfer (e.g., Alexander & Murphy, in press; Murphy & Woods, 1996). A great part of the challenge of teaching educational psychology is helping students see the power of prior knowledge operating in their own lives—not just as a key term in a chapter on cognitive views of learning or as the answer to a multiple-choice question. To facilitate learning and transfer for novices, some slowing down of action, some taking apart to make the task smaller, then putting back together into wholes is necessary. This is not the same as beginning with basics and later building more complexities. It is more like a musician who practices scales and routines, but also performs whole pieces and improvises—with the music becoming more complex as the musician develops. Finally, learning is socially mediated (e.g., Bandura, 1997; Vygotsky, 1978). Thus, the involvement of others in learning is necessary and powerful.

Quite a bit has been written lately about the need to prepare teachers by making their learning to teach more authentic. Rather than viewing most teacher preparation courses as opportunities to learn skills and principles that will be applied later in teaching, many teacher educators and standards boards are calling for preparation that situates the learning of skills and principles in real-life teaching contexts (cf. Anderson et al., 1995; Darling-Hammond, 1994; Goodlad, 1994; Guyton & Rainer, 1996; Holmes Group, 1996; Leinhardt, 1988; Putnam & Borko, 1997; Shulman, 1990). The question is, "How?"

Putnam and Borko (1997) concluded that "there is not just one way, or even one best way, to situate teacher learning in practice. Rather there are different ways to situate learning, each suited particularly well to different components of teacher learning" (pp. 1283–1284). Writing about educational psychology and teacher preparation, Anderson et al. (1995) suggested that one key to situating the learning of prospective teachers in practice is to design better tasks for teacher education students, as discussed in the following section.

TASKS FOR TEACHING EDUCATIONAL PSYCHOLOGY

Doyle (1983) defined *tasks* as the products students are asked to create, the resources provided, and the kinds of thinking that students are expected to apply to produce the outcomes using those resources. Tasks determine what academic content students will encounter, what they will do with that content, and how they will think about it. Tasks have a particular subject focus and also involve certain cognitive operations such as memorize, infer, classify, and apply. Hence, as students work on a task, they are learning content and practicing operations. Given that much of what students know and believe remains tacit, it is important that we design tasks that have the possibility of bringing knowledge and beliefs to the explicit level. Once at the explicit level, tasks are more likely to meaningfully influence teachers' knowledge and beliefs.

Designing Tasks

Anderson et al. (1995) described five considerations for designing meaningful tasks for teacher education:

1. "A set of tasks should provide multiple representations of key ideas across situations" (Anderson et al., p. 152). If we take as an example the topic of cooperative learning, this might mean designing tasks that allow multiple opportunities for prospective teachers to observe productive and problematic interactions in groups. To do so, however, raises issues of depth versus breadth in coverage and also questions about cooperation across different courses in teacher preparation programs. Can enough time be devoted to peer learning within and across courses, or will students encounter superficial discussions of structures and strategies in several different courses?

2. "A set of tasks (though not necessarily every task) should feel authentic, representing as much as possible the complexity of teaching without overwhelming students" (Anderson et al., p. 152). The key here is to ask students to take several dimensions into account at once as they make decisions about teaching, then analyze the possible implications of the decisions. It can be difficult to find the right balance of authenticity, complexity, and pace that allows novices to sort through the issues and practice responses. Some simplifying or slowing down may be necessary. Simulations, microteaching, videotaping, and teaching laboratory experiences can be good, initial-learning situations, allowing prospective teachers to focus on manageable segments of the design, monitoring, or assessment of student learning activities (Howey, 1996).

3. "Tasks should be designed to help make explicit prospective teachers' beliefs and conceptions, and to engage them in explaining their own beliefs and considering alternative points of view" (Anderson et al., p. 152). Strauss (1996) agreed that, to extend and elaborate prospective teachers' mental models, we must first find ways to make explicit what was formerly implicit. Possibilities for accomplishing these kinds of tasks are described in an upcoming section.

4. "Tasks should create opportunities for public interaction among the students and between the instructor and students" (Anderson et al., p. 152). This consideration invites a recommendation to use cooperative learning in the teacher preparation classes. Certainly many teacher preparation programs include such an element. However, unless the planning and execution of cooperative learning strategies are informed by knowledge about productive group interaction, it is likely that participation in cooperative learning in college classes will be miseducative. Experiences that simply reinforce prior beliefs—that group learning is mostly for social or motivational objectives or that work in groups is just a way to divide the labor (with some people always doing more or less than their share)—will not help prospective teachers understand and use peer learning (see Woolfolk Hoy & Tschannen-Moran, 1999, for a model to guide the design of cooperative learning).

5. "Grading and assessment should be congruent with other considerations" (Anderson et al., p. 152). A major factor that affects how students
will use a task is how they will be assessed—what is the performance to
be exchanged for a grade (Doyle, 1983). The following section describes
some assignments and projects that both support and challenge students'
implicit understandings of teaching and learning.

Example Tasks for Educational Psychology

Assignments and assessment focus attention. If the goal of an educational psychology course is to help prospective teachers create warranted
practice, then classroom tasks and assessments should focus attention on
this goal. Knowing that prior knowledge and beliefs affect what is learned
and that many students believe that they "don't have time to learn this
stuff," how can assignments reveal prior beliefs and motivate students to
do the work necessary to expand or change knowledge and beliefs?

Examining Beliefs.   Lately, both authors have experimented with
tasks that help students examine their assumptions about teaching and
learning. At the beginning of a course, the first author asks students to draw
concept maps of good teaching and learning. First, we have to explore
what a concept map is and how to complete one, and how to label nodes
and relationships among elements of the map. Students work individually, explain their maps to a partner, and then modify their maps if they
choose. We return to this exercise at the end of the course, redrawing
maps and comparing new ideas to original work. Students must write
about their current understandings of teaching and learning, what (if anything) has changed, and what readings, experiences, or reflections led to
the changes.

Another approach, employed by the second author, is to have students
write philosophies of learning at the beginning of the course. As part of
these philosophies, prospective teachers are encouraged to examine their
preexisting knowledge and beliefs about how students learn, how to motivate students, and the best methods for assessing learning. The preservice
teachers are then encouraged to modify their understandings as the
course proceeds; at the end of the course, students are required to resub-
mit their learning philosophies. As part of this final submission, prospective teachers must reflect on any changes or modifications they have made
in their philosophies.

Blumenfeld et al. (1996) described an approach to teaching educational psychology based on planning and writing rationales for plans. They
used planning as a way to encourage prospective teachers' problem solving about how to apply psychological principles in designing learning

experiences for particular groups of children. By designing specific activities for particular children and relating these designs to psychological principles of learning and instruction, Blumenfeld et al. (1996) helped students examine their beliefs. "The process of planning and writing rationales helps make preservice teachers' thinking explicit. By making explicit what often remains implicit, preservice teachers can confront and reexamine their assumptions and understanding about educational psychology" (p. 51).

Renninger (1996) designed an educational psychology course that focuses on developing prospective teachers' understanding of learning. Within the course are a number of assignments and activities that encourage students to examine their beliefs about learning. For example, on the first day of the course, students are asked to decide whether they believe learning is more like snorkeling or carpentry. Students meet with others who share their metaphor and discuss reasons for their choice, then work in small groups (that include advocates of both metaphors) to develop a model of learning. The groups share their models with the class and then the class as a whole identifies characteristics of learning that are repeated in many models. Finally, the students reflect on what they have learned about learning through the exercise and how they learned it. Renninger (1996) noted:

> The task is designed to demonstrate to students that each of them has ideas (sometimes some rather fixed ideas) about how learning works and that there are any number of different perspectives on this subject—that when they use the word learning, they must remember that it does not necessarily mean the same thing to the other people in the room, let alone the authors they will be reading, the teachers and researchers with whom they will be corresponding, or the students they will be tutoring. (p. 65)

Students return to these models on the last day of class. They are asked to amend the models based on their current beliefs about learning. These beliefs are also reflected in their final paper for the course—an explanation of their own theory of instruction. For example, one student wrote, "My focus shifted from being teacher/theory centered to student-centered. . . ." (Renninger, 1996, p. 66).

Identifying Key Ideas. Lately there have been many attempts by educational psychologists to describe the nature and value of the field (e.g., American Psychological Association Board of Educational Affairs, 1995; Bereiter, 1994; Berliner, 1992; Bredo, 1994; Calfee, 1992; Derry, 1991; Goodenow, 1992; Mayer, 1991; Pintrich, 1994; Prawat & Floden, 1994; Wittrock, 1992). We believe that students should be confronting these same issues. The first author told her undergraduate students that they had the opportunity to join the struggle. For their major assignment, they were asked to do the following with their textbook:

> Based on the chapters assigned (9, 10, 11, 13, 14) *identify 5 to 7 principles of educational psychology* that you believe capture the most important ideas in and across the chapters. Do not overlook any of the chapters. A principle is a generalization that relates two or more concepts and has solid research support. For example, a principle from the first half of the course might be: *What people learn and remember is determined in great part by what they already know.*
>
> In your paper you should:
>
> 1. State each principle clearly
>
> 2. Provide a rationale for why it is important and how it is supported by research.
>
> 3. Give at least one extended example of how you would apply the principle to teaching a particular subject and grade level. (If you do not intend to teach, you may substitute an application that fits your intended occupation.)
>
> You may work with others in the class and turn in a jointly written paper. If one paper has multiple authors, however, I rely on you to verify that all authors contributed equally and deserve the same grade.

Needless to say, students initially moaned, but later said that they learned more from this than from any other assignment because it forced them to integrate and justify. Those who chose to work together seemed to benefit even more. A number of students stepped outside the confines of the chapter structure to identify idea themes that ran through several chapters, such as "The design of teaching and the means for assessing learning should be consistent with the learning goals." What moved this statement beyond an empty generality was the detailed example of how this principle might be applied in a 6th-grade class on hypothesis testing in science. To identify principles and example applications required the students to make explicit their implicit understandings and assumptions about teaching, learning, and testing.

Creating Examples.   Students can work in groups to present an example of a particular model of teaching or management. The students are required to work in groups, present the example to the class, and then write about the experience individually—explaining why their presentation was a good example of the model in question and what *else* they might have done to apply the model, and why that might have worked. Asking students to research and enact direct instruction or cooperative learning can challenge implicit beliefs about what these approaches are or how they function. Students who believe that direct instruction is ineffective may question these beliefs as they attempt to design good examples of direct teaching. Students who believe that putting children in cooperative groups will automatically lead to learning may realize that the connection between grouping and learning is not dependable when they are asked to enact what can go wrong with group work.

Analyzing Cases.   Students can work alone or together to analyze cases (video, print, or field-experienced based) with the expectation that they will use assigned readings as resources as they prepare to explain (orally or in writing, as a group or individually) the connections between their analyses and the research and theory presented in the readings. If these are rich and complex cases that can be revisited as students deepen their understanding—reconsidering the situation, for example, after studying aspects of motivation and again after examining the research on management—all the better (Harrington & Garrison, 1992; Shulman, 1992; Wasserman, 1993). In designing a sequence of cases, we may need to heed the warning by Rocklin (1996) that different levels of complexity may be appropriate for more and less experienced students.

A number of teacher educators recommend the use of cases to develop analytical capabilities and to situate teaching skills and principles in practice (Kennedy, 1988; Leinhardt, 1990; Putnam & Borko, 1997; Sykes & Bird, 1992). Putnam and Borko (1997) suggested that case teaching is particularly promising for exploring problems of pedagogy and for grounding theoretical ideas about teaching and learning in slices of classroom life. Both cases of problematic teaching situations and cases of exemplary teaching could be helpful in developing prospective teachers' knowledge. Through analysis of problem cases, prospective teachers practice framing issues, generating alternative solutions, making choices about actions, and considering the implications of their choices (Putnam & Borko, 1997). For example, video and hypertext cases might allow students to explore the complexity of cooperative learning by analyzing different tasks, goals, group compositions, strategies, and interactions—noting how changes in one of these dimensions affect other dimensions. The limitation with analysis, as Kennedy (1988) noted, is that practicing teachers cannot end with generating and evaluating alternatives—they must act. Here a second kind of case, samples of exemplary teaching, might be necessary to provide images of action (Leinhardt, 1988, 1990).

Textbooks as Resources.   We believe that texts can be useful in helping students examine and expand beliefs about teaching. Many of the criticisms of textbooks—that they are linear and solitary (whereas learning is non-linear and social), that they encourage students to memorize and regurgitate facts, that they rigidly define the course, and that they are based on a discredited transmission view of learning (Berliner, 1994)—seem to be criticisms of the uses of text. Why can't reading, understanding, and applying a textbook be social? Why assess in ways that require regurgitation? Why let a text define the content or sequence of a course? At the least, a textbook can be the basis for discussion, giving students a common experience on which to base their debate. If they are allowed to explore their interpretations of the reading, the students can experience firsthand the personal construction of knowledge as they discover that others read different information in the text. By seeing and discussing the power of preconceptions and implicit beliefs in interpreting texts, the prospective teachers may begin to examine the implicit understandings they have taken for granted as true.

Assessing Knowledge and Belief Change

Years and years of research have been dedicated to techniques for assessing changes in knowledge, especially factual knowledge. Indeed, knowledge assessments range from traditional assessments such as multiple choice or completion to performance assessments like writing narrative essays or reciting a poem. By comparison, few researchers have attempted to measure changes in beliefs of individuals or more subjective understandings. Although we would not suggest that it is necessary to partial knowledge from beliefs or vice versa, we do assert that teacher educators should try to assess the more subjective understandings that preservice teachers possess about teaching and learning. Somewhat different than factual knowledge assessments, however, belief or subjective knowledge assessments should measure the conceptions of the prospective teacher at multiple phases during the learning process. At a minimum, preservice teachers' understandings should be measured at the beginning and end of the educational psychology course. An even better practice would be to measure change at multiple intervals during the course. Some examples might include philosophies of teaching and learning, concept maps, or the reading of controversial topics, and the use of Likert scales or open-ended questions could be used to monitor change. Although there is no way to measure how preservice teachers' actions will change after their training has ended, such assessments will help teacher educators monitor moderate changes in knowledge and beliefs during training.

CONCLUSIONS AND CAUTIONS

The preceding are just a few ideas about tasks that encourage prospective teachers to understand, value, and use educational psychology while supporting and extending their beliefs and intuitions about teaching and learning. The goals of many of the tasks are to support students as they confront and test their beliefs, offer extensions and alternatives to those beliefs, and create situations that allow students to try out beliefs in action. Another important goal is to build a foundation for a sense of efficacy that will not be dismantled by the reality shock of actual teaching. In her educational psychology text, the first author tries to communicate this goal to readers:

> Becoming an expert teacher takes time and experience, but you can start now by becoming a good beginner. You can develop a repertoire of effective principles and practices for your first years of teaching so that some activities quickly become automatic. You can also develop the habit of questioning and analyzing these accepted practices and your own teaching so you can solve new problems when they arise. You can learn to look behind the effective techniques identified in research to ask why: Why did this approach work with these students? What else might be as good or better? The answers to these questions and your ability to analyze the situations are much more important than the specific techniques themselves. As you ask and answer questions, you will be refining your personal theories of teaching. My goal in writing this book is to help you become an excellent beginning teacher, one who can both apply and improve many techniques. Even more important, I hope this book will cause you to think about students and teaching in new ways, so that you will have the foundation for becoming an expert with experience. (Woolfolk, 2001, p. 18)

Attending to the developmental level of our students challenges us to identify key ideas and defensible enabling rules. Rather than covering every theory, we might spend more time with fewer approaches (Alexander et al., 1996). We also must make it clear that we know and expect the rules will cease to be rules and become points for reflection as the novice teachers gain experience and a basis for reflecting on practice. A final caution, as Pajares and Bengston (1995) reminded us, we do a disservice to students if we communicate to them that formal psychological principles supersede or replace knowledge of subjects being taught in becoming a good teacher.

REFERENCES

Adler, P. S., & Borys, B. (1996). Two types of bureaucracy: Enabling and coercive. *Administrative Science Quarterly, 41*, 61–89.

Alexander, P. A. (1996). The past, present, and future of knowledge research: A reexamination of the role of knowledge in learning and instruction. *Educational Psychologist, 31*, 89–92.

Alexander, P. A., & Dochy, F. J. R. C. (1995). Conceptions of knowledge and beliefs: A comparison across varying cultural and educational communities. *American Educational Research Journal, 32*, 413–442.

Alexander, P. A., & Murphy, P. K. (1998). The research base for APA's Learner-Centered Psychological Principles. In N. Lambert & B. McCombs (Eds.), *How students learn: Reforming schools through learner-centered education.* Washington, DC: American Psychological Association.

Alexander, P. A., & Murphy, P. K. (in press). Learner profiles: Valuing individual differences within classroom communities. In P. L. Ackerman, P. C. Kyllonen, & R. D. Roberts (Eds.), *The future of learning and individual differences research: Processes, traits, and content* (pp. 25–60). Washington, DC: American Psychological Association.

Alexander, P. A., Murphy, P. K., Buehl, M. M., & Sperl, C. T. (1998). The influence of prior knowledge, beliefs, and interest in learning from persuasive text. In T. Shanahan & F. Rodriguez-Brown (Eds.), *Yearbook of the National Reading Conference* (Vol. 47, pp. 167–181). Chicago, IL: National Reading Conference.

Alexander, P. A., Murphy, P. K., Guan, J., & Murphy, P. A. (1998). How students and teachers in Singapore and the United States conceptualize knowledge and beliefs: Positioning learning within epistemological frameworks. *Learning and Instruction, 8,* 97–116.

Alexander, P. A., Murphy, P. K., & Woods, B. S. (1996). Of squalls and fathoms: Navigating the seas of educational innovation. *Educational Researcher, 25*(3), 31–36, 39.

Alexander, P., Schallert, D., & Hare, V. (1991). Coming to terms: How researchers in learning and literacy talk about knowledge. *Review of Educational Research, 61,* 315–343.

Allington, R. (1980). Teacher interruption behaviors during primary-grade oral reading. *Journal of Educational Psychology, 71,* 371–377.

Alloway, N. (1984). *Teacher expectations.* Paper presented at the meeting of the Australian Association for Research in Education, Perth, Australia.

American Psychological Association Board of Educational Affairs. (1995, December). *Learner-centered psychological principles: A framework for school redesign and reform* [Online]. Available: http://www.apa.org/ed/lcp.html.

Anderson, L. M. (1994). *Reforming our courses and rethinking our roles.* Paper presented at the annual meeting of the Midwestern Association for the Teaching of Educational Psychology, Chicago, IL.

Anderson, L. M., Blumenfeld, P., Pintrich, P., Clark, C., Marx, R., & Peterson, P. (1995). Educational psychology for teachers: Reforming our courses, rethinking our roles. *Educational Psychologist, 30,* 143–157.

Anning, A. (1988). Teachers' theories about children's learning. In J. Calderhead (Ed.), *Teachers' professional learning* (pp. 128–145). London: Falmer.

Armor, D., Conroy-Oseguera, P., Cox, M., King, N., McDonnell, L., Pascal, A., Pauly, E., & Zellman, G. (1976). *Analysis of the school preferred reading programs in selected Los Angeles minority school* (RN. R-2007-LAUSD). Santa Monica, CA: Rand Corporation. (ERIC Document Reproduction Service No. 130 243)

Ashton, P. T. (1985). Motivation and teachers' sense of efficacy. In C. Ames & R. Ames (Eds.), *Research on motivation in education: Vol. 2. The classroom milieu* (pp. 141–174). Orlando, FL: Academic Press.

Ashton, P. T., Olejnik, S., Crocker, L., & McAuliffe, M. (1982, April). *Measurement problems in the study of teachers' sense of efficacy.* Paper presented at the annual meeting of the American Educational Research Association, New York.

Ashton, P. T., & Webb, R. B. (1986). *Making a difference: Teachers' sense of efficacy and student achievement.* New York: Longman.

Atkinson, R. C., & Shiffrin, R. M. (1968). Human memory: A proposed system and its control processes. In K. Spence & J. Spence (Eds.), *The psychology of learning and motivation* (Vol. 2, pp. 89–195). New York: Academic Press.

Babad, E. (1995). The "Teachers' Pet" phenomenon, students' perceptions of differential behavior, and students' morale. *Journal of Educational Psychology, 87,* 361–374.

Ball, D. (1989, March). *Breaking with experience in learning to teach mathematics: The role of a preservice methods course*. Paper presented at the annual meeting of the American Educational Research Association, New Orleans, LA.

Bandura, A. (1997). *Self-efficacy: The exercise of control*. New York: W. H. Freeman.

Barone, T., Berliner, D. C., Blanchard, J., Casanova, U., & McGowan, T. (1996). A future for teacher education: Developing a strong sense of professionalism. In J. Sikula (Ed.), *Handbook of research on teacher education* (2nd ed., pp. 1108–1149). New York: Macmillan.

Bennett, N., & Carre, C. (1993). *Learning to teach*. London: Routledge & Kegan Paul.

Bereiter, C. (1994). Implications of postmodern science or science as progressive discourse. *Educational Psychologist, 29*, 3–12.

Berliner, D. C. (1992). Telling the stories of educational psychology. *Educational Psychologist, 27*, 143–162.

Berliner, D. C. (1994, April). *Some thoughts on why the textbook in educational psychology will still be around after we are all gone*. Paper presented at the annual meeting of the American Educational Research Association, New Orleans, LA.

Berliner, D. C. (1994). The wonders of exemplary performance. In J. N. Mangieri & C. C. Block (Eds.), *Creating powerful thinking in teachers and students*. Ft. Worth, TX: Harcourt Brace.

Berman, P., McLaughlin, M., Bass, G., Pauly, E., & Zellman, G. (1977). *Federal programs supporting educational change: Vol. VII. Factors affecting implementation and continuation* (RN. R-1589/7-HEW). Santa Monica, CA: The Rand Corporation. (ERIC Document Reproduction Service No. 140 432)

Bird, A. (1991, April). *Making conversations about teaching and learning in an introductory teacher education course*. Paper presented at the annual meeting of the American Educational Research Association, Chicago, IL.

Bird, T., Anderson, L. M., Sullivan, B. A., & Swindler, S. A. (1992). *Pedagogical balancing acts: A teacher educator encounters problems in an attempt to influence prospective teachers' beliefs*. East Lansing, MI: National Center for Research on Teacher Learning.

Blumenfeld, P. (1994, October). *How educational psychology helps educators*. Paper presented at the annual meeting of the Midwestern Association for the Teaching of Educational Psychology, Chicago, IL.

Blumenfeld, P., Hicks, L., & Krajcik, J. S. (1996). Teaching educational psychology through instructional planning. *Educational Psychologist, 31*, 51–62.

Book, C., Byers, J., & Freeman, D. (1983). Student expectations and teacher education traditions with which we can and cannot live. *Journal of Teacher Education, 34*(1), 9–13.

Borko, H., & Putnam, R. (1996). Learning to teach. In D. Berliner & R. Calfee (Eds.), *Handbook of educational psychology* (pp. 673–708). New York: Macmillan.

Braun, C. (1976). Teacher expectation: Sociopsychological dynamics. *Review of Educational Research, 46*(2), 185–212.

Bredo, E. (1994). Reconstructing educational psychology: Situated cognition and Deweyian pragmatism. *Educational Psychologist, 29*, 23–36.

Britzman, D. (1991). *Practice makes practice: A critical study of learning to teach*. Albany, NY: State University of New York Press.

Brookhart, S. M., & Freeman, D. J. (1992). Characteristics of entering teacher candidates. *Review of Educational Research, 62*, 37–60.

Brophy, J. E. (1982, March). *Research on the self-fulfilling prophecy and teacher expectations*. Paper presented at the annual meeting of the American Educational Research Association, New York.

Brophy, J. E., & Good, T. (1986). Teacher behavior and student achievement. In M. Wittrock (Ed.), *Handbook of research on teaching* (3rd ed., pp. 328–375). New York: Macmillan.

Brown, D. F., & Rose, T. D. (1995). Self-reported classroom impact of teachers' theories about learning and obstacles to implementation. *Action in Teacher Education, 17*(1), 20–29.

Brown, S., & McIntyre, D. J. (1993). *Making sense of teaching.* Buckingham, England: Open University Press.

Bullough, R., & Knowles, J. (1991). Teaching and nurturing: Changing conceptions of self as a teacher in a case study of becoming a teacher. *Qualitative Studies in Education, 4,* 121–140.

Burley, W. W., Hall, B. W., Villeme, M. G., & Brockmeier, L. L. (1991, April). *A path analysis of the mediating role of efficacy in first-year teachers' experiences, reactions, and plans.* Paper presented at the annual meeting of the American Educational Research Association, Chicago, IL.

Bussis, A., Chittenden, E., & Amarel, M. (1976). *Beyond the surface curriculum: An interview study or teachers' understandings.* Boulder, CO: Westview.

Calderhead, J. (1988). Learning for introductory school experience. *Journal of Education for Teaching, 14*(1), 74–83.

Calderhead, J. (1996). Teachers: Beliefs and knowledge. In D. Berliner & R. Calfee (Eds.), *Handbook of educational psychology* (pp. 709–725). New York: Macmillan.

Calderhead, J., & Robson, M. (1991). Images of teaching: Student teachers' early conceptions of classroom practice. *Teaching and Teacher Education, 7,* 1–8.

Calfee, R. (1992). Refining educational psychology: The case of the missing links. *Educational Psychologist, 27,* 163–176.

Chambliss, M. J. (1995). Text cues and strategies successful readers use to construct the gist of lengthy written arguments. *Reading Research Quarterly, 30*(4), 778–807.

Chinn, C. A., & Brewer, W. F. (1993). The role of anomalous data in knowledge acquisition: A theoretical framework and implications for science instruction. *Review of Research, 63*(1), 1–49.

Civil, M. (1992, April). *Prospective elementary teachers' thinking about mathematics.* Paper presented at the annual meeting of the American Educational Research Association, San Francisco, CA.

Clandinin, D. J. (1986). *Classroom practice: Teacher images in action.* London: Falmer.

Clandinin, D. J., & Connelly, F. (1987). Teachers' personal knowledge: What counts as personal in studies of the personal. *Journal of Curriculum Studies, 19,* 487–500.

Clark, C., & Peterson, P. (1986). Teachers' thought processes. In M. Wittrock (Ed.), *Handbook of research on teaching* (3rd ed., pp. 255–296). New York: Macmillan.

Cochran-Smith, M., & Lytle, S. L. (1990). Research on teaching and teacher research: The issues that divide. *Educational Researcher, 19*(2), 2–10.

Cooper, H. M., & Good, T. (1983). *Pygmalion grows up: Studies in the expectation communication process.* New York: Longman.

Crow, N. (1988, April). *A longitudinal study or teacher socialization: A case study.* Paper presented at the annual meeting of the American Educational Research Association, New Orleans, LA.

Darling-Hammond, L. (1994). *Professional development schools: Schools for developing a profession.* New York: Teachers College Press.

Derry, S. (1991). Beyond symbolic processing: Expanding horizons for educational psychology. *Journal of Educational Psychology, 84,* 413–418.

Doyle, W. (1983). Academic work. *Review of Educational Research, 53,* 159–199.

Doyle, W. (1986). Classroom organization and management. In M. C. Wittrock (Ed.), *Handbook of research on teaching* (3rd ed., pp. 392–431). New York: Macmillan.

Dweck, C., & Bempechat, J. (1983). Children's theories of intelligence: Consequences for learning. In S. Paris & G. Olson (Eds.), *Learning and motivation in the classroom* (pp. 239–256). New York: Wiley.

Eisenhart, M., Borko, H., Underhill, R., Brown, C., Jones, D., & Agard, P. (1993). Conceptual knowledge falls through the cracks: Complexities of learning to teach mathematics for understanding. *Journal for Research in Mathematics Education, 24,* 8–40.

Elbaz, F. L. (1983). *Teacher thinking: A study of practical knowledge.* London: Croom Helm.

Featherstone, H. (1993). Learning from the first years of classroom teaching: The journey in, the journey out. *Teachers College Record, 95*(11), 93–112.

Feiman-Nemser, S., & Buchmann, M. (1989). Describing teacher education: A framework and illustrative findings from a longitudinal study of six students. *The Elementary School Journal, 89,* 365–377.

Fenstermacher, G. (1979). A philosophical consideration of recent research on teacher effectiveness. In L. Shulman (Ed.), *Review of research in education* (pp. 157–185). Itasca, IL: Peacock.

Fenstermacher, G. (1994). The knower and the known: The nature of knowledge in research on teaching. In L. Darling-Hammond (Ed.), *Review of research in education* (Vol. 20, pp. 1–54). Washington, DC: American Educational Research Association.

Finn, J. (1972). Expectations and the educational environment. *Review of Educational Research, 42,* 387–410.

Fiske, S. T. (1993). Social cognition and social perception. *Annual Review of Psychology, 44,* 155–195.

Florio-Ruane, S., & Lensmire, T. J. (1990). Transforming future teachers' ideas about writing instruction. *Journal of Curriculum Studies, 22,* 277–289.

Garner, R., & Alexander, P. A. (1991, April). *Skill, will, and thrill: Factors in adults' text comprehension.* Paper presented at the annual meeting of the American Educational Research Association, Chicago, IL.

Garner, R., & Alexander, P. A. (Eds.). (1994). *Beliefs about text and instruction with text.* Hillsdale, NJ: Lawrence Erlbaum Associates.

Glickman, C., & Tamashiro, R. (1982). A comparison of first-year, fifth-year, and former teachers on efficacy, ego development, and problem solving. *Psychology in Schools, 19,* 558–562.

Goldman, A. I. (1986). *Epistemology and cognition.* Cambridge, MA: Harvard University Press.

Good, T. L. (1983). Classroom research: A decade of progress. *Educational Psychologist, 18,* 127–144.

Good, T. L. (1988). Teacher expectations. In D. Berliner & B. Rosenshine (Eds.), *Talks to teachers* (pp. 159–200). New York: Random House.

Good, T., & Brophy, J. (1997). *Looking in classrooms* (7th ed.). New York: HarperCollins.

Goodenow, C. (1992). Strengthening the links between educational psychology and the study of social contexts. *Educational Psychologist, 27,* 177–196.

Goodlad, J. I. (1994). *Educational renewal: Better teachers, better schools.* San Francisco: Jossey-Bass.

Graham, S., & Weiner, B. (1996). Theories and principles of motivation. In D. C. Berliner & R. C. Calfee (Eds.), *Handbook of educational psychology* (pp. 63–85). New York: Macmillan.

Grant, G. E. (1992). The sources of structural metaphors in teacher knowledge: Three cases. *Teaching and Teacher Education, 8,* 433–440.

Green, T. (1971). *The activities of teaching.* New York: McGraw-Hill.

Greeno, J. G., Collins, A. M., & Resnick, L. B. (1996). Cognition and learning. In D. Berliner & R. Calfee (Eds.), *Handbook of educational psychology* (pp. 15–46). New York: Macmillan.

Greenwood, G. E., Olejnik, S. F., & Parkay, F. W. (1990). Relationships between four teacher efficacy belief patterns and selected teacher characteristics. *Journal of Research and Development in Education, 23*(2), 102–106.

Guskey, T. (1984). The influence of change in instructional effectiveness upon the affective characteristics of teachers. *American Educational Research Journal, 21*, 245–259.

Guskey, T. (1989). Attitude and perceptual change in teachers. *International Journal of Educational Research, 13*, 439–453.

Guskey, T., & Passaro, P. (1994). Teacher efficacy: A study of construct dimensions. *American Educational Research Journal, 31*, 627–643.

Guyton, E., & Rainer, J. (Eds.). (1996). Constructivism in teacher education [Special Issue]. *Action in Teacher Education, 18*(2).

Hall, B., Burley, W., Villeme, M., & Brockmeier, L. (1992). *An attempt to explicate teacher efficacy beliefs among first year teachers.* Paper presented at the annual meeting of the American Educational Research Association, San Francisco, CA.

Harrington, H., & Garrison, J. (1992). Cases as shared inquiry: A dialogical model of teacher preparation. *American Educational Research Journal, 29*, 715–735.

Hewstone, M. (1989). Changing stereotypes with disconfirming information. In D. Bar-Tal, C. Graumann, A. Kruglanski, & W. Stroebe (Eds.), *Stereotyping and prejudice: Changing conceptions* (pp. 207–223). New York: Springer-Verlag.

Hollingworth, S. (1989). Prior beliefs and cognitive change in learning to teach. *American Educational Research Journal, 26*, 160–189.

Holmes Group. (1996). *Tomorrow's schools of education.* East Lansing, MI: Author.

Holt-Reynolds, D. (1992). Personal history-based beliefs as relevant prior knowledge in coursework: Can we practice what we teach? *American Educational Research Journal, 29*, 325–349.

Housego, B. (1992). Monitoring student teachers' feelings of preparedness to teach, personal teaching efficacy, and teaching efficacy in a new secondary teacher education program. *Alberta Journal of Educational Research, 38*(1), 49–64.

Howey, K. (1996). Designing coherent and effective teacher education programs. In J. Sikula (Ed.), *Handbook of research on teacher education* (2nd ed., pp. 143–170). New York: Macmillan.

Hoy, W. K., & Woolfolk, A. E. (1990). Socialization of student teachers. *American Educational Research Journal, 27*, 279–300.

Hussey, E. (1990). The beginnings of epistemology from Homer to Philolaus. In S. Everson (Ed.), *Epistemology* (pp. 11–38). Cambridge, England: Cambridge University Press.

Johnson, D. W., & Johnson, R. T. (1988). Critical thinking through structured controversy. *Educational Leadership, 45*, 58–64.

Kagan, D. (1990). Ways of evaluating teacher cognition: Inferences concerning the Goldilocks principle. *Review of Educational Research, 60*, 419–469.

Kagan, D. (1992). Implications of research on teacher belief. *Educational Psychologist, 27*, 65–90.

Kagan, D., & Tippins, D. J. (1991). How student teachers describe their pupils. *Teaching and Teacher Education, 7*, 455–466.

Kennedy, M. M. (1988). Inexact sciences: Professional development and the education of expertise. In E. Z. Rothkoph (Ed.), *Review of research in education* (Vol. 14, pp. 133–167). Washington, DC: American Educational Research Association.

Knowles, J. G. (1992). Models for teachers' biographies. In I. Goodson (Ed.), *Studying teachers' lives* (pp. 99–152). New York: Teachers College Press.

Korthagen, F. A. (1993). Two modes of reflection. *Teaching and Teacher Education, 9*, 317–326.

Leinhardt, G. (1988). Situated knowledge and expertise in teaching. In J. Calderhead (Ed.), *Teachers' professional learning* (pp. 146–168). London: Falmer.

Leinhardt, G. (1990). Capturing craft knowledge in teaching. *Educational Researcher, 19*(2), 18–25.

Lortie, D. (1975). *Schoolteachers: A sociological study*. Chicago: University of Chicago Press.

Mayer, R. (1991). Cognition and instruction: Their historic meeting within educational psychology. *Journal of Educational Psychology, 84*, 405–412.

McDiarmid, G. W. (1993). Changes in beliefs about learners among participants in eleven teacher education programs. In J. Calderhead & P. Gates (Eds.), *Conceptualizing reflection in teacher development* (pp. 113–143). London: Falmer.

McLaughlin, J. (1991). Reconciling care and control: Authority in classroom relationships. *Journal of Teacher Education, 40*(3), 182–195.

Morine-Dershimer, G. (1993). Tracing conceptual change in preservice teachers. *Teaching and Teacher Education, 9*, 15–26.

Moser, P. K., & vander Nat, A. (1987). *Human knowledge: Classical and contemporary approaches*. New York: Oxford University Press.

Murphy, P. K. (1998). *Toward a multifaceted model of persuasion: Exploring textual and learner interactions*. Unpublished doctoral dissertation, University of Maryland, College of Education, College Park, MD.

Murphy, P. K., & Woods, B. S. (1996). Situating knowledge in learning and instruction. *Educational Psychologist, 31*, 141–145.

Nespor, J. (1987). The role of beliefs in the practice of teaching. *Journal of Curriculum Studies, 19*, 317–328.

Nisbett, R., & Ross, L. (1980). *Human inference: Strategies and shortcomings of social judgment*. Englewood Cliffs, NJ: Prentice-Hall.

Ohmart, H. (1992). *The effects of an efficacy intervention on teachers' efficacy feelings*. Unpublished doctoral dissertation, University of Kansas, Lawrence, KS.

Oosterhof, A. (1999). *Developing and using classroom assessments* (2nd ed.). Columbus, OH: Merrill.

Pajares, F. (1992). Teachers' beliefs and educational research: Cleaning up a messy construct. *Review of Educational Research, 62*, 307–332.

Pajares, F. (1993). Preservice teachers' beliefs: A focus for teacher education. *Action in Teacher Education, 15*(2), 45–54.

Pajares, F., & Bengston, J. K. (1995). The psychologizing of teacher education: Formalist thinking and preservice teachers' beliefs. *Peabody Journal of Education, 70*, 83–98.

Pajares, F., & Graham, L. (1998). Formalist thinking and language arts instruction: Teachers' and students' beliefs about truth and caring in the teaching conversation. *Teaching and Teacher Education, 14*, 855–870.

Parkay, F. W., Greenwood, G., Olejnik, S., & Proller, N. (1988). A study of the relationship among teacher efficacy, locus of control, and stress. *Journal of Research and Development in Education, 21*(4), 13–22.

Peterson, P., Fennema, E., Carpenter, T., & Loef, M. (1989). Teachers' pedagogical content beliefs in mathematics. *Cognition and Instruction, 6*, 1–40.

Pintrich, P. (1994). Continuities and discontinuities: Future directions for research in educational psychology. *Educational Psychologist, 29*, 137–148.

Prawat, R. S. (1992). Teachers beliefs about teaching and learning: A constructivist perspective. *American Journal of Education, 100*, 354–395.

Prawat, R. S., & Floden, R. E. (1994). Philosophical perspectives on constructivist view of learning. *Educational Psychologist, 29*, 37–48.

Putnam, R. T., & Borko, H. (1997). Teacher learning: Implications of new views of cognition. In B. J. Biddle, T. L. Good, & I. F. Goodson (Eds.), *The international handbook of teachers and teaching* (Vol. 2, pp. 1223–1296). Dordrecht, The Netherlands: Kluwer.

Renninger, A. (1996). Learning as the focus of an educational psychology course. *Educational Psychologist, 31*, 63–76.

Rentel, V. (1994). Preparing clinical faculty members: Research on teachers' reasoning. In K. Howey & N. Zimpher (Eds.), *The professional development of teacher educators* (pp. 109–128). Norwood, NJ: Ablex.

Resnick, L. B. (1981). Instructional psychology. *Annual Review of Psychology, 32,* 659–704.

Richardson, V. (1994). The consideration of belief in staff development. In V. Richardson (Ed.), *Teacher change and the staff development process: A case in reading instruction* (pp. 90–108). New York: Teachers College Press.

Richardson, V. (1996). The role of attitudes and beliefs in learning to teach. In J. Sikula (Ed.), *Handbook of research on teacher education* (2nd ed., pp. 102–119). New York: Macmillan.

Richardson, V., Anders, P., Tidwell, D., & Lloyd, C. (1991). The relationship between teachers' beliefs and practices in reading comprehension instruction. *American Educational Research Journal, 28,* 559–586.

Richardson, V., & Kile, S. (1992, April). *The use of videocases in teacher education.* Paper presented at the annual meeting of the American Educational Research Association, San Francisco, CA.

Richardson-Koehler, V. (1988). Barriers to effective supervision of student teachers. *Journal of Teacher Education, 39*(2), 28–34.

Rocklin, T. (1996). Context effect in teaching educational psychology. *Educational Psychologist, 31,* 35–40.

Rokeach, M. (1968). *Beliefs, attitudes, and values: A theory of organization and change.* San Francisco: Jossey-Bass.

Rosenshine, B., & Stevens, R. (1986). Teaching functions. In M. Wittrock (Ed.), *Handbook of research on teaching* (3rd ed., pp. 376–391). New York: Macmillan.

Rosenthal, R. (1987). Pygmalion effects: Existence, magnitude and social importance. A reply to Wineburg. *Educational Researcher, 16,* 37–41.

Rosenthal, R. (1994). Interpersonal expectancy effects: A 30-year perspective. *Current Directions in Psychological Science, 3,* 176–179.

Rosenthal, R. (1995). Critiquing Pygmalion: A 25-year perspective. *Current Directions in Psychological Science, 4,* 171–172.

Rosenthal, R., & Jacobson, L. (1968). *Pygmalion in the classroom.* New York: Holt, Rinehart & Winston.

Ross, D. D., Johnson, M., & Smith, E. (1991, April). *Developing a professional teacher at the University of Florida.* Paper presented at the annual meeting of the American Educational Research Association, Chicago, IL.

Ross, J. A. (1994). The impact of an inservice to promote cooperative learning on the stability of teacher efficacy. *Teaching & Teacher Education, 10,* 381–394.

Saklofske, D., Michaluk, B., & Randhawa, B. (1988). Teachers' efficacy and teaching behaviors. *Psychological Report, 63,* 407–414.

Schon, D. A. (1983). *The reflective practitioner.* New York: Basic Books.

Shuell, T. (1986). Cognitive conceptions of learning. *Review of Educational Research, 56,* 411–436.

Shuell, T. (1990). Phases of meaningful learning. *Review of Educational Psychology, 60,* 531–548.

Shuell, T. (1996). The role of educational psychology in the preparation of teachers. *Educational Psychologist, 31,* 15–22.

Shulman, L. (1990). Reconnecting foundations to the substance of teacher education. *Teacher College Record, 91,* 300–310.

Shulman, L. (1992). Toward a pedagogy of cases. In J. Shulman (Ed.), *Case method in teacher education* (pp. 1–30). New York: Teachers College Press.

Simon, H. (1995). The information processing view of the mind. *American Psychologist, 50,* 507–508.

Smylie, M. A., (1988). The enhancement function of staff development: Organizational and psychological antecedents to individual teacher change. *American Educational Research Journal, 25,* 1–30.

Snow, R. E. (1995). Pygmalion and intelligence. *Current Directions in Psychological Science, 4,* 169–171.

Spector, J. E. (1990, April). *Efficacy for teaching in preservice teachers.* Paper presented at the annual meeting of the American Educational Research Association, Boston, MA.

Sternberg, R., Conway, B., Ketron, J., & Bernstein, M. (1981). People's conceptions of intelligence. *Journal of Personality and Social Psychology, 41,* 37–55.

Stipek, D. J. (1996). Motivation and instruction. In D. C. Berliner & R. C. Calfee (Eds.), *Handbook of educational psychology* (pp. 85–117). New York: Macmillan.

Strauss, S. (1993). Teachers' pedagogical content knowledge about children's minds and learning: Implications for teacher education. *Educational Psychologist, 28,* 279–290.

Strauss, S. (1996). Confessions of a born-again constructivist. *Educational Psychologist, 31,* 15–22.

Strauss, S., & Shilony, T. (1994). Teachers' mental models of children's minds and learning. In L. Hirschfeld & S. A. Gelman (Eds.), *Mapping the mind: Cognition and culture* (pp. 455–473). New York: Cambridge University Press.

Swann, W. B., & Snyder, M. (1980). On translating beliefs into action: Theories of ability and their implications in an instructional setting. *Journal of Personality and Social Psychology, 38,* 879–888.

Sykes, G., & Bird, T. (1992). Teacher education and the case idea. In G. Grant (Ed.), *Review of research in education* (Vol. 19, pp. 457–521). Washington, DC: American Educational Research Association.

Tschannen-Moran, M., Woolfolk Hoy, A., & Hoy, W. K. (1998). Teacher efficacy: Its meaning and measure. *Review of Educational Research, 68,* 202–248.

Vosniadou, S. (1994). Capturing and modeling the process of conceptual change. *Learning and Instruction, 4,* 45–69.

Vygotsky, L. S. (1978). *Mind in society: The development of higher psychological processes.* Cambridge, MA: Harvard University Press.

Wasserman, S. (1993). *Getting down to cases.* New York: Teachers College Press.

Watters, J. J., & Ginns, I. S. (1995, April). *Origins of and changes in preservice teachers' science teaching efficacy.* Paper presented at the annual meeting of the National Association of Research in Science Teaching, San Francisco, CA.

Weiner, B. (1986). *An attributional theory of motivation and emotion.* New York: Springer.

Weinstein, C. (1988). Preservice teachers' expectations about the first year of teaching. *Teaching and Teacher Education, 4,* 31–41.

Weinstein, C. (1989). Teacher education students' perceptions of teaching. *Journal of Teacher Education, 40*(2), 53–60.

Weinstein, C., Woolfolk, A., Dittmeier, L., & Shanker, U. (1994). Protector or prison guard: Using metaphors and media to explore student teachers' thinking about classroom management. *Action in Teacher Education, 16*(1), 41–54.

Willower, D. J., Eidell, T. L., & Hoy, W. K. (1967). *The school and pupil control ideology* (Penn State Studies Monograph No. 24). University Park, PA: Pennsylvania State University.

Wilson, S. M. (1990). The secret garden of teacher education. *Phi Delta Kappan, 72,* 204–209.

Wilson, S. M. , & Wineberg, S. S. (1988). Peering at history through different lenses: The role of disciplinary perspectives in teaching history. *Teachers College Record, 84,* 525–539.

Wittrock, M. C. (1992). An empowering conception of educational psychology. *Educational Psychologist, 27,* 129–142.

Woolfolk, A. E. (2001). *Educational psychology* (8th ed.). Boston: Allyn & Bacon.

Woolfolk, A. E., & Brooks, D. (1983). Nonverbal communication in teaching. In E. Gordon (Ed.), *Review of research in education* (Vol. 10, pp. 103–150). Washington, DC: American Educational Research Association.

Woolfolk, A. E., & Brooks, D. (1985). The influence of teachers' nonverbal behaviors on students' perceptions and performance. *Elementary School Journal, 85,* 514–528.

Woolfolk, A. E., & Hoy, W. K. (1990). Prospective teachers' sense of efficacy and beliefs about control. *Journal of Educational Psychology, 82,* 81–91.

Woolfolk Hoy, A., & Tschannen-Moran, M. (1999). Implications of cognitive approaches to peer learning for teacher education. In A. O'Donnell & A. King (Eds.), *Cognitive perspectives on peer learning* (pp. 257–284). Mahwah, NJ: Lawrence Erlbaum Associates.

Yinger, R. (1987, April). *By the seat of your pants: An inquiry into improvisation in teaching.* Paper presented at the annual meeting of the American Educational Research Association, Washington, DC.

Zeichner, K., & Gore, J. (1990). Teacher socialization. In W. R. Houston (Ed.), *Handbook of research on teacher education* (pp. 329–348). New York: Macmillan.

CHAPTER EIGHT

Nine Prospective Teachers and Their Experiences in Teacher Education: The Role of Entering Conceptions of Teaching and Learning

Linda M. Anderson
Michigan State University

Much research on learning by teachers has investigated their conceptions about teaching and learning (Calderhead, 1996; Pajares, 1992; Prawat, 1992; Richardson, 1996). One line of research on the conceptions of teachers has focused on prospective teachers' learning within teacher-education programs—specifically, how entering conceptions about teaching and learning influence whether, what, and how prospective teachers learn from formal, university-based teacher education (Borko & Putnam, 1996; Brookhart & Freeman, 1992; Calderhead, 1991; Calderhead & Robson, 1991; Feiman-Nemser & Remillard, 1996; Freeman, 1996; Goodman, 1988; Hollingsworth, 1989; Holt-Reynolds, 1992; Kagan, 1992; Levin & Ammon, 1992; Powell, 1992; Wubbels, 1992).

As a teacher educator, I am regularly reminded that my students do indeed come to their preparation program with strong beliefs about teaching and learning, and that I and my colleagues must continually ask ourselves how our students are making sense of the teacher-education program in light of their entering conceptions. To learn more about this phenomenon, we conducted three studies in the National Center for Research on Teacher Learning (NCRTL) at Michigan State University. One result of our work is a collection of case studies of the learning of prospective teachers, with analyses focused on ways that entering conceptions of teaching and learning affected and interacted with their experiences in and learning from teacher-education courses or programs. The purpose of this chapter is to present those cases in brief form and highlight insights from our research about the conceptions of teaching and learning of prospective teachers.

BACKGROUND

The Nature of Beliefs and Conceptions

The teacher-education literature abounds with research on an aspect of teachers' and prospective teachers' thinking and knowledge that I label *conceptions* or *beliefs* about teaching and learning, but which has been labeled by other researchers in other ways, including *perspectives* (John, 1991), *lay theories* (Holt-Reynolds, 1994), *worldviews* (Powell, 1996), *constructs* (Powell, 1992), *images* (Calderhead & Robson, 1991; Johnston, 1992), *metaphors* (Bullough & Stokes, 1994), and *implicit theories* (Clark & Peterson, 1986). As Pajares (1992) pointed out, these many labels suggest a messy construct in the field.

Within the research described here, we defined *conceptions* (which earlier in our project we called *beliefs*) to mean propositions and networks of ideas that a teacher holds to be reasonable, whether those propositions were expressed overtly by the teacher or held implicitly and inferred from statements and actions. Elements of beliefs or conceptions include conceptual categories that define what is reasonable or important to notice, differentiate, and attend to (e.g., differences among students or features of classroom activity); empirical claims (e.g., children whose parents read to them as preschoolers will learn to read at an earlier age); prescriptive guidelines (e.g., teachers should never lecture to students about science until after they have engaged in a hands-on activity); and educational values (e.g., cooperation is preferable to competition in the classroom; Bird, Anderson, Sullivan, & Swidler, 1993).

Our research was about change in any or all of these elements of conceptions. However, our use of the term *conceptual change* differed from its use by others (e.g., Carey, 1985), who defined it as a shift between incommensurable ideas. When we began the project, many teacher educators who wrote about belief or conceptual change also seemed to be describing replacement of an old idea with a newer, opposing idea (specifically, replacement of traditional views of teaching and learning with constructivist views of teaching for understanding, as described later). Within the project, however, we defined *conceptual change* to include not only a shift between incommensurable ideas, but also more subtle elaboration and refinement of entering ideas toward more complex views of teaching, which might or might not stand in opposition to earlier views.

When we initiated the research project in 1991,[1] we reasoned that conceptions about teaching and learning served an important function for teachers and prospective teachers. Like all humans, teachers respond to complexity in their daily lives in part through belief or conceptual systems that help them organize and select among myriad aspects of the scene before them. Belief systems function as filters, highlighting certain information as relevant to the goals of the situation and deeming other information less important. Belief systems also function to explain what is perceived and render it sensible—that is, to help the perceiver understand how and why an event occurred as it did or allow the perceiver to predict what will happen next. Finally, belief systems include knowledge about possible and desirable actions associated with goals and situations, thus providing a basis for judging actions as reasonable or not, depending on how they advance the goals held by the person in a given situation. Belief systems, like other forms of knowledge, are often organized around situations (Brown, Collins, & Duguid, 1989). Thus, an individual may hold different beliefs about appropriate actions and their justifications for different situations, and how situations are perceived and differentiated is also determined in large part by the associated belief systems.

The definition of *belief* or *conceptual systems* in the project was influenced by early writing about beliefs and attitudes (e.g., Rokeach, 1968) as well as more recent work on conceptual change (Carey, 1985; Posner, Strike, Hewson, & Gertzog, 1982), schema theory (Anderson & Pearson, 1984), epistemological beliefs and development (Belenky, Clinchy, Goldberger, & Tarule, 1986; Perry, 1970), anthropological theories (Goodenough, 1981), and folk theories (Bruner, 1986, 1990; for a more recent discussion of folk pedagogy, see Bruner, 1996).

At the time we began the project, we found appealing the characterization of conceptual ecologies (Toulmin, 1972) as a way to synthesize these many other authors and ideas. Toulmin argued for a view of knowledge change as gradual evolution in thinking rather than paradigmatic revolution as suggested by Kuhn (1970). Toulmin did not disagree with the notion that knowledge is organized and systemic, but he warned against seeing bodies of knowledge as too systematic. Instead of being tightly coupled systems, in which a change in one idea would necessarily precipitate change in another idea, he said that bodies of knowledge were more like a "conceptual aggregate, or 'population,' within which there are—at most—localized pockets of logical systematicity" (Toulmin, 1972, p. 128).

---

[1]The early conceptualization of beliefs within the project as described here was developed with Tom Bird. Portions of this section are adapted from an unpublished manuscript coauthored with him (Anderson & Bird, 1992).

Similarly, we have conceptualized the conceptions of teachers as organized into loosely coupled systems in which there is potential for interaction among all components and across all situations, but that interaction is not necessarily predictable and is usually limited in scope. The special challenge of the teacher educator, then, is to figure out how to provoke change in some components or situations and then assist its spread through the system by helping prospective teachers consider potential connections and discrepancies in their beliefs.

The Role of Beliefs and Conceptions in Preservice Teacher Education

Literature on prospective teachers' learning from teacher education often describes a core tension that we documented within our research project. In our first study, we described it in this way:

> Prospective teachers' own past experiences as learners and students tend to shape beliefs that pose challenges in many teacher education courses (Holt-Reynolds, 1992; Lortie, 1975; Pajares, 1993; Zeichner & Gore, 1990). Some prospective teachers' images of teaching and learning reflect conventional educational experiences, where teachers tell and knowledge is received and reproduced. When their teacher educators offer alternative points of view, such as the idea that teachers mediate and assist students' active constructions of meaning and transformation of knowledge, these less familiar ideas and images are not easily or quickly understood or accepted. Like any learners, prospective teachers can learn only by drawing upon their own beliefs and prior experiences to understand new ideas, but their beliefs and knowledge may not support their learning about new views of learning and teaching advocated by many teacher educators. (Anderson & Bird, 1995, p. 480)

Reflected in this statement is the assumption that one important goal for teacher educators is to introduce new ways of teaching that reflect reform-based recommendations for curriculum, instruction, and assessment standards based on constructivist views of teaching and learning and often called *teaching for understanding* (Cohen, McLaughlin, & Talbert, 1993; Kennedy, 1991; Prawat, 1992).

Contrasts between teaching for understanding and traditional views of teaching were easy to find in the literature of the early 1990s and usually featured the elements selected by McLaughlin and Talbert (1993):

> This vision of practice [i.e., teaching for understanding] signals a sea change in notions of teaching and learning; constructivist ideas about teachers co-

constructing knowledge with learners replace traditional views of teacher as knowledge transmitter and behavioral engineer. In this view of teaching and learning, teachers' central responsibility is to create worthwhile activities and select materials that engage students' intellect and stimulate them to move beyond acquisition of facts to sense making in a subject area. Rather than reproduce facts, teachers expect their students to explain their ideas, support their conclusions, and persist when they are stumped. (McLaughlin & Talbert, 1993, p. 2)

Many writers during this time made the case that changes in teaching practice toward the vision articulated by McLaughlin and Talbert required changes in the beliefs or conceptions of teachers. Although belief change alone would not guarantee change in practice, new forms of practice could not be implemented on anything other than a superficial level when teachers did not understand and accept the underlying premises of a constructivist view of learning and associated principles of teaching (Anderson, 1989; Cohen, 1989; Fosnot, 1989; Kennedy, 1991).

Conducting teacher education with teaching for understanding as the goal is quite challenging if prospective teachers come to teacher education with a different view of teaching in mind. The conventional wisdom in the early 1990s was that most prospective teachers came into teacher education having served a long apprenticeship of observation (Lortie, 1975) in mostly traditional classrooms where, supposedly, they only saw teachers in front of classrooms maintaining order and presenting information. As a result, it was commonly predicted, they would bring beliefs that would be incommensurable with and interfere with their learning about the newer, teach-for-understanding perspective.

The conventional wisdom of the time about the consequences of this apprenticeship of observation was expressed by McDiarmid (1990), writing about his attempts to present a model of elementary mathematics teaching for understanding—a model quite different from the math instruction most of his students had experienced. McDiarmid found it difficult to create significant change in the views of his students about teaching in one semester. He remarked: "Although the students appear to reconsider their beliefs [about teaching and learning], such changes may be superficial and short-lived" (p. 12), and "the strength of each individual belief about teaching, learning, learners, subject matter knowledge, and context is formidable. Interwoven, the strands constitute a web of remarkable resilience; severing one strand barely diminishes the overall strength of the whole" (p. 18).

Others at that time also expressed their pessimism about the possibilities of countering the strengths of prospective teachers' entering conceptions about what would be involved in teaching, what they needed to learn, and, therefore, what they should attend to (and discount) in teacher-education coursework (e.g., see Britzman, 1986; Brookhart & Freeman, 1992; Buchmann, 1987; Calderhead, 1991; Calderhead & Robson, 1991; Knowles & Holt-Reynolds, 1991; Lanier & Little, 1986; Powell, 1992; Wubbels, 1992). In this somewhat discouraging atmosphere, we initiated our research project to learn more about the ways that teacher education might influence change in prospective teachers' beliefs about teaching in general and beliefs about teaching for understanding in particular.

In addition to wanting to learn about how teacher educators influenced change, we also wanted to understand better the nature of conceptual change that occurred during teacher education. In particular, we asked whether and when it involved a drastic shift from one set of beliefs to another incommensurable set, as compared with a more gradual and evolutionary form of conceptual change, which was less likely to involve complete replacement of entering ideas and more likely to involve elaboration and reorganization.

Our research strategy was to select promising sites where teacher educators were, first of all, committed to teacher education as intervention into belief systems, recognizing that the underlying entering conceptions of prospective teachers were important and influential in their learning. Furthermore, we selected sites where the teacher educators involved had a track record of some success in promoting belief change or, at least, were operating with some defensible hypotheses in mind about how to promote change. Another important element in our research strategy was to focus on individual prospective teachers, to study them closely across time to try to trace qualitative changes in their belief systems, and not simply to note preinstruction versus postinstruction changes on a list of discrete and narrowly defined beliefs.

As a result of these design decisions, data collection in each study was intensive and extensive, including transcripts of whole-class and small-group discussions, informal and structured interviews with a focus sample of prospective teachers, and analyses of writing of the students for the class. In two of the three studies, one of the researchers was also the teacher educator whose course was being studied; in the third case, the teacher educators participated in the design and monitoring of the study. However, the noninstructional researchers were careful not to share with instructors anything that prospective teachers told us until after the class or program ended, and the prospective teachers were no longer being evaluated by the teacher educators. Further details about the conduct of each study are available in the primary article or paper about that study, described later.

THE NCRTL RESEARCH PROJECT ON TRANSFORMING BELIEFS ABOUT TEACHING, LEARNING, AND LEARNERS

Although we were interested in sites where teacher educators wanted to promote a vision of teaching for understanding, we expected that would take different forms depending on the nature of the course or program studied, any subject-matter specialization, and other factors such as the amount of time available (i.e., in a one-semester course, an instructor selects some elements of teaching to emphasize and not others). Therefore, we were not looking for sites that fit a particular model of teacher education, that emphasized particular aspects of teachers' beliefs, or that sought a particular form of conceptual change. In fact, we expected that differences in approaches and emphases across research sites would make for a more informative collection of studies. As a result, the teacher educators in the three sites held somewhat different conceptions of prospective teachers' conceptions, different hypotheses about how to promote conceptual change, and emphasized different aspects of teaching. However, they were alike in that they were committed to some form of conceptual change, and their course or program goals could be related to the current reform movement toward teaching for understanding.

Each study is described in terms of: (a) the goals of the teacher educator for conceptual change by the prospective teachers; (b) hypotheses about features of pedagogy that would promote the desired change; (c) descriptions of three prospective teachers from each study, and how their conceptions changed over time; and (d) conclusions from the study.

STUDY 1: THE "EXPLORING TEACHING" COURSE (ANDERSON & BIRD, 1995; BIRD ET AL., 1993)

Teacher Educator's Goals

"Exploring Teaching" was a course required for all prospective elementary teachers. In this study, Anderson and Bird studied a section taught by Bird, who described his goals this way:

> Bird expected many students to hold, and he wanted to challenge, the image of a classroom in which the teacher is the constant and prominent center of students' attention, where teaching and learning are mainly or exclusively matters of telling and remembering, and where worthwhile learning occurs only at the teacher's insistence and direction. . . . He wanted to introduce the possibility that subject matters might hold some interest for students, that a

class might be a place where students are focused on their projects involving the subject matter, and that a teacher might do good work by organizing, guiding, and supporting such activity. (Bird et al., 1993, p. 257)

Hypotheses About Features of Pedagogy That Would Promote the Desired Conceptual Change

Bird taught the course through a series of classroom cases that presented different images of teaching to his students. Each of three cases was presented in a 2- to 3-week segment of class that began with a videotape of the lesson or classroom featured in the case, followed by discussion about the initial impressions of the college students of the case. Then students read an article about some ideas that the case might illustrate or exemplify. Following further work in class with the case and the reading, students wrote a paper in which they commented on the case of teaching from perspectives as a teacher (as they imagined a teacher might respond), as the experienced student they were, and as the author whose ideas they had studied in relation to the case. In keeping with ideas prevalent at the time, we hypothesized that the use of cases along with the assignment to take on various perspectives would not only surface conceptions of prospective teachers, but also provoke some dissatisfaction with them and provide plausible alternatives (Posner et al., 1982).

Cases of Three Prospective Teachers in Study 1

We collected data about nine students from this class, then featured three who differed in terms of their initial conceptions of teaching and learning: Kay, Jessica, and Jill.[2] Because we hypothesized that the use of classroom cases would prompt changes in their beliefs about possible teacher roles, we focused on their responses to each of three different cases: (a) a tra-

[2]In each of the first two studies, we reported about only three of eight or nine prospective teachers for whom we had data. (Initial selection of the eight or nine prospective teachers balanced salient categories like gender, major, etc., among those students who had volunteered. In both cases, the majority of the class members volunteered.) We selected only three cases to report in order to highlight interesting contrasts in entering conceptions without having to report too many cases for the reader to keep straight. The prospective teachers selected were not so extreme that they would be unfamiliar to most experienced teacher educators in typical settings. That is, we strove to select contrasting cases that were within the typical range of prospective teachers that we had known. When one of the original eight or nine cases turned out to be so unusual as to seem outside the mainstream, we did not select that person to feature in the report. While he or she might have been interesting for other purposes, our goal was to illustrate a range of entering conceptions and kinds of conceptual change that teacher educators could expect to encounter within the kinds of institutions where we conducted the studies.

ditional, direct instruction lesson; (b) an open classroom with student-initiated projects; and (c) a math lesson taught through student–student dialogue where the teacher facilitated the dialogue of students about content but did not appear to teach directly. (The latter two cases might be considered as examples of teaching for understanding, although they were not presented with that label.) To characterize conceptions of prospective teachers, we described the most central and sturdy idea around which other ideas and examples were organized; then we analyzed reactions of each student to each case for traces of or changes in those central ideas about teaching and the roles of teachers. Details of data collection and analysis are reported in Anderson and Bird (1995).

Entering Conceptions. We labeled Kay's central conceptions about teaching, "Teacher leadership creates student participation which causes learning." We reported that:

> Kay portrayed teachers as active, visible leaders of lessons, implying that if the teacher did not orchestrate lessons well, providing the necessary information and impetus for student participation, then no learning would result. . . . She implied that the content to be learned should be transmitted from the teacher to the student, . . . [which occurs only] when the teacher works actively to get all of the students engaged with the work. (Anderson & Bird, 1995, pp. 484–485)

She believed that good teachers provided accurate and timely feedback to students. Kay's entering conception was in many ways traditional and teacher-centered, but those labels do not convey the extent to which Kay also emphasized student participation in their own learning.

In contrast, we labeled Jessica's entering conception as "Teachers' indirect guidance helps students think for themselves, which is a worthy goal in and of itself." She believed that learners should discover knowledge for themselves rather than the teacher telling them, and that teachers could support this student-centered learning by asking guiding questions and encouraging students to explain their thinking. In her image, teachers should avoid telling students answers or implying that their thinking was not correct. Thus, Jessica's conception contrasted to Kay's conception in a number of ways.

Compared with Kay and Jessica, Jill was in many ways more like the typical elementary prospective teacher as portrayed in the research literature: She focused on being nice to children and making learning fun for them. We labeled her conception as "Teachers should create interesting relevant experiences to make school learning tolerable and useful." We described her in this way:

Jill portrayed teachers as creators of interesting activities that would cam-
ouflage the dullness of content while preparing students for the future.
Everything done should seem relevant to future work, even if . . . only promotion to the next school grade. . . . Jill emphasized "hands-on" activities. . . . [S]he took an almost anti-intellectual stance, implying that if one
couldn't do something actively with what one was learning (besides think
about it), then the learning was probably not worthwhile. (Anderson &
Bird, 1995, p. 487)

Similarities in Their Entering Conceptions.   Despite the obvious
differences in the three prospective teachers' entering conceptions about
teaching and learning, they shared one component of their conceptual
ecology relevant to learning to teach: "None expressed doubts about her
initial views of teaching. As each looked ahead to her professional education, she expected to learn about those aspects of teaching most central
to her own image of the teacher she expected to become" (Anderson &
Bird, 1995, p. 488). Indeed, this is exactly what happened.

***How Entering Conceptions Were Evident in Each Student's Expe-
rience of the Course.***   Kay found much to admire in both the direct-
instruction case and the open-classroom case, in both cases focusing on
the ways that the teacher was an evident leader of the class, prompting
and sustaining participation by the students. In her analyses of the cases,
Kay drew on the same aspects of teaching that were central in her entering conception. She was more ambivalent about the third case, but here
again justified her response in familiar terms. She liked the way the
teacher prompted student participation (i.e., a lot of student-to-student
talk about the content), but she faulted the teacher for not providing
enough direct feedback about correctness of answers, echoing themes
evident in her entering conception.

In Kay's end-of-term interview, she said virtually the same thing as in
her beginning-of-term interview, portraying her ideal teacher as an active,
direct instructor. Although we did not ask students to use ideas or terminology from the course in the interviews, we did note when they referred
to course content. In Kay's final interview, she drew heavily on the reading that accompanied the first case of the direct and more traditional
instructor, but not on the other readings or cases. We concluded that "the
case that seemed most memorable and useful to Kay at the end of the term
was the case that was most like her own initial image of teaching" (Anderson & Bird, 1995, p. 495).

Not surprisingly, Jessica found much to praise in the second case (open
classroom), focusing on the teacher's indirect, facilitative role; this was in
keeping with her entering conceptions, but ignoring the main point (from

the instructor's perspective) of the accompanying reading—that the teacher was supporting the engagement of the students with the subject matter and creating personal relationships through the curriculum. Thus, Jessica noticed those features of the case that she already believed at the beginning of the course to be important, and she ignored other features that represented new or alternative interpretations.

Like Kay, Jessica was less enthusiastic about the third case of rather unconventional mathematics teaching, but praised it because the teacher was (in Jessica's view) letting the students discover something for themselves. Again, she did not notice the feature of the case that the instructor had intended, the consensual construction of meaning in a learning community where subject-matter understanding was highly valued. Instead, she attended to an aspect of instruction that she already considered important.

Jill struggled with the assignments in the class throughout the term, and her papers reflected her struggle. However, like Kay and Jessica, what she emphasized in her papers was congruent with her entering conceptions: Student affect, comfort, and interest were very salient to her. In her final paper, she concluded with a statement that she apparently believed (or hoped) was derived from the course content, but that sounded much like statements she had made in her first interview about the importance of personal experience and the power of children to learn from their experiences. In her final interview, she would not answer most of the questions, but instead took the opportunity to complain that the course had not offered enough real experiences for her, again reflecting her entering conception that good teaching means providing real-life, hand-on experience that learners will enjoy.

Conclusions From Study 1

We asked whether the students had accomplished the goal of the instructor of acquiring new options for teaching, expanding their conceptions of what kind(s) of teaching they might learn and practice. We concluded:

> It was as if [the three students] approached the study of the cases as an opportunity to fill in the missing details in their existing schemas of teaching, to learn how to do whatever they already imagined they should learn to do . . . [When the students responded to the cases], they did not do so by expanding their belief systems for what it is possible to notice, consider, and value in teaching. Rather, they interpreted each case through the lens of their initial images of teaching. (Anderson & Bird, 1995, p. 495)

Thus, we ended this first study in the research project reminded of the power of entering conceptions to shape perception and learning and a desire to learn more about teacher-education pedagogy that engaged the entering conceptions of students. We also were eager to do more regular and detailed tracings of conceptions and interpretations of course experiences over time, which meant conducting interviews more frequently, rather than relying only on course writing of students as the primary indicator of their interpretation of course content. Our questions had shifted from "Do conceptions change when you teach in certain ways (e.g., with cases and perspective-taking assignments)?" to "How do entering conceptions play out in the week-to-week experience of students in a course? How does that experience affect what is learned?"

STUDY 2: THE CONTENT-AREA READING COURSE (ANDERSON & HOLT-REYNOLDS, 1995; HOLT-REYNOLDS, 1994)

Teacher Educator's Goals

On one level, course goals were to teach prospective secondary teachers instructional methods when using text in content areas. However, the instructor, Holt-Reynolds, knew that any teaching method is evaluated by teachers according to their underlying conceptions about learning and how teachers help students learn. She knew from her own earlier research (Holt-Reynolds, 1992) that secondary prospective teachers often came to the content-area reading course with beliefs that kept them from understanding rationales behind the teaching methods, and therefore limited the usefulness and effectiveness of those methods in practice.

Holt-Reynolds predicted that prospective teachers would enter with certain related beliefs that she hoped to change. In particular, she predicted that they would believe:

1. The learning by secondary students is primarily a function of their motivation or interest. (Holt-Reynolds wanted prospective teachers to shift to an explanation for learning that focused on construction of meaning of students, and acknowledged that failure to learn is sometimes due to instructional problems, not to personality or motivational problems resident in the students.)

2. Effective secondary teaching is primarily a matter of being enthusiastic and showing students that you care while you transmit content. (Holt-Reynolds wanted prospective teachers to shift to a belief that teachers make purposeful, principled decisions about what students should learn and how the learning should be arranged. In particular, she wanted them to see teachers as mediators between current knowledge of students and the subject matter to be learned.)

3. Listening to teachers and reading textbooks are the most important ways that secondary students learn content. (Holt-Reynolds wanted prospective teachers to shift to a belief that other activities by students, such as small-group discussions, writing, and analysis activities, can also teach content when they provoke student thinking and meaning-making.)

Hypotheses About Features of Pedagogy That Would Promote the Desired Conceptual Change

Holt-Reynolds hypothesized that changing beliefs first required her to elicit and actively engage entering beliefs. She hypothesized that one way to accomplish this in a university-based course was to use in-class student-experience activities. She knew from earlier research that the student voice (based on prospective teachers' recent experiences as secondary and college students) spoke more loudly to the emerging teacher voice than did the college professor. Therefore, the easiest, perhaps only, way for a professor to affect the teacher voice was through the student perspective. She had developed a number of instructional activities to accomplish her goals, as well as a conceptual scheme for describing her instruction (described in Holt-Reynolds, 1994). She welcomed the opportunity to participate in a study to test her practical theory about how and what her students learned from her class, especially how they changed the three beliefs previously described.

Cases of Three Prospective Teachers in Study 2

We collected data on eight students from the class across the semester and then selected three who posed interesting contrasts: Jenna, Kayla, and Perry (see footnote 8.2 for explanation of selection).

Entering Conceptions. Jenna, a prospective secondary history teacher, began the course with conceptions of teaching and learning that almost exactly matched the predictions of Holt-Reynolds. Her images of teaching were organized around the theme of interestingness, and she attributed success of teachers largely to personality and enthusiasm. She expected that textbooks would be boring, as would most lectures, and because their use was inevitable, student boredom would be the most critical problem she would face as a teacher.

Kayla, a prospective secondary mathematics teacher, also expressed entering conceptions that matched the predictions of Holt-Reynolds: "Kayla portrayed teachers as the central figures in classrooms, who promoted learning by presenting information to mostly passive students; better teachers revealed better organization in their presentations, and they did not bore students" (Anderson & Holt-Reynolds, 1995, p. 11). Kayla was discouraged about her own experiences as a mathematics student (especially her college courses, which she found difficult and frustrating) and had strong beliefs about what she did not want to do as a teacher (frustrate students by failing to explain clearly—a shortcoming of her math professors). Thus, she was like Jenna in that she did not want to bore students, and she felt it was important to be kind and interesting, but she emphasized good explanations more than did Jenna. Kayla's focus on clear explanations matched the prediction of Holt-Reynolds in that her students would see content as given, to be passed on from teacher or text with little need for teachers to mediate it.

Perry, like Jenna, was a prospective history teacher. At first we thought he was similar to other students in his entering focus on interestingness. However, his use of the construct *interest* was different from many students (although this was not apparent to the instructor or researchers until careful analysis of his interviews after the class ended). We described his entering conceptions this way:

> He saw the solution for boring lessons not in terms of teacher personality or enthusiasm, but rather in terms of the activities that teachers created to engage students with the material. It was activities that needed to be interesting, not teachers, and the way that activities could be made interesting was to adjust them to the students, rather than expecting students to change as a result of instruction. [He gave the example of assigning more "practical" math or writing assignments for lower-tracked classes.] (Anderson & Holt-Reynolds, 1995, p. 13)

For Perry, the critical factor was doing the activity, not being interested in the content or even in the process, although some attractive hook was necessary to get the student to engage initially.

In some ways, Perry's entering conception seemed closer to the goal conception of Holt-Reynolds than other students because it emphasized the role of activities for students. On more careful analysis, however, we realized that Perry's view was different from both the goal of the instructor and from most other students' entering conceptions, in that Perry seldom referred to any aspect of students' mental states or mental responses to content. As a teacher, he would design activities that appear interesting and relevant enough to get students to cooperate; once the students came in contact with the content through the activities, they would learn. He portrayed learning as passive. Whether students connected to the content, either affectively (through interest and enthusiasm) or intellectually (through understanding), did not seem salient to Perry.

Similarities in Their Entering Conceptions. Like the three focal students in Study 1, these three students began the semester with some clear ideas about the kind of teacher they each wanted to become (or, in Kayla's case, to avoid becoming). None of them expressed doubt that they knew what they should learn to become a teacher, and each expected that the course would help them learn to do better what they already believed to be important.

How Entering Conceptions Were Evident in Each Student's Experience of the Course. Jenna and Kayla transformed key components of their conceptions about teaching and learning in the directions intended by Holt-Reynolds and consequently learned about content-area reading methods in ways that seemed genuine and rich. Perry, in contrast, did not appear to change targeted components of his conception of teaching. Closer analyses of the three students' week-to-week experiences in the course and interpretation of course content helped us understand these differences.

Jenna enthusiastically engaged with the activities that Holt-Reynolds intended would lead to reflection on her experiences as a student in the class. For example, following one activity in which students read a nonsense passage but were still able to answer the questions about it, Jenna could explain to the interviewer that the activity showed her how a student could read, and even memorize, but not really understand ideas. She interpreted several other in-course experiences as teaching her the importance of "not having to tell a student everything and instead doing something to help them learn for themselves," suggesting that she was beginning to develop a view of learning as construction and teaching as mediation (Holt-Reynolds' goal). At one point, when an interview began with an open-ended question about what had stood out about the class the preceding week, Jenna enthusiastically described a class discussion about "what is learning?" and acknowledged that she was uncertain but now thought the question worth considering.

By the end of the semester, Jenna's conception of teaching incorporated many of the elements Holt-Reynolds had intended and reflected a more constructivist view of learning and mediational view of teaching. When interviewed a year later after student teaching, her description of her practice and its supporting rationales still reflected this change. Furthermore, she attributed many of her good ideas and success in student teaching to the methods she had learned and the new view of teaching she had developed in the content-area reading class.

Kayla was like Jenna in that her account of the course and in-class student-experience activities revealed a high level of engagement and reflection, and she appeared to understand the course ideas as Holt-Reynolds intended. For example, she interpreted the nonsense-passage activity in similar ways to Jenna. More important, perhaps, was a change in her conception of herself as a mathematics learner: The more she learned about a new way to conceive of learning and instruction, the more she believed that her past problems in math classes could have been due to poor instruction, not to her being dumb in math. She said, "It made me realize . . . what kind of teaching I got. It made me see that it didn't work even though the teachers were satisfied with my grade." Like Jenna, her poststudent-teaching interview still reflected the new conceptions a year later, and she attributed a successful student teaching experience to the new ideas about teaching that she gained from this course.

Perry attended class and always participated, and his grades on written work were good. However, his interviews revealed that he either did not mentally engage with the student-experience activities or he interpreted them in different ways than intended. For example, contrast his interpretation of the nonsense-passage activity to that of Jenna and Kayla, whose responses were exactly what the instructor hoped to hear. Perry interpreted the result—that you could correctly answer questions based on nonsense passage due to knowledge of language conventions—in a positive light, saying that it showed how capable learners are: "[Y]ou can understand things, it shows that even if you don't know what they're talking about you have certain skills, and you can understand some things that are going on." In response to the same class discussion about "what is learning?" that had excited Jenna, Perry questioned why the instructor was spending so much time on something so obvious, saying, "I don't know if it matters all that much." Our conclusion from Perry's interviews was that he seemed perplexed not about the nature of learning, but about why one would ever worry about defining it.

Perry seemed to experience the course as a series of activities and assignments that served as models of teaching techniques that he might someday use, but not as an occasion to talk about why those techniques could help students learn. In his final interview of the semester, and then again after his student teaching semester, Perry indicated that he had learned some teaching methods that he might use when he wanted to go beyond the basics, but otherwise he did not attribute any significant learning to the course. We concluded that his entering conceptions about teaching and learning remained mostly intact, with the only notable change the addition of a few details about methods he might try some day.

Conclusions From Study 2

Two of the three students changed their conceptions as intended by the teacher. Why were Jenna and Kayla responsive to the class in ways that Perry was not? One conclusion we drew was that the predictions of Holt-

Reynolds about her students' entering conceptions were accurate for Jenna and Kayla but not for Perry. This mattered because Holt-Reynolds designed class activities to target directly certain beliefs that she expected her students to bring (e.g., the belief that the most important thing is for a teacher to be interesting and kind, and then students will learn).

In particular, it seemed critical that the entering conceptions brought to the course contained some slot for inside-the-head student experience. For example, Jenna featured student interest (or boredom) prominently in her entering conception. So did Kayla, who also highlighted student experiences of frustration due to failure to understand and remember. The in-class student-experience activities helped Jenna and Kayla add and rearrange conceptual categories for inside-the-head experiences; that is, they came to see that student construction of knowledge was a more powerful way to think about student experiences than interest. Only then could the prospective teachers begin to reconsider teaching practices they had assumed were connected to inside-the-head experiences, leading them eventually to see that teacher mediation was a more powerful way to think about instruction than be interesting and enthusiastic.

The instructional strategies of Holt-Reynolds assumed that the prospective teachers came equipped with conceptions that highlighted students' inside-the-head experiences in school, and that her job was to help them expand, rearrange, and reprioritize those conceptions. With Jenna and Kayla (and most other students in the class that we studied), the assumptions and predictions of Holt-Reynolds were very accurate. However, Perry came to the course with few concerns or questions about what happened inside of students' head when they learned, and thus he did not find the course activities compelling. For others in the class, those activities provoked self-examination of ideas about learning and eventual reconstruction of their conceptions of teaching. In Perry's case, there was apparently no rearrangement of beliefs because the assumed point of entry into his conceptions was not available.

STUDY 3: LEARNING TO TEACH SCIENCE IN AN ELEMENTARY EDUCATION PROGRAM (ANDERSON, SMITH, & PEASLEY, IN PRESS)

In this study, we collected data across 1 year in a teacher-education program that led to elementary certification with a special emphasis on science teaching (Krajcik, Blumenfeld, & Starr, 1993). The faculty in this program collaborated with the researchers in selecting focal students, designing interviews, and regular debriefings about the program, but they did not participate in data collection or analysis in the same ways that Bird or Holt-Reynolds had.

Teacher Educators' Goals

Several themes permeated all courses and defined the conceptions of teaching and learning advocated by the program: learning as active construction of connected knowledge through situated activity; learners as diverse in several ways, including prior knowledge about science; instruction as engagement of diverse students and facilitation of learning through design of tasks and multiple-content representations that build on key ideas and their connections; and curriculum as malleable and interwoven, organized around driving questions, rather than static and linear, organized around materials and texts (Krajcik et al., 1993).

Hypotheses About Features of Pedagogy That Would Promote the Desired Conceptual Change

In many ways, the program reflected the characteristics that Wideen, Mayer-Smith, and Moon (1998) attributed to teacher-education programs that successfully impact the beliefs of prospective teachers. The faculty agreed on the major themes and collaborated to integrate them across courses and semesters. The students were part of a small cohort that took all courses together and were supported extensively by the program faculty as they undertook teaching responsibilities in schools. Our purpose in studying this program was twofold: to learn more about how a cohort-based program with coherent thematic emphases throughout all its courses would create opportunities for prospective teachers to examine and reorganize their conceptions, and to learn more about how individual students responded to those opportunities.

Cases of Three Prospective Teachers in Study 3

We collected data about five students during their first year in the program; three students who completed student teaching with the program are featured here: Joanna, Mindy, and Greg.[3] Because the program emphasized the development of an integrated knowledge base about teaching in general, and about teaching science in particular, we traced

---

[3]Sampling in the third study differed somewhat from the first two. We initially interviewed all students in the cohort with the exception of one who was ill during interviews, and then we selected five to follow closely across the rest of the year because they appeared at the beginning of the year to differ in interesting ways. As was the case in the first two studies, we defined *differed in interesting ways* as reflecting a typical range that would seem familiar to most other teacher educators. The three cases reported here were selected from the five because the other two did not complete the program due to financial, personal reasons, or both.

development of integrated conceptions of science teaching defined in terms of Darling-Hammond's "devilishly difficult dialectic" (1996b, p. 8): Good teaching entails simultaneous, integrated attention to individual learners (who bring diverse background knowledge and preferences) and content learning (where high standards are held for every learner).

Entering Conceptions. Joanna began her teacher-education program with a strong emphasis on learners and the quality of their experiences during science lessons. In particular, she wanted to encourage student inquiry and curiosity. In her initial interview, she played down the importance of science content learning, saying that "fact is not so important" as engaging in inquiry and becoming interested in science. She imagined that she would teach in a nondirective manner, responding to student-initiated questions by providing interesting demonstrations and relating the science to the lives of students.

Mindy also valued the enthusiasm and interest of students more than content learning. However, in contrast to Joanna, she talked less about what she wanted students to do in her classroom than she talked about herself and her role. To Mindy, the key to effective science teaching was to be charismatic and present riveting lessons that would "blow them away." Her image of herself teaching was to sit in the middle of a circle of students who responded by saying "Wow!" when she taught them about the wonders of science. She wanted students to be active and interested, but she portrayed students as active in response to her teaching, not so much as active agents who came with their own questions and curiosities (as did Joanna).

Greg contrasted to Joanna and Mindy in several ways. He definitely wanted students to learn about science content and believed that the way to accomplish this was for teachers who were experts in science to deliver good presentations that could be understood by children. He talked about connecting as something that good teachers did for students, not something that students did for themselves. "He portrayed science as a body of knowledge that was inaccessible to students except when teachers predigested it for them and presented it in a simplified, systematic way" (Anderson et al., in press). Greg did not refer to student inside-the-head experiences (e.g., feeling interested and raising questions because of felt curiosity) as much as did Joanna and Mindy.

Similarities in Their Entering Conceptions. Just as in the other two studies, although the three prospective teachers differed in the particular conceptions of teaching and learning that they brought to their program, they were alike in their confidence about what they needed to learn in their teacher-education program and in their image of the kind of teacher they would become.

How Entering Conceptions Were Evident in Each Students' Experience of the Program. In analyzing change during the year, we focused on the integration of concerns about learners (as individuals, with attention to the quality of their experience in the classroom) and about content learning (as meeting high standards by all students for knowledge of science), as this integration is described by Darling-Hammond (1996b). We wanted to know whether and how this integration—or its opposite, seeing the two elements in opposition to one another—developed over the year and how entering conceptions affected or were changed by such development. We concluded that, by the end of the year, Joanna and Mindy each had begun to integrate these two concerns in their conceptions of teaching, although they had arrived at that point via different paths. In contrary, Greg ended the year with the two concerns in opposition and did not seem to have made much progress toward an integrated conception. He definitely had undergone conceptual change, just not in directions desired by program faculty.

In the fall term, Joanna looked different from the image she had created in her initial interview. Instead of planning lessons around the curiosities expressed by students and playing an indirect, supportive teacher role, she developed lessons that had clear content-learning goals and she made several direct presentations of content. References to learners and their experiences were limited in her accounts of her fall teaching. Although her lessons and approach to planning were influenced by program requirements and the preferences of her cooperating teacher, Joanna did not express any regret that she was teaching in ways contrary to her initial image. Indeed, she found exciting new ideas from her education courses about content representations and ways of thinking about understanding as making connections among content ideas.

By the end of the fall, however, Joanna was beginning to question the relative emphasis she placed on content learning versus learners, saying she had concentrated too hard on what the teacher did to teach content and not enough on the response of the students. In the spring term, she continued to raise questions about how to teach so that students were engaged, making connections to their own unique prior knowledge and finding interest and relevance in the lessons, while making sure that everyone acquired the content knowledge. In particular, she struggled with questions about when teachers should tell information to students, and when they should intervene when students did not learn content from activities and indirect teacher facilitation.

By the end of the year, Joanna was articulating a new image of good science teaching and a new goal for herself: Teach so that all students are involved and making sense of science in light of their own experiences and prior knowledge, but keep pushing for content understanding too.

She continued talking about this learner–learning balance through her student teaching. Although her practice was far from fluent at that point, she had apparently made an important conceptual shift. Joanna was considered a very successful student teacher and was offered a teaching job the next year in a nearby district.

Mindy also ended the year expressing a similar image of her goals as a science teacher—balancing content learning and learner concerns—but she arrived by a different path than Joanna. During the fall, her lessons reflected her initial images of teaching, which were not only teacher-centered but also very Mindy-centered, with a focus on her presence and charisma, which would inspire the enthusiasm and interest of students. During the fall term, Mindy began to talk about program ideas more related to content learning, such as the importance of good content representations. She also began to say that she should let students "do more on their own" instead of always being so "take-charge."

During the first part of the spring term, Mindy, acting on her new resolve, talked like a completely different teacher. Not only was she no longer center stage in all her lessons, but she had almost removed herself from the stage completely and emphasized the initiative and inquiry of students. However, by the end of the year, even more change was evident: Mindy was raising questions about how she could teach so that students learned content as well as participating with enthusiasm and interest in science activities. Like Joanna, she headed into student teaching determined to learn more about how to strike that balance. At the end of her student teaching, she was still not fluent enough to accomplish her goal all of the time, but she appeared to have changed her image of science teaching toward the integration of learner and learning concerns. She was considered a successful student teacher (even winning an award) and accepted a job in a nearby district for the next year.

Greg also changed his conception during the year, but did not end with a desire to accomplish the difficult integration of learner–learning concerns. Greg spent his fall term teaching science as he had described it in his initial interview: content presentations that he intended would simplify complex ideas so that fourth graders could understand them. He felt that his fall lessons were disasters and blamed this on the requirements of the programs for lesson plans, which he believed pushed him into an overly scripted lesson to which students did not respond. In several other ways, he was bitter about what he perceived as unreasonable demands placed on him by the program to teach in ways that he did not believe were important.

During the spring term, his lessons looked quite different compared with the fall. Instead of usually presenting content to students, he set up activities so that they could mess around and become interested in the science, after which there might be teacher presentations. Although he still hoped that students would learn the content, he was ready to modify his goals if involvement of students was compromised through an emphasis on content learning. In contrast to Joanna and Mindy, Greg did not articulate a desire to accomplish both at the same time, but rather saw them as conflicting goals that he might have to choose between. He associated teacher planning with too heavy an emphasis on content learning; he said that he did less planning than (he believed that) the program wanted so that he could remain flexible in response to the students.

In the end, Greg shifted his conceptions of teaching and learning from one in which teachers make simplified presentations and students learn through reception to one in which students get enthusiastic when they engage in science activities; the students might learn from those activities or the teacher might present content, but not if such presentations threatened student involvement. Greg requested a kindergarten class for his student teaching and did an acceptable job, but taught very little science there. Because he still had university courses to take the next year, we do not know if or when he obtained a teaching position.

Conclusions From Study 3

We asked of our data, "What counts as progress in prospective teachers' conceptual development, and how do you know it when you see it?" One conclusion is that sometimes progress is evident only in retrospect, when the conceptual history of the prospective teacher is taken into account. Each prospective teacher made swings during the year in their prevailing conception of teaching, as if they were trying on new ideas but only knew how to do so by shifting from one extreme to another. Viewed out of context at any given point in the year, each of these three prospective teachers could have appeared to be just as far from the program goals as they appeared at the beginning of the year, although headed in different wrong directions than in September. However, when viewed over the longer term, the shifts in each prospective teachers' emphases and practices look more like necessary detours on a unique path toward their personal construction of a more complex conception of teaching.

Joanna and Mindy presented an interesting comparison because they ended up in a similar place conceptually despite starting from different places and differing in the speed with which they tried out new ideas, reflected on them, and tried to reconcile old and new ideas. Joanna picked up on program ideas and began to articulate the learner–learning integration goal earlier than Mindy. Indeed, Mindy was a concern to program faculty during much of the year, due to what seemed like excessive confidence in her own abilities to teach. However, she did sort out her various experiences and, with the support and pushing of program faculty, she ended up also determined to learn a more complex kind of practice than she had originally envisioned. We did not see this as a sudden conversion at the end of the year, but rather as the cumulative effect of her experiences during the year, including those lessons that appeared to reflect only one or a few program ideas and that therefore did not signal a lot of progress toward program goals if viewed alone and out of context.

Greg also posed an interesting case because he suggested why a program, even one with as many strengths and resources as the one we studied, is not necessarily a strong influence on what and how someone learns to teach. Perhaps in Greg's case, more time and continued support would have resulted in his experiencing the same kind of conceptual change as Joanna and Mindy. (After all, at the end of the year, he sounded in many ways like Joanna at the beginning of the year.) However, his affective reactions to the program were so negative that it is hard to imagine that more of the same would have had a different effect.

One possible explanation for the differences is the same explanation offered in Study 2. Like Jenna and Kayla, Joanna and Mindy revealed in their initial interviews that some kind of student inside-the-head experience was important to them and figured prominently in their entering conceptions. Also like Jenna and Kayla, during the year they developed additional ways of thinking about inside-the-head experiences, adding construction of knowledge and connecting content ideas to the original set of feeling interested and excited to know more. For Joanna and Mindy, developments in their views of learning and the nature of inside-the-head student experiences appeared to precede changes in their ideas about teaching. For example, we noted that great leaps in the complexity of their talk about teaching, such as articulation of the need for learner–learning integration, came only after they began to talk in interviews about student learning in more constructivist ways. Whether there are conceptual causal links between new views of learning and teaching, or whether both these changes indicate increasing ownership and understanding of program ideas and vocabulary, or some other explanation, we cannot say.

Greg, like Perry in Study 2, did not emphasize student inside-the-head experiences in his initial interviews. By the end of the year, he was beginning to emphasize student interest and enthusiastic engagement, so perhaps he had developed a sense of the importance of inside-the-head experiences. In the meantime, however, the coursework and expectations of the program may not have made a great deal of sense to him.

The similarities in these cases across Studies 2 and 3 led us to suggest that:

> [T]he ease with which different prospective teachers adopt certain ideas about *teaching* is related to the extent to which they already have a place for

"inside the students' heads" phenomena in their initial conceptions of *learning*. . . . If this pattern is indeed often true, then these cases suggest that although teacher educators sometimes disparage prospective teachers' faith in the power of . . . enthusiasm and interest, that faith may well provide a starting point for prospective teachers' learning about many ideas that we hold dear, such as constructivist views of learning and associated teaching strategies. (Anderson et al., in press)

CONCLUSIONS FROM THE SET OF STUDIES

Cases cannot be used to support claims about population trends, but they can suggest new insights into and questions about complex phenomena that may be obscured and oversimplified by studies seeking generalizability with larger numbers. Taken together, the nine cases suggest the following about the influence and mutability of entering conceptions of prospective teachers in a university-based teacher-education program:

1. They counter earlier portrayals of conceptions of prospective teachers as fairly uniform and organized around traditional images of teaching as telling and learning as passive reception based on educational experiences in fairly traditional and teacher-centered classrooms (e.g., Cohen, 1989). The nine student cases presented here demonstrate that the entering ideas of prospective students about teaching and learning are quite variable. Even when a teacher educator has a great deal of experience with particular subject matter and a given population, as did Holt-Reynolds in Study 2, there may be prospective teachers like Perry who appear on the surface to be typical in many respects, but whose entering conceptions lead to unexpected interpretations of course or program content—interpretations that are not apparent unless someone probes the thinking of the prospective teacher in some depth. The challenge this presents to teacher educators is to plan courses and programs according to their best predictions about entering conceptions while continually monitoring interpretations of students with an open mind to the likely diversity of underlying conceptions.

2. Even when entering conceptions of prospective teachers appear to be discrepant with the goal conceptions of teacher educators, they are not necessarily obstacles to the learning of prospective teachers if they offer a point of entry—an opening where new ideas that the teacher educator wants to present will fit because they match a function valued by the prospective teacher. This was the case with Jenna, Kayla, Joanna, and Mindy, whose entering notions about the importance of interest and teacher enthusiasm could easily be predicted to be obstacles (because so

often a focus on making it interesting seems to interfere with the thinking of prospective teachers about teaching for understanding). However, in the hands of skillful teacher educators, entering beliefs about the power of interest and enthusiasm were the starting points for more powerful frames for thinking about instruction, and the prospective teachers did not feel that their initial ideas were discredited, only expanded.

This conclusion represents a shift away from hypotheses of the early 1990s about the need to provoke conceptual change by convincing prospective teachers that their entering ideas were unsatisfactory (Kennedy, 1991). For example, a common reference in the teacher-education literature about how to change the beliefs of teachers was in Posner et al. (1982) and their model for conceptual change by provoking dissatisfaction with current conceptions, posing a plausible alternative, and so forth.

3. Notwithstanding the first point about diversity among conceptions of prospective teachers, these nine cases also suggest there may be common dimensions of these conceptions with predictable consequences when teaching about certain ideas. The best example is the one just offered, that it matters whether prospective teachers have a prominent place in their entering conceptions for inside-the-head student experiences of any sort when the course or program content emphasizes ways that learners construct meaning and new learning.

This conclusion suggests that, in addition to further research about how prospective teachers think about what goes on inside the heads of learners, we also need research that identifies other dimensions of entering conceptions that might be critical for other common and fundamental ideas in teacher education (such as ideas about the nature of disciplinary knowledge or the nature and mutability of human intelligence). Teacher educators would be wiser teachers if they understood more about the subtle interactions among various dimensions of the entering conceptions of their students and the particular ideas they emphasize in their courses and programs.

4. Progress in changing the conceptions of teaching and learning of prospective teachers is not necessarily dramatic or immediately obvious. As was demonstrated by Joanna and Mindy, different prospective teachers take different paths to similar ends. Sometimes progress in conceptual development requires a conceptual detour that may appear to teacher educators to be backsliding but is, in retrospect, necessary to sort out new ideas and construct a more complex way of thinking about teaching. This suggests that many studies that concluded that teacher education has no effect on the conceptions of prospective teachers may have been using too restricted or decontextualized criteria for change and development.

5. As noted earlier, scholarship of the late 1980s and early 1990s was pessimistic about the effects of teacher education on the long-held con-

ceptions of prospective teachers (e.g., Britzman, 1986; Lanier & Little, 1986; McDiarmid, 1990; Zeichner & Tabachnik, 1981). However, more recent scholarship suggests that teacher-education programs with certain characteristics can and do influence these conceptions of teaching and learning (Darling-Hammond, 1996a; Graber, 1996; Grossman, 1991; Levin & Ammon, 1992; Wideen et al., 1998).

Although the three studies in the NCRTL project focused more on students than on pedagogy, they also contribute to this latter body of literature. When teacher education was effective in promoting desirable conceptual development—the cases of Jenna, Kayla, Joanna, and Mindy—there was a set of pedagogical or program characteristics that helped explain the success in part (e.g., teacher educators created opportunities for prospective teachers to examine, elaborate, and revise their conceptions, then supported that revision in a variety of ways). However, as the cases of Perry and Greg remind us, those same pedagogical and program characteristics are not sufficient when the entering conceptions of students lead to interpretations of course content and experiences that did not support the desired conceptual development. Teacher educators must attend not only to general pedagogical and program characteristics, but they must also listen to the interpretations of prospective teachers and use of the program content and recognize that conceptual change is dynamic, gradual, nuanced, and diverse. In that regard, we are no different from any other teacher.

ACKNOWLEDGMENT

The ideas expressed here were influenced greatly by colleagues who codesigned and coauthored the three studies and who continue to share ideas about teacher education and prospective teachers' learning: Thomas Bird, Diane Holt-Reynolds, and Deborah Smith. In addition, four graduate students also contributed to the work presented in this chapter: Kathy Peasley, Steven Swidler, Barbara Sullivan, and Curtis Maine. The NCRTL was funded primarily by the Office of Educational Research and Improvement, U.S. Department of Education. The opinions expressed in this chapter do not necessarily reflect the position, policy, or endorsement of the Office or Department.

REFERENCES

Anderson, L. M. (1989). Implementing instructional programs to promote meaningful, self-regulated learning. In J. E. Brophy (Ed.), *Advances in research on teaching* (Vol. 1, pp. 311–341). Greenwich, CT: JAI.

Anderson, L. M., & Bird, T. (1992). *Transforming teachers' beliefs about teaching, learning, and learners.* Unpublished manuscript, Michigan State University at East Lansing, MI.

Anderson, L. M., & Bird, T. (1995). How three prospective teachers construed three cases of teaching. *Teaching and Teacher Education, 11*(5), 479–499.

Anderson, L. M., & Holt-Reynolds, D. (1995). *Prospective teachers' beliefs and teacher education pedagogy: Research based on a teacher educator's practical theory* (Research Rep. 95-6). East Lansing, MI: National Center for Research on Teacher Learning, Michigan State University.

Anderson, L. M., Smith, D. C., & Peasley, K. (in press). Integrating learner and learning concerns: Prospective elementary science teachers' paths and progress. *Teaching and Teacher Education.*

Anderson, R. C., & Pearson, P. D. (1984). A schema-theoretic view of reading. In P. D. Pearson (Ed.), *Handbook of reading research* (pp. 255–292). New York: Longman.

Belenky, M. F., Clinchy, B. M., Goldberger, N. R., & Tarule, J. M. (1986). *Women's ways of knowing: The development of self, voice, and mind.* New York: Basic Books.

Bird, T. D., Anderson, L. M., Sullivan, B. A., & Swidler, S. A. (1993). Pedagogical balancing acts: A teacher educator encounters problems in an attempt to influence prospective teacher beliefs. *Teaching and Teacher Education, 9*(3), 253–267.

Borko, H., & Putnam, R. (1996). Learning to teach. In D. C. Berliner & R. C. Calfee (Eds.), *Handbook of educational psychology* (pp. 673–708). New York: Macmillan.

Britzman, D. P. (1986). Cultural myths in the making of a teacher: Biography and social structure in teacher education. *Harvard Educational Review, 56,* 442–472.

Brookhart, S. M., & Freeman, D. J. (1992). Characteristics of entering teacher candidates. *Review of Educational Research, 62*(1), 37–60.

Brown, J. S., Collins, A., & Duguid, P. (1989). Situated cognition and the culture of learning. *Educational Researcher, 18,* 32–42.

Bruner, J. (1986). *Actual minds, possible worlds.* Cambridge, MA: Harvard University Press.

Bruner, J. (1990). *Acts of meaning.* Cambridge, MA: Harvard University Press.

Bruner, J. (1996). *The culture of education.* Cambridge, MA: Harvard University Press.

Buchmann, M. (1987). *Teaching knowledge: The lights that teachers live by.* East Lansing, MI: National Center for Research on Teacher Education, Michigan State University.

Bullough, R. V., & Stokes, D. K. (1994). Analyzing personal teaching metaphors in preservice teacher education as a means for encouraging professional development. *American Educational Research Journal, 31*(1), 197–224.

Calderhead, J. (1991). The nature and growth of knowledge in student teaching. *Teaching and Teacher Education, 7,* 531–535.

Calderhead, J. (1996). Teachers: Beliefs and knowledge. In D. C. Berliner & R. C. Calfee (Eds.), *Handbook of educational psychology* (pp. 709–725). New York: Macmillan.

Calderhead, J., & Robson, M. (1991). Images of teaching: Student teachers' early conceptions of classroom practice. *Teaching and Teacher Education, 7,* 1–8.

Carey, S. (1985). *Conceptual change in childhood.* Cambridge, MA: MIT Press.

Clark, C. M., & Peterson, P. L. (1986). Teachers' thought processes. In M. Wittrock (Ed.), *Handbook of research on teaching* (3rd ed., pp. 255–296). New York: Macmillan.

Cohen, D. K. (1989). Teaching practice: Plus ça change. . . . In P. W. Jackson (Ed.), *Contributing to educational change: Perspectives on research and practice* (pp. 27–84). Berkeley, CA: McCutchan.

Cohen, D. K., McLaughlin, M. W., & Talbert, J. E. (Eds.). (1993). *Teaching for understanding: Challenges for policy and practice.* San Francisco: Jossey-Bass.

Darling-Hammond, L. (1996a). The changing context of teacher education. In F. B. Murray (Ed.), *The teacher educator's handbook: Building a knowledge base for the preparation of teachers* (pp. 14–62). San Francisco: Jossey-Bass.

Darling-Hammond, L. (1996b). The right to learn and the advancement of teaching: Research, policy, and practice for democratic education. *Educational Researcher, 25*(6), 5–17.

Feiman-Nemser, S., & Remillard, J. (1996). Perspectives on learning to teach. In F. B. Murray (Ed.), *The teacher educator's handbook: Building a knowledge base for the preparation of teachers* (pp. 63–91). San Francisco: Jossey-Bass.

Fosnot, C. W. (1989). *Inquiring teachers, inquiring learners: A constructivist approach to teachers*. New York: Teachers College Press.

Freeman, D. (1996). "To make the tacit explicit": Teacher education, emerging discourse, and conceptions of teaching. *Teaching and Teacher Education, 7*(5/6), 439–454.

Goodenough, W. (1981). *Culture, language, and society*. Menlo Park, CA: Benjamin Cummings.

Goodman, J. (1988). Constructing a practical philosophy of teaching: A study of preservice teachers' professional perspectives. *Teaching and Teacher Education, 4*, 121–137.

Graber, K. C. (1996). Influencing student beliefs: The design of a "high impact" teacher education program. *Teaching and Teacher Education, 125*, 451–466.

Grossman, P. L. (1991). Overcoming the apprenticeship of observation in teacher education coursework. *Teaching and Teacher Education, 7*(4), 345–357.

Hollingsworth, S. (1989). Prior beliefs and cognitive change in learning to teach. *American Educational Research Journal, 26*(2), 160–189.

Holt-Reynolds, D. (1992). Personal history-based beliefs as relevant prior knowledge in coursework: Can we practice what we teach? *American Educational Research Journal, 29*, 325–349.

Holt-Reynolds, D. (1994, April). *Learning teaching, teaching teachers*. Paper presented at the American Educational Research Association, New Orleans, LA.

John, P. D. (1991). A qualitative study of British student teachers' lesson planning perspectives. *Journal of Education for Teaching, 17*(3), 301–320.

Johnston, S. (1992). Images: A way of understanding the practical knowledge of student teachers. *Teaching and Teacher Education, 8*(2), 123–136.

Kagan, D. M. (1992). Professional growth among preservice and beginning teachers. *Review of Educational Research, 62*(2), 129–169.

Kennedy, M. M. (1991). *An agenda for research on teacher learning*. East Lansing, MI: National Center for Research on Teacher Learning, Michigan State University.

Knowles, J. G., & Holt-Reynolds, D. (1991). Shaping pedagogies through personal histories in preservice teacher education. *Teachers College Record, 93*(1), 87–113.

Krajcik, J. S., Blumenfeld, P. C., & Starr, M. L. (1993). Integrating knowledge bases: An upper elementary teacher preparation program emphasizing the teaching of science. In P. Rubba (Ed.), *Excellence in educating teacher of science. Yearbook of the Association for Education of Teachers in Science*. Columbus, OH: Clearinghouse for Science, Mathematics, and Environmental Education. (Eric ED Document Reproduction Service No. 355 111)

Kuhn, T. (1970). *The structure of scientific revolutions* (2nd ed.). Chicago: University of Chicago Press.

Lanier, J. L., & Little, J. W. (1986). Research on teacher education. In M. C. Wittrock (Ed.), *Handbook of research on teaching* (3rd ed., pp. 527–569). New York: Macmillan.

Levin, B. B., & Ammon, P. (1992). The development of beginning teachers' pedagogical thinking: A longitudinal analysis of four case studies. *Teacher Education Quarterly, 19*(4), 19–37.

Lortie, D. (1975). *Schoolteacher: A sociological study*. Chicago: University of Chicago Press.

McDiarmid, G. W. (1990). Challenging prospective teachers' beliefs during early field experience: A quixotic undertaking? *Journal of Teacher Education, 41*(3), 12–20.

McLaughlin, M. W., & Talbert, J. E. (1993). Introduction: New visions of teaching. In D. K. Cohen, M. W. McLaughlin, & J. E. Talbert (Eds.), *Teaching for understanding: Challenges for policy and practice.* San Francisco: Jossey-Bass.

Pajares, F. (1993). Preservice teachers' beliefs: A focus for teacher education. *Action in Teacher Education, 15*(2), 45–54.

Pajares, M. F. (1992). Teachers' beliefs and educational research: Cleaning up a messy construct. *Review of Educational Research, 62*(3), 307–332.

Perry, W. G. (1970). *Forms of intellectual and ethical development in the college years.* New York: Holt, Rinehart & Winston.

Posner, G., Strike, K., Hewson, P., & Gertzog, W. (1982). Accommodation of a scientific conception: Toward a theory of conceptual change. *Science Education, 66*, 211–227.

Powell, R. R. (1992). The influence of prior experiences on pedagogical constructs of traditional and non-traditional preservice teachers. *Teaching and Teacher Education, 8*, 225–238.

Powell, R. R. (1996). Epistemological antecedents to culturally relevant and constructivist classroom curricula: A longitudinal study of teachers' contrasting world views. *Teaching and Teacher Education, 12*(4), 365–384.

Prawat, R. S. (1992). Teachers' beliefs about teaching and learning: A constructivist perspective. *American Journal of Education, 100*(3), 354–395.

Richardson, V. (1996). The role of attitudes and beliefs in learning to teach. In J. Sikula, T. J. Buttery, & E. Guyton (Eds.), *Handbook of research on teacher education* (2nd ed., pp. 102–119). New York: Macmillan.

Rokeach, M. (1968). *Beliefs, attitudes, and values: A theory of organization and change.* San Francisco: Jossey-Bass.

Toulmin, S. (1972). *Human understanding: The collective use and evolution of concepts.* Princeton, NJ: Princeton University Press.

Wideen, M., Mayer-Smith, J., & Moon, B. (1998). A critical analysis of the research on learning to teach: Making the case for an ecological perspective on inquiry. *Review of Educational Research, 68*(2), 130–178.

Wubbels, T. (1992). Taking account of student teachers' preconceptions. *Teaching and Teacher Education, 8*(2), 137–149.

Zeichner, K., & Gore, J. (1990). Teacher socialization. In W. R. Houston (Ed.), *Handbook of research on teacher education* (pp. 329–348). New York: Macmillan.

Zeichner, K. M., & Tabachnik, B. R. (1981). Are the effects of teacher education "washed out" by school experience? *Journal of Teacher Education, 32*(3), 7–11.

CHAPTER NINE

Folk Psychology, Folk Pedagogy, and Their Relations to Subject-Matter Knowledge

Sidney Strauss
Tel Aviv University

As this chapter is being written, controversy swirls in the state of Massachusetts. The topic of oftentimes acrimonious and sanctimonious debate concerns how well teacher-education departments prepare teachers for their profession. The debate has been used as a stick to beat the drums of a gubernatorial race. The head of the education division in the state of Massachusetts resigned purportedly out of indignation that a topic of such importance was getting used for political purposes. Boston newspapers were filled with op-ed articles and letters to the editor for and against college departments of education, teachers, and the ways in which departments of education prepare future teachers.

Bad news travels fast. *The New York Times* picked up on the topic and published an opinion piece praising a decision by the New York State legislature allowing the possibility of certifying teachers without their having studied in departments of education in universities and colleges. The program, "All Things Considered," on National Public Radio (NPR) had programs on the topic. Late-night television comedians have been having a heyday skewering everyone in sight involved in these matters. Much ink has been spilled. Many words have been uttered. Education has been in the headlines.

However, unlike the adage of advertising people, not all publicity is good publicity even if your name is spelled correctly. What prompted the rush to judgment were some worrisome findings. A teacher certification exam, new in Massachusetts, was failed by close to 60% of those graduating students who are prospective teachers. The examination tested the general cultural knowledge of teachers (basic arithmetic skills and their knowledge about grammar) and the knowledge they have about the subject matter they are going to teach.

This not encouraging finding was seized by many as an indication of what they always knew: Teachers are not a bright lot, and teacher-education departments fail in their mission to improve teachers to an even minimal level. Others rushed to defend both the future teachers and their college teachers. Few were apathetic to the issues that were part of the maelstrom.

In the vortex of debate was what certification tests should include, which is another way of asking what should be in an examination that purports to predict teacher effectiveness. Debate also centered on whether the particular test used this time was adequate. Surprisingly few questioned whether teachers should be examined to be licensed, although they received their Bachelor of Arts (BA) degrees from accredited colleges and universities. Perhaps this is because professions such as medicine and law have licensing examinations after applicants have completed their university studies. If that holds for medicine and law, why shouldn't it for education?

There was also some discussion about whether licensed teachers who are currently teaching should be examined, with their teaching licenses being renewed if they passed the examination or revoked were they to fail it—a practice that holds for continuing certification in the medical field. There have been objections to this possibility. No surprises there. Some protested the threat to job security. Others questioned whether a test of the sort used to license new teachers in the state of Massachusetts captures the knowledge and skills teachers have and use as effective practicing teachers. So here we are back again to the enormously complex question: What does an effective teacher know and know how to do that an examination can capture?

One of the problems about certification examinations for licensing teachers is that there is no consensus about how to answer that question. Should one know contemporary theories of learning? Of classroom management? Should one have considerable and deeply organized subject-matter knowledge? Should one demonstrate actual teaching, especially when children are having difficulties with material, so that the examiners can evaluate how a teacher analyzes the nature of these difficulties and addresses them in classroom instruction? Should classroom presence, a close relative to leadership and charisma, be a feature of such an examination?

In the debate about the certification examination, the unanswered question was and remains one of anatomy: What is at the heart of teaching? Nobody has an agreed-on answer to that question no matter how complex that answer is. I pose here one part of an answer to the anatomy query. The partial answer is that adults—teachers in the case at hand—have folk psychology conceptions of the mind, psychological causality, and learning. These conceptions are reflected in the way teachers speak about their teaching and in the way they teach. The first purpose of this chapter is to address the nature of this folk psychology as it applies to teachers.

Among the content tested in the licensing examination was teachers' subject-matter knowledge (SMK). Conventional wisdom holds that the deeper the teachers' SMK, the better teachers of that subject matter they should be. My second purpose in writing this chapter is to question the conventional wisdom.

To recap, this chapter is divided into two parts. In the first, I describe what I believe is at the heart of adult cognition that concerns teaching: teachers' folk psychology of the mind and learning, and folk pedagogy. The second part gets at how a part of teachers' folk psychology, the part that relates to learning, is related to their SMK.

FOLK PSYCHOLOGY AND FOLK PEDAGOGY

Folk psychology deals with the way laypersons represent the psychological world (Olson & Bruner, 1996). These laypersons have not studied the cognitive sciences, psychology, and related fields that deal directly with the human psyche. In contrast, psychologists of various stripes are experts in the area of the human psyche.

One part of the psychological world is the domain of cognition. Part of human cognition touches on the nature of the human mind, psychological causality, and how learning takes place in the mind. Although adult laypersons have not formally studied psychology or allied fields, they have notions about the nature of the psychological world of a human being.

Work by Rips and Conrad (1989) was among the first to not test the ideas of psychologists about human cognition, but instead to test laypersons' notions of human cognition. Work in this area has come to be termed *theories of mind*. This quite young area of theory building and research has four principal foci. One concerns the language of young children. Research has shown that young children use words that indicate an understanding of mind (e.g., think, believe, etc.; Astington & Pelletier, 1997; Bartsch & Wellman, 1995). The second focus is on the ability of children to solve false-belief tasks (Perner, 1991; Wellman, 1990). The third focus concerns the use of metaphors in language as expressions of our understandings of the mind (Reddy, 1978; Sfard, 1998). The fourth focus is the concern of this chapter: how adults conceive of the mind and its functioning (Strauss, 1993, 1996, 1997).

I once assumed that the folk psychology of laypersons was completely different than the folk psychology of experts who conduct research in domains such as cognitive aspects of psychology, the cognitive sciences as practiced in laboratories that test the wet mind (the brain sciences), laboratories that deal with artificial intelligence, philosophy of the mind, and so on. After all, cognitive scientists spend much of their lives constructing theoretical models that describe the mind and how it works and conducting research to test those models. Laypersons do none of this. We should expect, then, that the folk psychology views about the mind, learning, and so on held by cognitive scientists and laypersons are different.

For me, this assumption about the nature of the differences between cognitive scientists and laypersons lasted until I attended a colloquium arranged for a potential donor for the establishment of a Center for the Study of Learning at Tel Aviv University. It was there that I realized that scientists and laypersons may have the same implicit, intuitive folk psychology notions about the mind and learning. But that gets me ahead of my story.

The meeting was intended to show the donor various aspects of learning that are being explored these days, and the format of the colloquium was that several faculty members from the learning sciences presented their work with discussions afterward—a sort of tutorial about the areas they were investigating.

The first speaker, a biochemist working on learning at the level of the neuron, spoke about how proteins are produced when an impulse passes through a neuron and how these proteins go to a particular site in the cell. Once at the site, the protein breaks up in a matter of milliseconds. However, if another impulse passes through the cell, the protein is once again synthesized and sent to the same site. This can happen repeatedly. After many impulses have passed through the neuron, part of the cell sends information to the nucleus that, in turn, sends information to a relevant part of the cell to constantly produce that protein and send it to the same site. This description was how learning of the short- and long-term types can be described at the biochemical level of a single neuron. It was a bottom–up model of learning.

The second speaker was an artificial intelligence (AI) expert. He spoke about how expert systems learn: They can seek solutions in a problem space; when the solution does not work, they seek other solutions. Expert systems are able to modify their behavior when presented with problems. In short, expert systems are adaptive and learn. This speaker's model, different from that of the biochemist, was a top–down model of learning.

A third speaker, a philosopher, encouraged the audience to consider different kinds of learning (e.g., ride a bike; make a friend; keep a friend; solve a linear algebra problem; take apart a carburetor, clean it, and reassemble it; understand why a colleague behaved badly; understand how large bureaucracies work and do not work; etc.). He suggested that these different kinds of learning, not being identical, need different models to describe them.

Others spoke at the same meeting. It struck me during the presentations that each speaker had developed a model of learning in the areas of their expertise. Each of the models was different from the others. In fact, there did not seem to be any overlap among the models they had constructed, which is quite expected.

Yet despite these differences, there was one area of commonality among these scientists. They all taught the audience in the same manner. Because people teach to cause learning in others (more about that later), these scientists had the same implicit, intuitive folk psychology understandings of learning. Not surprisingly, these understandings were quite unrelated to their scientific models of learning.

Given this and similar experiences and some reflection about them, I believe that even experts in the area of learning hold folk psychology views of learning when they teach others. To be sure, scientists hold explicit views that are strikingly different from that of laypersons about the mind and learning. However, when they teach and speak about teaching, their intuitive understandings of learning come into play. They are indistinguishable from those of the layperson. The line separating cognitive scientists and laypersons concerning their folk psychology understandings about the mind and learning, then, are blurred beyond recognition when they teach and speak about teaching.

My work has carried me to investigate teachers' folk psychology notions of the mind since 1989, and I do so out of the conviction that they are at the heart of teachers' teaching. Put strongly, the idea is that the way teachers understand the minds of children and learning (that part of their folk psychology) guides their actual teaching and the way they speak about their teaching. So if I am interested in teacher preparation and in-service teacher education, I ought to know what that understanding looks like. For if I do not, I will be in the position of preparing teachers for teaching without understanding what I believe to be fundamental to their understanding of teaching. I now turn to the first part of this chapter: teachers' folk psychology.

TEACHERS' FOLK PSYCHOLOGY ABOUT CHILDREN'S MINDS AND LEARNING

The study of teachers' folk psychology involves determining the nature of the psychological entities that guide the way that teachers teach and interpret the world of learning of children. These psychological entities have been described in various ways: theories (Schon, 1983), knowledge (Shulman, 1986), and mental models (Johnson-Laird, 1983; Norman, 1983). I use the mental models (MMs) construct as an heuristic. I tested neither Johnson-Laird's nor Norman's version of MMs. Instead, I used their notions of MMs as a means to test teachers' mental representations of children's minds and learning.

The claim here is that MMs are powerful organizers of people's understandings of aspects of their world (Gentner & Stevens, 1983; Johnson-Laird, 1983). In the same vein, Norman (1983) claimed that a major purpose of a mental model is to enable a user of that model to predict the operation of a target system that has operations. An example he offered concerned people's MMs of the operation of a calculating machine. In research I have conducted with my colleagues and students, the target system is children's minds and learning. Norman proposed that MMs have three functional factors of importance, which I summarize in terms of children's minds and learning: (a) people's MMs reflect their beliefs about children's minds and learning; (b) there is a correspondence between parameters and states of the MM and the aspects and states of children's minds and learning; and (c) the MM has predictive power in that it allows people to understand and anticipate the behavior of children's minds and how learning takes place in them.

In addition to the aforementioned, MMs are implicit in that they are hidden, internal, and inaccessible by direct observation. They are inferred from what is observable, external, and explicit. Implicit MMs cannot be seen directly; instead, they are inferred from explicit, observable behaviors. The relations between implicit MMs and explicit behaviors are that the former organizes the latter and, through the latter, we come to know the former.

Teachers' implicit MMs of children's minds and learning, then, are the psychological entities described in this chapter.

Types of Mental Models

The nature of professionals' beliefs and theories has occupied the concerns of Schon (1983) and his coworkers who, among other ideas, devised a classification system of the kinds of theories professionals have. Although Schon claimed that teachers have theories, I believe the psychological entity we should be addressing is MMs. However, to stay true to Schon's terminology, I write about theories when discussing his work.

Among the theories Schon (1983) suggested are part of professionals' repertoire are two that I addressed in my research: teachers' espoused and in-action MMs. Espoused theories are those theories professionals display when they speak about how they practice their profession. In-action theories are those theories professionals show when they practice their profession. Both kinds of theories are implicit. They are between the lines of what people do and say. We studied teachers' implicit espoused and in-action MMs (not theories).

Schon's taxonomy of professional knowledge is intended to describe the theories of professionals. But the theories of professionals who practice different professions do not have the same content; for example, there is no reason to expect that the content of, say, the in-action theory of design of an architect will be the same as a teacher's in-action theory of children's learning. As a consequence, we must look elsewhere for those aspects of professionals' theories that are central to teachers. Shulman (1986) provided us with those aspects, and it is to his work that I now turn.

Teachers' Cognition

Shulman and his coworkers (Shulman, 1986; Wilson, Shulman, & Richert, 1987) proposed a taxonomy of kinds of knowledge teachers employ. Among the kinds of teacher knowledge Shulman proposed are pedagogical-content knowledge (PCK) and SMK (more about that later).

In broad strokes, PCK refers to the professional knowledge of teachers about how to make subject matter understandable to children. PCK includes the knowledge of teachers of students' preconceptions about subject matter, which concepts and skills are particularly difficult for children to learn, what makes them difficult, ways to make these difficult concepts and skills easier, and how these are different at different ages. In shorthand form, it is the knowledge teachers have about the minds of children (folk psychology), how their minds work when learning takes place (folk psychology), and the roles of instruction in fostering learning (folk pedagogy).

Let us now look at the two kinds of MMs about learning held by teachers: espoused and in-action MMs.

Teachers' Espoused Mental Models. We tapped teachers' implicit espoused MMs by interviewing novice and experienced high school teachers who teach the sciences and the humanities (Strauss & Shilony, 1994). We used a semistructured clinical interview format in which we posed the same initial question to teachers and then followed up their answers with other questions. The initial question we posed to teachers asked how they teach material that is difficult for children to learn. Because teachers teach for learning to take place, we could infer their MMs of children's minds and learning from their statements. Teachers' statements were classified and organized, and it is that organization that constituted our description of teachers' espoused MMs of children's minds and learning.

The espoused MMs found among the teachers by Strauss and Shilony (1994) and subsequently replicated by Strauss, Ravid, Zelcer, and Berliner (1999), Strauss, Ravid, Magen, and Berliner (1998), Strauss and Rosenberg-Meltser (1996), and Polansky (1996) bears a family resemblance to 1960s information-processing models such as that of Atkinson and Shiffrin (1968). This model has been presented elsewhere (Strauss, 1993, 1996, 1997; Strauss, Ravid, et al., 1998) so I do not elaborate on it here. Suffice it to say that it is based on a view that knowledge is outside the minds of children, and the task of the teacher is to get it inside the mind so that it will eventually arrive at a location where it will stick. That's the place where the glue is.

For learning to occur, the content must first enter the minds of children, and teachers conceive of children as having openings of a certain size that allow information to enter. Teachers believe that good pedagogy involves serving up knowledge in chunk sizes that can get through the openings. For example, teachers said that what makes some subject matter difficult is that it is complex and, as a result, it may not be able to get in the mind. Here teachers see their task as reducing this complexity by breaking the material into component parts so that it will be able to enter the openings of the mind. I have more to say about this later on. However, even were the material to be of the right complexity, it may never enter the mind if the affective states of the child are not primed to receive the content.

Teachers believe that once content gets through, it must somehow connect up with already existing knowledge by means of analogies, associations, familiar examples, and so on. Accordingly, teachers believe they should facilitate connection making between new and old knowledge. If there is no existing knowledge to get connected to, the new knowledge can get driven into memory through repetition, rehearsal, and practice. This new knowledge now becomes part of already learned knowledge. How does the new knowledge affect the prior knowledge? Teachers believe that there are changes in the amount and organization of prior knowledge: The prior knowledge gets broadened and generalized, it is at higher levels of abstraction than what was in previous knowledge, and more.

Figure 9.1 illustrates this remarkable rich and structured espoused MM. It contains 11 general categories of knowledge teachers hold about children's minds, learning, and instruction. Notice that the category "Characteristics of Subject Matter Content" has levels of complexity as one of its components. Each category has a number of components, only some of which appear in the figure.

Teachers' In-Action Mental Models. Work initiated by Mevorach (1994) and subsequently replicated and extended by Mevorach and Strauss (in press) and Strauss, Mevorach, and Litman (1998) investigated teachers' in-action mental models of the learning of children. This MM is gleaned from the way teachers actually teach.

Participants in the Mevorach and Strauss (in press) study were 24 first-grade teachers of varying teaching experience. We videotaped an arithmetic lesson given by each teacher, where the teacher taught new material on the process of adding two numbers that generate a third number. We developed a category system that enabled us to analyze the videotaped data and to describe the MM. I present here the general description of the categorization system.

Categorization System. We devised a two-tier category system that allows a classification of the instruction of teachers and enables us to infer the MMs teachers hold about the minds of children.

The first tier classified the explicit teaching behaviors of teachers, and we found that they were organized into units that bear a resemblance to those described by both Flanders (1970) and Cazden (1988). The first tier has four units:

1. The teachers' and pupils' behaviors; for example, the teacher asks a question. Each behavior at this level is meaningless.

2. An event is the combination of several behaviors on the part of the teacher and pupils; for example, the teacher asks a question, a pupil answers the question, and the teacher remarks about the answer. Behaviors from the first unit gain meaning in the events.

3. An episode includes several events; for example, there are several events where the teacher asks—pupil answers—teacher responds type, where the aim of the episode is to, say, define the subject being presented.

4. A lesson is comprised of a number of events, where the lesson has a particular purpose; for example, introducing the subject matter: addition.

The second tier is more inferential and is based on the explicit behaviors of the teachers that we observed in the first tier. This tier is our addition to previous work on teachers teaching. Others have documented the first tier's behaviors (Cazden, 1988; Flanders, 1970), but we are the first to suggest that an implicit MM organizes them. This is our contribution, and I believe it points to a way that the cognitive sciences can be put to use to describe cognition of teachers.

The Units of the Second Tier Comprise Teachers' In-Action MM. These units are:

1. Cognitive goals that teachers want their pupils to achieve; for example, connecting the new material being taught to what the pupils already know.

CHILDREN'S MINDS

| HOW NEW CONTENT GETS TO BE LEARNED | WHAT IS KNOWN, ALREADY LEARNED |

(1) Characteristics of Subject Matter
- Level of abstraction
- Complexity
- Size of unit
- Amount of material
- Kind of discipline

(2) Teacher as Intermediary
- Teaching knowledge, tools
- Guiding, directing
- Creating learning opportunities
- Organizing material for teaching
- Fitting the material to the learner

(3) Instruction
- Teaching through stories
- Play
- Explanations
- Asking questions
- Discussions

(4) Child's Environment
- Family, home
- Teachers
- Technology
- Mass communication

(5) Characteristics of the Learner
- Abilities
- Intelligence
- Personality, maturity
- Experience as a learner
- Level of abstraction in learning

(6) Means
- Physical experience
- Senses
- Reading material
- Activity
- Paying attention
- Activity
- Emotional involvement

(7) Elements
- Knowledge
- Reading
- Writing
- Arithmetic
- Vocabulary
- Reading comprehension
- Concepts
- Subject matter knowledge and skills

(8) Characteristics
- Kind of knowledge
- Amount of knowledge
- Knowledge organization

(9) Processes
Relating new content to already-learned content through:
- Associations
- Comparisons
- Analogies
- Adaptations
- Internalization
- Assimilation

Driving new content into Memory through:
- Rehearsal
- Memorization

(10) Products of Learning
- Change in knowledge in memory
- Growth of amount of knowledge in memory
- Change in knowledge organization in memory
- Expansion

(11) Demonstrates New Knowledge
- Knowledge retrieval
- Solving new problems
- Being able to evaluate

FIG. 9.1. Teachers' espoused mental model of children's minds and learning.

The child's mind is the box and, through instruction, teachers attempt to get material into the mind and moved along the mind in such a way that it stays there for a long time, which is another way of saying that it gets learned.

On the left side of the figure are categories that are not part of learning as such, but they do influence it. There are five categories here: (1) *Characteristics of the Material* to be taught (e.g., it is complex); (2) the *Teacher as Intermediary* between the material and the learner (e.g., the teacher breaks a problem into parts for the children); (3) aspects of *Instruction* (e.g., asking questions); (4) aspects of the *Child's Environment* (e.g., mass communication); and (5) *Characteristics of the Learner* (e.g., abilities, intelligence).

We now move from the categories that are not learning as such to the sixth (6) category that involves how the material enters the child's mind. We have labeled that category *Means* because this category's components are the means by which material external to the mind enters it. This category gets at the seam between the external world and the mind. The openings have flaps next to them allowing material to enter when they are up or preventing the material from entering if they are down. As previously mentioned, these flaps are regulated by the affective system, that is, if the child is interested and motivated or not.

The mind has five categories: (7) *Already Learned Knowledge* that exists in the mind. These are concepts, skills, and so forth that have already been learned; (8) *Characteristics of Already Learned Knowledge*, such as amount of knowledge; (9) *Mental Processes* that allow new material that just entered the mind to become part of the already learned knowledge or, in other words, to become learned. An example would be analogies between new and old knowledge. The next category, (10) *Products of Learning* deals with what happens to the old knowledge when the new knowledge gets learned, for example, it gets expanded. And there is a category of the mind that involves they ways the learner (11) *Demonstrates Uses of the New Knowledge*, for example, the learner can solve problems that are similar to those just learned.

227

2. Cognitive processes that teachers think lead to these cognitive goals; for example, retrieval of already learned material from memory.

3. Assumptions about how teaching in a particular way leads to these cognitive processes that, in turn, lead to the cognitive goals; for example, mentioning a prior lesson leads to the retrieval of already learned material from memory.

4. The mother of all assumptions (meta-assumptions) about learning and teaching; for example, knowledge is stored and can be retrieved.

I now illustrate some aspects of these units. Teachers occasionally say something like this to their class: "We are now going to begin our history lesson. Where did we leave off last time"? On the surface, this familiar way of opening a lesson seems to be a rather meager beginning, but it actually has a quite deep and rich MM underlying it.

The teacher, by asking the children this seemingly trifling question, believes that children remember where the last history class ended, which is to say that that knowledge is stored somewhere in their minds. This is a meta-assumption. She also believes that that knowledge can be located and retrieved. This, too, is a meta-assumption. She is interested in the children searching for, locating, and retrieving that knowledge, which are cognitive processes. The cognitive goal she wants her students to achieve is retrieving the knowledge of their last history lesson. She believes that her teaching, which begins by asking about the last lesson, can cause the cognitive processes of searching, locating, and retrieving that knowledge. This is what we have termed an *assumption*.

So what appears on the surface to be a rather innocent and insignificant question has considerable power packed into it. That power is the in-action MM that gives rise to such a question.

The point here is that teachers have a folk psychology MM of children's minds and learning that is inferred from their folk pedagogy. This is the case for both espoused and in-action MMs. For the espoused MM, teachers speak about how they teach (folk pedagogy) for learning to take place (folk psychology). We infer their espoused MM of children's minds and learning (folk psychology) from the ways they speak about their teaching (folk pedagogy). For the in-action MM, teachers teach for learning to take place, and we interpret the way they teach (folk pedagogy) to see what their MMs of learning are (folk psychology). The espoused and in-action MMs are quite different from each other epistemologically. They are as different from each other as are declarative and procedural knowledge.

Part of teachers' in-action MM is a notion of psychological causality.

Psychological Causality

What are hallmarks of folk psychology? At the heart of any model of the mind and its workings, especially when learning takes place, is a notion of causation. Philosophers have wrestled with this particularly prickly area and have written about three aspects of causation. The first is its ontology, where one tries to account for the nature of causality, the kinds of causality, what is and what is not a causal relation, and more. The second deals with epistemological considerations. Here philosophers describe how causal relations are discovered, how they can be tested and confirmed, when we can assert a causal claim, and what kinds of causal inferences may be valid. The third deals with conceptual analyses. This area concerns itself with the meaning of the term *cause*. How shall one define it? How is it different from other, but related, terms? What is their use in our language, and more.

Discussions of psychological causality generally include the notion of intentionality, which sets psychological causality apart from physical causality. I believe that intentionality has two important facets: physical impermeability and psychological action at a distance.

The physical impermeability of the mind is central to psychological causality. We believe that we cannot literally enter the minds of children or mix our minds with theirs in ways that physical objects can penetrate other physical objects, as when we put our finger in clay or place a rock in water, or in ways that physical objects can mix, as when a soluble powder mixes in water or when cold and hot water mix.

That leads to the second facet, psychological action at a distance. This means, in the case of the psychological realm, that although teachers stand outside of the minds of children, they can cause learning to occur in those minds. By way of contrast, examples of action at a distance in physics are magnets' influence on metals and the attraction that celestial bodies have on each other in their trajectories through the heavens. Psychological action at a distance is caused by, for example, speaking (persuading, questioning, summarizing, cajoling, pleading, and describing) and showing (demonstrating, modeling, authenticating, and validating) in particular ways. Through questioning, summarizing, and so forth, we believe we can cause learning in children, although we are acting on their minds at a distance.

The part of the assumption of psychological causality that underlies teachers' MMs is that, although we cannot directly and physically enter the mind to cause learning, we can cause learning outside others' minds by speaking, giving instructions, and so forth. From a distance, minds can influence other minds. How teachers choose to influence the minds of others is deeply related to their MMs of the structure of the mind and how learning takes place in it.

In summary, I attempted to show in this first section that teachers have espoused MMs and in-action MMs. They are different from each other epistemologically. They constrain the ways that teachers speak about how they teach and the ways they actually teach. The espoused MM that guides the way teachers speak about how they teach and the in-action MM that steers the way they actually teach belie their folk psychology because they teach for learning to occur. I use MMs as ways to describe those folk pedagogies. Furthermore, I argue that these espoused and in-action MMs of folk pedagogy are embedded in their folk psychology understandings of the minds of children and how learning takes place in their minds.

The second part of the chapter deals with SMK and its relation to the MMs of teachers. Remember that the Massachusetts state teacher examination had considerable SMK items, which fits the conventional view of teaching—that is, teachers with deep and extensive SMK will teach differently and better than teachers with more shallow and less extensive SMK. I intend to challenge that view.

SUBJECT-MATTER KNOWLEDGE

The area of teachers' SMK has many aspects, only two of which we briefly discuss here: definitions of what subject matter (SM) of disciplines is, and how that subject matter is organized mentally by teachers (i.e., what their SMK is).

Definitions of Subject Matter of Disciplines

The psychological description of SM of disciplines, and its related pedagogy, has a century-long history (Shulman & Quinlan, 1996). Among the most influential contemporary scholars to study these issues was Schwab (1962). At the core of his ideas are two main aspects of the structure of SM in disciplines: its syntactic and substantive structure.

Syntactic Structure of SM and Knowing in a Discipline. The syntactic structure of disciplines concerns the way researchers obtain data, interpret it, and draw conclusions. In short, it deals with ways people in a field come to know and understand it. And the ways one knows and understands a discipline are discipline dependent. Knowing and understanding music are not the same as knowing and understanding physics or literature or psychology. Those special ways of knowing that characterize each discipline are part of teachers' SMK, and their understandings of it should influence how they teach.

Substantive Structure of SM in a Discipline. This structure pertains to the main concepts of a discipline and their relations. As an example, the main concepts in cognitive developmental psychology, from the structuralist viewpoint, are logicomathematical structures as the psychological entities that interpret the world and guide behaviors; assimilation and accommodation as invariant psychological functioning; disequilibrium as a mechanism of structural change; and so forth. For information-processing adherents, among the main concepts are knowledge organizations as the principal psychological entities that influence the interpretation of environmental data and that guide behaviors; attention mechanisms that influence the environmental information that gets acted on; and encoding, maturation, and automatization as mechanisms that foster learning.

Substantive structures influence researchers' views of the discipline and lead them to specific ways they choose what data to attempt to gain, interpret that data, and draw conclusions. In other words, substantive structures influence syntactic structures, and vice versa.

What constitutes a discipline or field has been a subject of intense investigation in the history and philosophy of science and the social sciences. What teachers understand to be the syntactic and substantive knowledge of disciplines comprise most of teachers' SMK. The research reported here is about how teachers come to mentally represent the SM of the discipline they teach, which is their SMK.

Relations Between Teachers' SMK and Their MMs

Teachers' SMK and their MMs are generally seen as two intertwined kinds of knowledge that teachers have and use when teaching and speaking about teaching. We untangle them, reexplore them, and then retwine them with somewhat different relations. In short, we propose to change the traditional ways of understanding their relations.

The claims we make are not intuitive and are not represented in current theory in the area. Theoretical elaboration has begun only recently (Strauss, 1993, 1996), and several studies have been conducted to put our claims to empirical test (Polansky, 1996; Strauss & Berliner, 1996; Strauss & Meltzer-Rosenberg, 1996; Strauss & Shilony, 1994).

The conventional stance about relations between SMK and teaching for children's learning is that the former has priority over and actually guides the latter. The following quote represents the current view.

> Recent research highlights the critical influence of teachers' subject matter understanding on their pedagogical orientations and decisions. . . . Teachers' capacity to pose questions, select tasks, evaluate their pupils' understanding, and make curricular choices all depend on how they themselves understand the subject matter. (McDiarmid, Ball, & Anderson, 1989, p. 198)

This quote is representative of the conventional view. Others who I believe adhere to this sentiment are Even (1993), Grossman, Wilson, and Shulman (1989), Gudmundsdottir (1991), and Stodolsky (1988).

The ideas behind this quote, although not stated explicitly, are that SMK is an important facet of teacher knowledge that comes to bear on their teaching, and SMK has priority over teaching strategies in that it guides many aspects of teachers' teaching, including posing questions, evaluating children's understanding, or, in short, how they make teaching decisions. Teachers with deep SMK teach differently than teachers who have shallow SMK.

My colleagues and I propose an alternative understanding of the nature of the relations between SMK and MMs. To illustrate that view, I show how teachers' espoused and in-action MMs have priority over their SMK when they speak about teaching and when they actually teach, respectively.

SMK and the Espoused MM

The argument goes as follows. Teachers teach subject matter to children for learning to take place, and it is teachers' espoused MMs of children's minds and learning that guide how they speak about their teaching. If teachers' SMK knowledge base is large or small, and if it is organized deeply or in a shallow manner, teachers will speak about how they teach in the same ways that belie their espoused MMs of children's learning. For example, part of teachers' espoused MMs of children's minds and learning is that a characteristic of material has different levels of complexity. Ideas about complexity and simplicity are profound and elusive, as shown so elegantly by Gell-Mann (1994). Teachers believe that complex material is difficult to learn and, as a consequence, one should break it up into component parts so that it will be easier to learn. This guides the way they speak about their teaching. Teachers will speak about the breaking up of subject matter if they have considerable or little SMK about the concepts in question and if that SMK is organized deeply or superficially. What this suggests, then, is that teachers' espoused MM overrides and has precedence over SMK when it comes to how teachers talk about how they teach. The way teachers speak about how they teach reflects their espoused MM of children's minds and learning.

In addition, what teachers say when they speak about what they teach is influenced by their SMK. Let us take two teachers as an example, one who has considerable knowledge that is deeply organized and one who has less knowledge that is superficially organized. Let us again use the example of breaking material into its component parts when teachers speak about realizing that the material being taught is too complex for the children. Both teachers will speak about breaking up the material into component parts. As already noted, this means that these teachers have the same espoused MM of the learning of children. But the places where they break up the material will be different depending on the SMK of the teachers. In other words, teachers carve the subject matter at its joints, and the joints are different, given the SMK of the teachers. I present the following example where the SMK of teachers is wh-constructions in English grammar.

Our prediction, then, is that teachers with high and low SMK organization will have the same espoused MM of children's minds and learning. That means that the MM has priority over their SMK because the SMK, as interpreted in the way teachers speak about teaching, is expressed in the framework of their espoused MM.

SMK and the In-Action MM

Here, too, the prediction is that the MMs of teachers are not influenced by their SMK organization, except that this time I am writing about teachers' in-action MM. This is the MM teachers have that guides their teaching. An illustration might be helpful here to make the point.

Recall the case of the teacher who begins her history lesson by asking the students to retrieve where they left off at the end of the last history lesson. I argued that this seemingly simple request, an almost everyday occurrence, reflects a powerful in-action MM about the minds of children and how learning takes place in them.

Among the units in the in-action MM are the cognitive goals the teacher sets for the students: retrieving knowledge. To briefly review this example, this means that the teacher has meta-assumptions; for example, knowledge exists in the minds of children and can be retrieved, and so forth. She also believes that cognitive processes, another unit in the in-action MM, can lead to the just mentioned cognitive goals: searching, locating, and retrieving. Finally, this teacher has a unit, termed *assumptions*, that leads her to believe that she can induce cognitive processes that, in turn, can achieve the desired cognitive goal in her pupils.

Now think about this for a minute. Why should the amount and level of SMK make a difference for that opening question? Should having deeply organized SMK or superficially organized SMK make a difference in how the previously mentioned units of the in-action MM operate? Should deep SMK about the structure of syntactic and semantic aspects of the SM change that initial question that started off the history lesson?

My answer to this question, as you have surely surmised by now, is that the level of SMK organization should not change that question one iota. Stated more fully, the SMK of teachers should not influence the way they teach. The question just described is one of myriad examples I could have chosen to make the same point.

However, the content that interests the teacher in her teaching (e.g., the principal causes of World War I, what historical evidence is and how it differs from evidence in a biology experiment, the nature of similarities and differences concerning explanations of historical and physical causality, a comparison of the same historical event from different historical perspectives—thus rendering it different historical events) does influence the teaching of teachers. But here the influence is on what is being taught and not how it is being taught. The former is influenced by the SMK of teachers about history, whereas the latter is influenced by their in-action MM of children's minds and learning. In an attempt to put this idea to an empirical test, we conducted several studies. In some of these studies, teachers of English as a second language were tested for their SMK about wh-constructions. These are very difficult constructions for Israeli children because the English form of wh-constructions is quite different than that in Hebrew. Relative clauses are part of the English language curriculum in Israel and are taught in Grades 9 and 10 and tested in the Israeli matriculation examination.

I now briefly present wh-constructions and then describe two studies that tested the relations between the SMK of teachers and their espoused and in-action MM.

WH-CONSTRUCTIONS

Wh-constructions are divided into two main parts: Wh-questions and wh-relative clauses.

Wh-Questions

These questions are divided into two kinds: direct and indirect questions.

Direct Wh-Questions. Wh-questions constitute one of the two major subtypes of interrogative clauses in English: yes–no (or truth) questions, which question the truth value of a sentence (e.g., Is it raining?), and wh- (or content) questions, which elicit information about a particular part of the sentence (e.g., What did he eat?). Both children acquiring English as their mother tongue and learners of English as a second foreign language must become aware of the changes in the structure of the interrogative sentence to produce grammatical wh-questions in English.

Subject and Nonsubject Questions. Direct wh-questions are further classified into subject questions (e.g., Who likes John? about the subject of the sentence) and nonsubject or object questions (e.g., Who(m) does John like? about an object in the sentence).

Indirect Wh-Questions. When a question is embedded in a main clause to create an indirect wh-question construction, subject-auxiliary inversion is forbidden. For example, compare the direct question sentence "How did you feel?" and the indirect question sentence, "I want to know how you felt." Although both posit the same question, the first has undergone subject-auxiliary inversion, whereas the second has not and resembles a declarative rather than a question sentence.

Wh-Relative Clauses

Relative clauses bear a resemblance to wh-questions in general, and specifically to indirect questions: They contain subordinate clauses that begin with a wh-word that replaces a syntactic element originating at some site in the clause, without subject-auxiliary inversion. Compare, for example, the indirect question construction, *They want to know whose book you prefer*, and the relative clause construction, *The man whose sister you married has disappeared*. In both sentences the wh-word refers to an NP, but in the first sentence this NP is questioned, whereas the second construction originates in the combination of the main clause, *The man has disappeared*, and the clause, *You married his sister* subordinated to *the man*.

Structure of the Wh-Constructions Test

We developed a research tool that could measure the depth of English teachers' SMK about wh-constructions. It contained 12 sentences with wh-words that they were asked to classify. Table 9.1 presents the classification of the test sentences according to the categories previously described. The test contained nine direct and indirect wh-questions and three sentences with relative clauses marked by wh-question words.

We now turn to our study of teachers' SMK of wh-constructions and their MMs of children's minds and learning of wh-constructions.

Assessment of SMK (Structure of the Wh-Constructions Test)

The teachers were presented with the list of 12 sentences and were asked to classify them fully according to whichever criteria they deemed correct. After the teachers classified the sentences according to the previously

TABLE 9.1
Classification of Wh-Sentences in the Test

Questions

Direct Questions

Subject Questions
Who saw the murder?
Whose students drink coffee every morning?
Which books belong to you?
Nonsubject Questions
Who did he see?
Whose papers does he always steal?
Which students do you like?

Indirect Questions

She told me which students she liked in that class.
He always mentions how many stories he writes every year.
They want to know whose book you prefer.

Relative Clauses

I didn't like the man who spoke first.
The books that we recommended were boring.
The man whose sister you married has disappeared.

mentioned instruction, the experimenter gave them another piece of paper and asked the teachers to categorize the sentences according to wh.

Criteria for Levels of SMK

The optimal classification of the sentences done by a linguist would divide questions (direct and indirect) from nonquestions (relative clauses), and then proceed to differentiate questions into direct and indirect, and direct questions into subject and nonsubject questions. This classification was not found among the teachers.

Teachers' highest classification consisted of two classes, each of which was further differentiated into two classes; thus, there were two levels down and four aspects across. The criterion for high SMK was the full classification and correct labels for each of the categories. The criterion for middle SMK was a classification with the first categorization (indicating knowledge that the sentences are wh-elements) and either no further classification or an incorrect classification. The criterion for low SMK was that the teachers did not even make the first-level classification, indicating that they did not use wh-elements as the content, despite that the experimenter asked them to classify according to wh.

RELATIONS BETWEEN TEACHERS' SMK
AND THE MENTAL MODELS

We conducted several studies to determine the nature of relations between the SMK of teachers and their MMs (Polansky, 1996; Strauss, Ravid, Zelcer, & Berliner, 1999; Strauss, Ravid, et al., 1988). I discuss two studies here: one concerned with espoused MMs and one dealing with in-action MMs.

Teachers' SMK and Their Espoused MMs

Strauss, Ravid, et al. (1998) presented the previous SMK organization test to teachers and found, for the expository purposes of this chapter, that the teachers were divided into two groups: high and low SMK teachers. There were 16 teachers in each of the two groups.

After each teacher was found to be either high or low on SMK organization, she participated in an interview whose purpose was to determine the nature of her espoused MMs. The findings of the study were just as I expected—teachers with high and low SMK organization of wh-constructions had the same espoused MMs.

Teachers' SMK and Their In-Action MMs

I briefly report a study that is currently underway. However, enough data have been collected and our data analyses are far enough along that I can report them with a modicum of confidence (Strauss, Ravid, & Haim, in press). As in the previous study, we found teachers with either high or low SMK about wh-constructions. We videotaped classes where they taught wh-constructions and analyzed them in terms of the teachers' in-action MMs using the category system of Mevorach (1994).

So far, our findings are that teachers with high and low SMK have the same in-action MM. In other words, although the teachers are different in terms of the depth of knowledge organization they have about wh-constructions, they are not different in terms of their in-action MM of the learning of children. It is this MM that guides the teaching of teachers. These findings are also in line with my expectations and are different from what adherents of the traditional view would expect.

What does all of this mean for the importance of SMK? The main argument here is that the nature of relations between the SMK of teachers and their MMs is different than what the conventional view holds. Traditionally, theoreticians and researchers claim that SMK has priority over much of classroom teaching. To return to McDiarmid et al. (1989), teachers' capacity to ask questions, make analogies, listen to children's answers to questions posed, and more is influenced by their SMK. In other words, the

SMK of teachers constrains their pedagogical decisions that are in the service of children's learning.

The alternative view posed here is that teachers' MMs and SMK are separate entities. Teachers' MMs deal with their beliefs about children's minds and learning. Teachers have SMK about their discipline. The structure of the minds of children and how learning occurs in those minds is independent of the level and extent of the SMK of teachers.

These are claims for keeping MMs and SMK conceptually separate, but they do have relations because SM is taught so that it is learned. A second part of the claim I am making is that the MM constrains and subordinates SMK. I argue that the MM is the framework within which teachers make pedagogical decisions. Teachers do not teach in a particular way if it is inconsistent with their MM of children's minds and learning.

Notice that we cannot make a parallel formulation about the SMK of teachers. That is, it sounds peculiar to say that teachers do not teach in a particular way if that way is inconsistent with their SMK. This is because how teachers teach is not dependent on their SMK. What they teach is, however.

My formulation of these ideas is that teachers do not teach in ways that are inconsistent with their MM of children's minds and learning. The MM (folk psychology), then, is the main organizing system that gives rise to how teachers teach (folk pedagogy). The content of what is taught depends on the SMK of a teacher, but that decision is dependent on decisions about how to teach. The SMK of teachers is, then, subordinated to their MM.

Implications for Teacher Education

There are two implications that follow from our theory building and the empirical results from our studies: (a) teaching teachers to be aware of their own MMs of children's minds and learning, and (2) teaching subject matter.

Teaching Teachers to Be Aware of Their MMs.   The MMs that we discovered among teachers are implicit and tacit. Teachers are not aware that they hold such MMs, let alone that these MMs guide how they teach. When teachers were taught about learning in their educational psychology courses, nobody taught the MMs they hold. I showed (Strauss, 1993, 1996) that preservice teachers have these MMs before they even take these university courses. Because teachers do not know they have an MM, they do not know that what they are being taught is an alternative to their tacit understanding of the mind and learning.

The recommendation here is to help teachers unearth these tacit MMs. In so doing, the teachers become aware of what they believe learning is—something that they have not given much thought to. When alternative views are presented, teachers can see them as genuine alternatives because they now know what they believe children's minds and learning are.

The conceptual-change literature in science teaching seems particularly relevant here. These studies demonstrate the amazing power of inadequate models children construct about the world of physics, even in the face of contradictory evidence. Thus, children hold the naive belief that water at 10° C, when mixed with water at 10° C, becomes water at 20° C even after they measure its temperature with a thermometer. They may hold beliefs that numbers can be added onto infinity but they cannot be divided infinitely, that hot and cold water mix in such a way that tiny hot globules and tiny cold globules exist side by side, or that sugar when stirred into tea releases sweetness as the sugar disappears. These naive beliefs are not taught, but they are constructed just as are the MMs of the mind we have discovered. They are apparently constructed without any formal instruction.

When the falsity of these models, theories, and beliefs are demonstrated in science classes, students often will answer test questions that reveal they have mature scientific knowledge—and continue outside of school to hold their original beliefs. This literature does, however, suggest ways that can help teachers overcome the inadequate models of their students. However, these methods are time-consuming and clearly not always effective. Nevertheless, if we wish teachers to consider a Piagetian constructivist understanding of learning, a social-constructivist model of learning in the Vygotskian tradition, or any other model of learning for that matter, a first step in that process would be to have them examine the MMs they already possess.

Teaching Teachers Subject Matter. Lest the reader interpret this chapter to mean that I have an axe to grind against SMK, I want to dispel that notion once again. I have written here, perhaps too many times, that the SMK of teachers is crucial to teaching. The deeper the SMK of teachers, the better they will be at what they teach. Nobody I know, and that includes myself, would claim that teachers' level of SMK is irrelevant to their teaching. Because of its importance for what teachers teach, it is obvious that teachers should be taught to have the deepest possible SMK.

To avoid any misunderstanding, I state for the last time that, as teachers gain deeper and more extensive SMK, they do not teach that SM differently. Only by elaborating on teachers' folk psychology (their MMs) will they teach differently. Then and only then can their folk pedagogy be defolked.

BACK TO THE BEGINNING

I began this chapter with a description of the state of Massachusetts examination for prospective teachers and the disappointment many felt at the poor test results found among those who were examined. In my anatomy question about the heart of teaching, I suggested that we should separate SMK and teachers' espoused and in-action MMs. The reasons for this are hopefully clear now.

In keeping with the tenor of this chapter's themes, I believe it is important to test the SMK of teachers about content they will be teaching because it indicates what teachers will teach. I also believe it is important to develop tools to measure aspects of teachers' professional knowledge about children's minds, how learning takes place in those minds, and how we can teach to influence that learning. Teachers should have professional knowledge about the aforementioned, knowledge that separates them from laypersons. Their folk psychology should be defolked, as I previously mentioned, so that their expanded professional knowledge about the mind and its workings could become more sonorous and diverse than they are now. Were that to happen, teachers would have richer, more varied, and more theory-grounded teaching strategies that could supplement and enrich their wisdom of practice.

What I described in these pages can be viewed as an initial attempt to make a description of teachers' espoused and in-action MMs about children's minds and learning. These are teachers' folk psychology and they lead to the ways teachers speak about how they teach and actually teach (i.e., their folk pedagogy). However, teachers must go beyond these folk psychology and folk pedagogy notions that have been found to be identical among teachers and nonteachers (Strauss & Meltser-Rosenberg, 1996) because they are only commonsense notions and not professional knowledge about the mind and its workings.

How to do this going beyond is the next phase of our work being done at Tel Aviv University. If our teacher-education courses fulfill our hopes that teachers will have richer and more explicit professional knowledge than what they have at present, we can then think about how to assess this knowledge via tests. In this way, teachers' folk psychology and folk pedagogy can be viewed as a baseline understanding of the mind and its workings, and teachers' new knowledge that goes beyond their folk psychology and pedagogy can be seen as professional knowledge that is not shared by nonteachers.

ACKNOWLEDGMENT

Some of the research reported in this chapter was supported by the Binational Science Foundation (Grant No. 92-00286), which was awarded to the present author and David C. Berliner. I would like to thank Eva Brand, Adee Matan, Miriam Mevorach, Gadi Rauner, Judy Steiner, Niva Wallenstein, and Gila Zimet for helpful discussions about this chapter and to Michal Avivi and Nili Laor Blasbalg for their help in various aspects of my work.

REFERENCES

Astington, J. W., & Pelletier, J. (1997). The language of mind: Its role in teaching and learning. In D. R. Olson & N. Torrance (Eds.), *Handbook of education and human development* (pp. 293–619). London: Blackwell.

Atkinson, R. C., & Shiffrin, R. M. (1968). Human memory: A proposed system and its control mechanisms. In K. W. Spence & J. T. Spence (Eds.), *The psychology of learning and motivation: Advances in research and theory* (Vol. 2, pp. 249–292). New York: Academic Press.

Bartsch, K., & Wellman, H. M. (1995). *Children talk about the mind.* New York: Oxford University Press.

Cazden, C. (1988). *Classroom discourse.* Portsmouth, NH: Heinemann.

Even, R. (1993). Subject matter knowledge and pedagogical content knowledge: Prospective secondary teachers and the function concept. *Journal for Research in Mathematics Education, 24,* 94–116.

Flanders, N. A. (1970). *Analyzing teaching behavior.* Reading, MA: Addison Wesley.

Gell-Mann, M. (1994). *The quark and the jaguar.* New York: W. H. Freeman.

Gentner, D., & Stevens, A. (Eds.). (1983). *Mental models.* Hillsdale, NJ: Lawrence Erlbaum Associates.

Grossman, P. L., Wilson, S. M., & Shulman, L. S. (1989). Teachers of substance: Subject matter knowledge for teaching. In M. C. Reynolds (Ed.), *Knowledge base for the beginning teacher* (pp. 23–36). New York: Pergamon.

Gudmundsdottir, S. (1991). Pedagogical models of subject matter. In J. Brophy (Ed.), *Advances in research on teaching* (Vol. 2, pp. 262–304). Greenwich, CT: JAI.

Johnson-Laird, P. (1983). *Mental models.* Cambridge, MA: Harvard University Press.

McDiarmid, G. W., Ball, D. L., & Anderson, C. W. (1989). Why staying one chapter ahead doesn't really work: Subject-specific pedagogy. In M. C. Reynolds (Ed.), *Knowledge base for the beginning teacher* (pp. 193–202). New York: Pergamon.

Mevorach, M. (1994). *Teachers' in-action mental model.* Unpublished doctoral dissertation, Tel Aviv University, Tel Aviv, Israel.

Mevorach, M., & Strauss, S. (in press). Teachers' in-action mental models of children's minds and learning. *Learning and Instruction.*

Norman, D. A. (1983). Some observations on mental models. In D. Gentner & A. Stevens (Eds.), *Mental models.* Hillsdale, NJ: Lawrence Erlbaum Associates.

Olson, D. R., & Bruner, J. S. (1992). Folk psychology and folk pedagogy. In D. R. Olson & N. Torrance (Eds.), *Handbook of education and human development* (pp. 9–22). London: Blackwell.

Perner, J. (1991). *Understanding the representational mind.* Cambridge, MA: Bradford Books/MIT Press.

Polansky, C. (1996). *Teachers' subject matter knowledge about finding the main idea in a text, their understandings of how that occurs in children, and their mental models of children's learning.* Unpublished master's thesis, Tel Aviv University, Tel Aviv, Israel.

Reddy, M. (1978). The conduit metaphor: A case of frame conflict in our language about language. In A. Ortony (Ed.), *Metaphor and thought* (2nd ed., pp. 164–201). Cambridge, England: Cambridge University Press.

Rips, L. J., & Conrad, F. O. (1989). Folk psychology of mental activities. *Psychological Review, 96,* 187–207.

Schon, D. A. (1983). *The reflective practitioner.* New York: Basic Books.

Schwab, J. (1962). The concept of the structure of a discipline. *Educational Record, 43,* 197–202.

Sfard, A. (1998). On two metaphors for learning and the dangers of choosing just one. *Educational Researcher, 27*(2), 4–13.

Shulman, L. S. (1986). Those who understand: Knowledge growth in teaching. *Educational Researcher, 12,* 4–14.

Shulman, L. S., & Quinlan, K. M. (1996). The comparative psychology of school subjects. In D. Berliner & R. Calfee (Eds.), *Handbook of educational psychology* (pp. 399–422). New York: Macmillan.

Stodolosky, S. (1988). *The subject matters: Classroom activity in math and social studies.* Chicago: University of Chicago Press.

Strauss, S. (1993). Teachers' pedagogical content knowledge about children's minds and learning: Implications for teacher education. *Educational Psychologist, 28,* 279–290.

Strauss, S. (1996). Confessions of a born-again structuralist. *Educational Psychologist, 31,* 12–21.

Strauss, S. (1997). Cognitive development and science education: Towards a middle level theory. In W. Damon (Series Ed.) & I. E. Sigel & K. A. Renninger (Vol. Eds.), *Handbook of child psychology: Vol. 4. Child psychology in practice* (2nd ed., pp. 327–399). New York: Wiley.

Strauss, S., & Berliner, D. (1996). *Teachers' mental models of children's minds and learning* (Final Report submitted to the United States–Israel Binational Science Foundation). Jerusalem, Israel.

Strauss, S., Mevorach, M., & Litman, T. (1998). *Effective and less effective junior high school mathematics teachers' in-action mental models.* Manuscript in preparation.

Strauss, S., Ravid, D., Zelcer, H., & Berliner, D. C. (1999). Teachers' subject matter knowledge and their belief systems about children's learning. In T. Nunes (Ed.), *Learning to read: An integrated view from research and practice* (pp. 259–282). London: Kluwer.

Strauss, S., Ravid, D., & Haim, O. (in press). *Relations between teachers' subject matter knowledge and their in-action mental models.*

Strauss, S., Ravid, D., Magen, N., & Berliner, D. C. (1998). Relations between teachers' subject matter knowledge, teaching experience, and their mental models of children's minds and learning. *Teaching and Teacher Education, 14,* 279–292.

Strauss, S., & Meltzer-Rosenberg, H. (1996). *Teachers' and non-teachers' mental models of children's minds and learning.* Unpublished manuscript, Tel Aviv University, Tel Aviv, Israel.

Strauss, S., & Shilony, T. (1994). Teachers' models of children's minds and learning. In L. A. Hirschfeld & S. A. Gelman (Eds.), *Mapping the mind: Domain specificity in cognition and culture* (pp. 422–473). New York: Cambridge University Press.

Wellman, H. M. (1990). *The child's theory of mind.* Cambridge, MA: Bradford Books/MIT Press.

Wilson, S. M., Shulman, L. S., & Richert, A. E. (1987). "120 different ways" of knowing: Representations of knowledge in teaching. In J. Calderhead (Ed.), *Exploring teachers' thinking* (pp. 104–124). London: Cassell Education.

CHAPTER TEN

The Fourth Folk Pedagogy

David R. Olson
Steven Katz
University of Toronto

In an earlier paper, Olson and Bruner (1996; Bruner, 1996) set out four folk or intuitive pedagogies that they found exemplified in the social interactions between the naïve and their caregivers, between child and parent or child and teacher for example, that could be taken as having a pedagogical intention. The first three pedagogies were distinguished in terms of their differing conceptions of competence and the pedagogical moves aimed at altering or enhancing that competence:

1. If competence is regarded as skill, for example, an appropriate pedagogy might call for demonstrations and practice.

2. If competence is regarded as the possession of knowledge, then an appropriate pedagogy might call for transmitting that knowledge through telling or teaching.

3. If competence is regarded as entertaining the appropriate shared beliefs, then conversational discourse may be an appropriate pedagogy.

The theories were used to explain not only teachers' choices of pedagogical strategy but also for some aspects of the evolution of culture. It is pedagogy that makes culture possible; without means for preserving and accumulating competencies, culture could not be created (Premack & Premack, 1996; Tomasello, Kruger, & Ratner, 1993). The four pedagogies articulated alternative forms of culture and the means adopted for passing them onto succeeding generations.

It was the fourth pedagogy that remained particularly problematic in the Olson and Bruner (1996) analysis. This fourth pedagogy acknowledged the existence of a cultural store of socially sanctioned knowledge, roughly what is known in contradistinction to the experiential skills, knowledge, and beliefs held by any individual knower. What is taken as known is sometimes referred to as *objective* knowledge in as much as it is distinguishable from more personal, subjective knowledge. However, objective also implies a form of knowledge that is free of subjectivity and therefore objectively or transcendentally true knowledge. In fact, etymologically speaking, *knowledge* means true belief. While abandoning this narrower conception of knowledge as the true, Olson and Bruner (1996) adopted the conception of what is known as those aspects of knowledge held as true by the larger society and hence they were able to distinguish between what any one person knows and what is known culturally speaking.

The problem for the fourth pedagogy was in assessing the pedagogical implications of such an assumption about knowledge. On the one hand, such an assumption threatened to collapse onto the second pedagogy, the view that knowledge existed, and it was the role of pedagogy to convey or transmit that knowledge. On the other hand, such an assumption threatened to collapse onto the third pedagogy, the pedagogy of discourse, in that the known could perhaps be little more than the set of collaborative discourses in which teachers and students were engaged. To say the least, the fourth pedagogy, the pedagogy that acknowledged the categorical distinction between what any living subject knows and what is taken as known, remained problematic.

In this chapter, we set out some of the properties and conditions of this fourth pedagogy by appealing to the concept of institutional knowledge as a way of bridging the gap between what is known subjectively and what is known collectively. We examine its utility by reference to a series of extensive interviews with teachers who are challenged to both meet the demands of the fixed-school curriculum and the needs of the individual children, with their varied interests, backgrounds, and understandings, who make up a class. These concerns pull teachers into different and often conflicting folk pedagogies. We begin with a brief review of the first three pedagogies.

FOLK PEDAGOGIES

For heuristic purposes, Fenstermacher and Soltis (1992) proposed the existence of a hypothetical wallet-size certificate known as the Educated Person (EP) card. The project fails, of course, for lack of a consensus as to what it means to be an educated person. What criteria need to be met to ensure receipt of an EP card? What defines the range of human competence acceptable to a specific society? Moreover, different conceptions of what it means to be competent entail different conceptions of what it means to teach and learn. It is this divergence, as noted earlier, that allows us to identify alternative folk pedagogical forms (Olson & Bruner, 1996).

Skills, Talents, and Abilities: The First Folk Pedagogy

If to be competent is to be able to do, then we are in the realm of the first folk pedagogy. The deliberate demonstration of a successful action by an expert to a novice is premised on the belief of the former that the latter can learn a novel skill by being shown. The novice proceeds to imitate the action, eventually advancing through repeated practice. Interactions between parents and their children are filled with instances of modeling that can be described as having a pedagogical intention. From the age of two, children show a remarkable proclivity for imitation, a feat that adults both recognize and take advantage of by providing what Bruner (1961) has called *noiseless exemplars*.

The image of competence emerging through practice is one well captured by the traditional craft apprenticeship. Induction of the novice into the ways of the expert follows a progressive route, one in which a complex skill is broken down into its constituent parts, each of which is demonstrated and practiced. Often imitative practices assume a natural or habitual position, a stance reflected in Kruger and Tomasello's (1996) phrase *expected learning*. Their account of Samoan life illustrates the ways in which immersion and participation provide opportunities for observation and imitation.

The delimiting theme in the first folk pedagogy, then, is the operational definition of *competence* as consisting of talents, skills, and abilities. It is what Ryle (1949) called *know how* as distinct from *know that*, the latter indicative of propositional knowledge. Indeed, notions of understanding and acquired declarative knowledge are nowhere to be found in the first folk pedagogy, hence the need for a second folk pedagogy.

Possessing Knowledge: The Second Folk Pedagogy

The Lockean metaphor, *mind as blank slate* or *mind as container* (Bereiter & Scardamalia, 1996), provides an appropriate characterization of the mental assumption underlying the second folk pedagogy. The minds of learners are considered devoid of the necessary facts, rules, and principles that must then be transferred in a unidirectional fashion from the instructor, text, or other resource. Astington (1997) reported the publication of a *Morning Smile* in a local newspaper that read, "Sign on school door: Free knowledge. Bring your own container" (p. 96). Thus, in keeping with the receptacle model of mind, teaching becomes an exercise in telling and learning an exercise in remembering. The sequential and hierarchical structure of didactic teaching exemplifies the second folk pedagogy.

If teaching is telling and learning is remembering, it follows that something must be told and something must be remembered. That something is propositional knowledge; for it to take on the status of a transferable commodity, it must achieve an existence independent of the individual knower. Knowledge considered in this light is certain and permanent. From what has been called a *dualist* (Perry, 1970) or *absolutist* (Chandler, Boyes, & Ball, 1990; Kuhn, 1991, 1992) perspective, knowledge is viewed as either right or wrong. It is not an exaggeration to say that knowledge is seen as a ". . . free-standing attribute of the environing world that only secondarily comes into the passive possession of those who, because they happen to be in the right place at the right time, automatically end up with some portion of the unmitigated truth directly embossed upon the recording equipment of their minds" (Chandler et al., 1990, p. 377). Disagreements between people are attributed to the lack of facts among one of the parties. The epistemic posture of defended realism (Chandler et al., 1990) is invoked in which a working distinction is made between facts and opinions. As the gospel of journalism states, "Comment is free, but facts are sacred."

The process by which knowledge is authenticated as the truth is thought to lie with the appropriate authorities (Kitchener, 1983; Kitchener & King, 1981; Kitchener, King, Wood, & Davidson, 1989; Kuhn, 1992; Perry, 1970). Belenky, Clinchy, Goldberger, and Tarule (1986) called this *silent knowing*, in which the individual accepts the authority's proclamation as to what is true. There is no belief that the knower can learn from his or her own experiences, and thus knowing does not belong to the individual.

Intimately bound to the process of knowledge acquisition is the nature of the evidence used to justify belief. Because truth is acquired from the appropriate authorities, justification for belief normally takes the form of what Belenky et al. (1986) termed *received knowing*. That is, evidence consists of returning the words of the authority, be it person or text. Many educators have experienced this in its purest form when, on asking a student to explain a certain phenomenon, they received this reply: "Because you said so."

In this second folk pedagogy, then, *competence* is defined in terms of an individual's acquisition of knowledge—knowledge best described in terms of God-given facts. It is probably the most widely practiced form of folk pedagogy, at least insofar as formal education is concerned. Through its ability to define the known, it purports to offer clear specifications as to what is to be taught, as well as an associated set of standards for assessing learning achievements. Formal testing is often the preferred vehicle for gauging the closeness of fit between what is told and what is remembered.

Subjective postures are sharply differentiated from objective facts. Personal belief, as noted earlier, is relegated to the substandard position of opinion or, worse, an erroneous account of the facts. Not so, as we see, in the third folk pedagogy.

Sharing Beliefs: The Third Folk Pedagogy

The signature theme of the third folk pedagogy is a new respect for the point of view of the child, an image well captured in the writings of the educational philosopher, John Dewey. Heavily influenced by Darwin's theory of evolution and the psychology of William James, Dewey (1902/1966) accepted that the human ability to think and learn had evolved for the same reason as all other capacities of living organisms—survival. As Phillips and Soltis (1991) wrote in their commentary on Dewey, ". . . thinking and learning are 'practical' capacities, in the exercise of which we actively interact with our surroundings" (p. 38). The active stance ascribed to the learner here stands in clear contrast to the passivity of second folk pedagogy that Dewey believed treated students in ways that disregarded the function of thinking and learning in the natural world (Dewey, 1902/1966).

In advancing his progressive ideals, Dewey saw knowledge emerging from a process of interpretation and clarification of meanings related to various aspects of experience in the world (Dewey, 1938). This central tenet unites both cognitive–developmental and sociocultural perspectives under the umbrella of the third folk pedagogy (Astington & Pelletier, 1996). Evolving out of Piagetian and neo-Piagetian theory, cognitive developmentalists emphasize the interaction of the child with the physical environment. Learning occurs as previously acquired cognitive structures are coordinated to form new superordinate structures. Initially, structures develop from concrete experiences, and thinking remains concrete until the coordination of superordinate structures allows for the emergence of abstract thought.

Sociocultural models emphasize the child's interactions with other people. Rooted in Vygotskian theory, cognitive development is regarded as a socially mediated process. The conversation metaphor (Applebee, 1996) is a popular one, as student and teacher engage in a dialogue in an attempt to construct meaning. Notions of communities of learners (Brown & Campione, 1994; Rogoff, Matusov, & White, 1996) and cognitive apprenticeships (Collins, Brown, & Newman, 1989) portray learning as the result of a coordination of perspectives between teacher and learner or among learners themselves.

In considering the point of view of the child, the third folk pedagogy acknowledges the mind as a place of privately held beliefs and ideas (Olson & Bruner, 1996). Children are seen as individuals capable of making sense both on their own (cognitive–developmental) and through discourse with others (sociocultural). Learning, then, can be conceptualized as a process of subjective interpretation, whereas teaching creates opportunities for intersubjective interchanges and for sharing beliefs through collaborative discourse.

By celebrating the subjective in its definition of competence, the third folk pedagogy necessarily advances a very different set of epistemological assumptions than those discussed in connection with the second folk pedagogy. Indeed, in recognizing that the known is neither God-given truth nor an indisputable fact of nature, subscribers to the third folk pedagogy view knowledge as fundamentally uncertain. Termed *multiplists* or *relativists* (Kuhn, 1991, 1992; Perry, 1970), these individuals see all opinions as valid and nothing as certain. After all, even experts disagree. Truth, on this view, varies from person to person, and knowledge is interpreted subjectively. Alternatively, they adopt the stance of skeptic in which ". . . all claims are challenged, every heart-felt belief is held up to ridicule, and all action is seen as permanently premature" (Chandler et al., 1990, p. 379).

For the unbridled relativists, the source of knowledge lies in personal, idiosyncratic processes such as individual opinion (Kitchener, 1983; Kitchener & King, 1981; Kitchener et al., 1989; Kuhn, 1992; Perry, 1970). Belenky et al. (1986) used the term *subjective knowing* to convey the delimiting role of intuition and gut feeling in the epistemological enterprise. Personal belief counts as evidence for knowing. To justify beliefs is to share them with others. In this way, teaching, as mentioned earlier, is collaboration, while learning is subjective interpretation. This third pedagogy is quite well reflected in the majority of chapters in this volume.

WHAT IS KNOWN AND THE FOURTH PEDAGOGY

The idea of a distinction between the knower and the known may strike a modern reader as anachronistic. As the second pedagogy spelled out, knowledge was once seen as a gift from God rather than a human achievement and, as such, could only be taught to others. Few still hold such a view of knowledge. Knowledge is the product of a subjective activity of learning or thinking something. As Smith (1990) pointed out: "Knowledge exists only in the activities and participation of subjects as knowers" and yet, "[to talk of] knowledge discards the presence of the knowing subject" (p. 66). That is, to talk of knowledge is to erase the subject, leaving what is then misleadingly thought of as objective knowledge. This was the mistaken assumption of the second pedagogy.

Yet the distinction between the knower and the known is ancient and was traced by Havelock (1982) to the beginnings of writing. Writing preserves knowledge independent of its author through time and across space. Writing then serves as an embodiment of the known. Olson (1994) adopted and expanded on this view arguing that written texts and the archival tradition in general provided the technology needed for the construction and accumulation of the known independently of the peculiarities of the individual knower. Bruner (1996), too, emphasized the importance of enduring artifacts, both in the form of texts and institutions in the creation of culture and in the development of an appropriate pedagogy. As Popper (1972) argued, such accumulated knowledge, which he referred to as *World 3*, was what made it possible for Newton's theory to outlive Newton and yet there is the possibility that hypotheses can die without harm to their holders. Knowledge could be seen as autonomous.

How are we to think of knowledge without a knower? Olson and Bruner (1996) acknowledged this possibility and insisted that any modern pedagogy had to come to terms with what is known and invent devices for connecting what is known with the learner's own knowledge and experience. Yet Olson and Bruner (1996) offered little account of just what this knowledge without a knowing subject could be. We propose, in this chapter, to fill that lacuna by appeal to the concept of institutional knowledge. Science is one such institution; schools are another. Both are institutions for the accumulation, preservation, and transmission of knowledge, of what is known. The first problem is in explaining in what sense there can be such a thing as institutional knowledge.

INSTITUTIONAL KNOWLEDGE

Not every belief held by a scientist is taken to be knowledge. Beliefs are subjected to a long and complex social process embedded in formally constituted institutions before they enter what we may loosely call the canon—the sanctuary of the known. These are not only social processes, that is, thinking processes carried on privately or collectively, but also involve the production of public artifacts that are subjected to the rituals of publication, replication, adoption, citation, and the like. These are the processes by means of which beliefs become knowledge. Although the outlines of these institutional processes were first set out in the writings of Max Weber and Durkheim early in the 20th century, the analysis was spelled out in regard to science in the writings of Michael Polanyi (1958).

Polanyi (1958) pointed out that, although each scientist follows his or her own hunches, intuitions, and judgments, individual work contributes to an enterprise as a whole that we call science. This corporate enterprise is made up not only of the individual contributions but also through such institutional practices as credentialling, publication, textbooks, professional societies, and the like. As Polanyi added:

nobody knows more than a tiny fragment of science well enough to judge its validity and value at first hand. For the rest he has to rely on views accepted at second hand on the authority of a community of people accredited as scientists [and] . . . anyone who speaks of science in the current sense and with the usual approval, accepts this organized consensus as determining what is 'scientific' and what is 'unscientific'. When I speak of science, I acknowledge both its tradition and its organized authority, and I deny that anyone who wholly rejects these can be said to be a scientist, or have any proper understanding and appreciation of science. (1958, pp. 163–164)

Recent research in the sociology of science by Latour and Woolgar (1986) and Dunbar (1993) indicated just how public institutions function in the formation and interpretation of such textual knowledge. The artifacts, what has been called the *world on paper* (Olson, 1994), are crafted in ways to not only express the beliefs of the authors, but to find an acceptable place in the tradition of which they are a part. Latour and Woolgar (1986) described the long and somewhat tortured route from private, subjective hunch expressed in such conjectural statements as "I wonder if . . ." and ending up, after many revisions, as canonical statements of truth: "The properties of were shown to be. . . ." As Smith (1990) pointed out and as previously mentioned, the final report removes all traces of subjectivity, that is of the private beliefs of individuals, to become statements taken as fact.

Indeed, Smith (1990) characterized fact as just the end product of these institutional procedures. "Facts are neither the statements themselves, nor the actualities these statements refer to. They are an organization of practices of inscribing an actuality into a text." And again, "A fact is constituted to be external to the particular subjectivities of the knowing" (Smith, 1990, pp. 69–70). An illustration may help to make this notion of fact comprehensible. In law, as we say, a person is innocent until proven guilty. Guilt is not simply a matter of what one actually did but rather the judgment offered by judge or jury. One is guilty, not because one did it, but because, through the cumbersome procedures of the courts, one is judged guilty. The same is true for fact. Facts are not simply what happened but what the institutional procedures and structures of science judge to be fact. Subjectivity, the feeling of knowing, like the feeling of guilt has little to do with it. Facts are institutional judgments; they constitute the known.

We are now in a position to elaborate on the fourth pedagogy that Olson and Bruner (1996) only hinted at. Facts like what is known and what is taken as known are the institutional expressions of knowledge. Education is a matter of introducing learners to these institutional facts and forms. Unlike the first three folk pedagogies, there is a radical discontinuity between the subjective experience and personal knowledge acquired by the child through their own efforts and through their participation in social life, and the institutional forms taken as the known in any advanced society.

Educational theory for much of the 20th century attempted to come to grips with this gap between what one knows subjectively and what is known collectively. Classical education theory accepted what we here call institutional knowledge as knowledge and attempted to transmit that knowledge to children. This was what Olson and Bruner (1996) called the *second pedagogy*. Educational reformers such as Dewey (1902/1966, 1938) took the other pole insisting on the primacy of subjective and communal experience as the ground of all knowledge. This was Olson and Bruner's (1996) third pedagogy. Neither theory satisfactorily recognizes let alone bridges the two. The fourth pedagogy brings into focus the often contradictory but legitimate claims of both persons and institutions, and acknowledges the difficulty, indeed impossibility, of achieving both.

It may be worth mentioning that psychological theory has not been helpful on this point. There are two disciplines of psychology. The first, the differential psychology based on intelligence and personality testing, serves primarily to predict the outcomes of institutional practices of the school. That is, intelligence tests serve to predict the outcomes of schooling while ignoring aspects of subjective experience. The second psychology, cognitive experimental psychology, attempts to come to terms with the mental activities of individuals, but with little relevance to the impacts of the institutional practices of schooling or culture generally. No psychological theories are currently available to coordinate these two, the institutional and the personal.

What the fourth folk pedagogy offers is a model in which the subjective and collective dimensions of the known can be recognized and related. Although theoreticians have been more or less content to operate almost exclusively in spheres defined by one or the other, the practical landscape of education does not enjoy the bounded consistency of abstract theory. Indeed, our recent work has brought us face-to-face with a situation characterized by folk pedagogical contradiction, a phenomenon exemplified at the levels of both educational policy and educational practice. We examine each of these in turn.

EDUCATIONAL POLICY

The Common Curriculum is the foundation of an approach to teaching and learning as set out by Ontario's Ministry of Education and Training in Canada. The mandated standard for all primary and junior classrooms in the province, this vision of education is most fully articulated in the document entitled, *The Common Curriculum: Policies and Outcomes, Grades 1–9* (Ministry of Education and Training, 1995). Essentially, two primary themes characterize the nature of this document: integrative–collaborative studies and outcome-based learning.

Integrative–collaborative studies promote a curriculum that empha-sizes connections and relationships among ideas, people, and things, as well as among academic disciplines. Teachers are expected to plan units that create authentic learning situations in which students collaborate with adults and other children in ". . . a constant search for meaning" (Ministry of Education and Training, 1995, p. 17). Learning is conceptual-ized as an outgrowth of existing knowledge, skills, and values, and tradi-tional subject boundaries are avoided in an effort to promote the view of life as an integrated whole in which people, things, events, processes, and ideas are interrelated. For our purposes, we can say that this portion of the document is essentially characterized by the third folk pedagogy.

Outcome-based learning, the second major theme of the document, is promoted as the vehicle for setting out clear learning expectations, along with performance standards, to help schools and teachers measure and report on student achievement. Specifically, the learning outcomes provided in the document are said to ". . . identify the observable/measurable knowl-edge, skills, and values that students are expected to have developed at cer-tain key stages of their schooling" (Ministry of Education and Training, 1995, p. 9). Seemingly ironic in the context of the integrative–collaborative dimen-sion of the document, subject-matter areas are resurrected for the presenta-tion of specific learning outcomes and become even more specialized in the discussion of provincial standards. Thus, the outcomes-based portion of the document is consistent with the second folk pedagogy.

What we have in *The Common Curriculum*, then, is the attempt of a policymaker at the simultaneous recognition of the subjective stance of the knower as a discourse participant on the one hand, and the claims of the institutionally known on the other. Anchored in what we have come to recognize as disparate folk pedagogies, the result is piecemeal product held together by an unspecified glue. However, policy is not practice and it is the latter with which we must be concerned if we are to argue for the utility of a fourth pedagogy. To this end, we set out to interview teachers with the hope of gaining an understanding of the folk pedagogical forms that play out in the practical arena of their professional lives.

EDUCATIONAL PRACTICE

Our methodology was informed by the distinction between teachers' espoused and in-use pedagogical content knowledge (Strauss, 1993, 1996). The former comes into play when teachers speak about how they would teach in a particular situation, whereas the latter occurs in practice, when teachers actually teach. Practice, according to Polanyi (1958), result-ed in the formation of tacit, as opposed to articulate, knowledge. Thus, a direct question such as "What is your philosophy of teaching?" may or may not be reflective of actual experience. Instead, the questions in our interview schedule asked teachers to tell us what they do in concrete terms. Each participant described the day of teaching that immediately preceded the interview, but also provided an account of a past, teaching unit thought best reflective of their stance as an educator.

Although the teachers in our study were all familiar with *The Common Curriculum*, they varied in the extent to which they actively attempted to integrate it into their practice. Closeness of fit between policy and practice was not a concern of the study, and the nonevaluative context of the interview offered teachers the opportunity to describe what they do beyond the boundaries of the particular curricular initiative. In fact, a frequent observation across our sample was that the lack of specificity in the directives of *The Common Curriculum* left much to the individual teacher (see Katz, 1998).

A bottom–up analytic perspective consisting of unitizing and categorizing (Lincoln & Guba, 1985) facilitated the interpretation of the interview data. The emergent picture is one of teachers whose professional lives are characterized by what we may appropriately term *folk pedagogical conflict*. Concern for the predetermined knowledge commodity and its transmission shares space with an equivalent concern for the subjectively charged dimension of individual student thought. By shares space we do not mean on an educational landscape populated by groups of teachers who consistently tend in one direction or the other. Rather, the simultaneity of existence that we refer to here is a property of the individual teacher. This distinction is important to bear in mind as we present prototypical interview evidence that exemplifies the second and third folk pedagogies.

CONCERN FOR THE KNOWN

Four major themes reflective of a concern for the known emerged from the interview data. *Expected Knowing*, *Communicating Expectations*, and *Measuring Outcomes* involve teacher-driven efforts aimed at the determination, transmission, and measurement of what students need to learn. The fourth theme, *Requisite Behavior*, captures the behavioral stance of students deemed necessary for the successful receipt of knowledge.

Expected Knowing

For some teachers, what students are expected to know is best described in terms of the absence of that very knowledge. Talk about knowledge gaps was not uncommon:

The kids are coming up with gaps in their learning. . .

The kids were just so far behind with so many gaps in their learning that it was quite shocking.

Often the identification of missing knowledge content was illustrated in concrete terms:

I gave them a page of different word uses. Instead of reading the word minute (small), the kids would automatically read it as minute (time).

The idea of possessive. "The boys' arrows", s', many told me that it was incorrect, that the apostrophe had to come before the s even though it was correct. They didn't know the idea of a possessive.

Some kids have no idea about short vowel and long vowel sounds. Spelling hop or hope is really hard for them.

One teacher described her students' lack of fraction terminology as follows:

I'd write a fraction on the board and I'd say, "tell me the parts of the fraction". The kids wouldn't put their hands up. Then one of the children said, "I always mix up which is which" and then everybody said "so do I, so do I". They just said that they knew one was called the denominator. . . . And then I said, "what about this kind of fraction?", and had fifteen over three, "what is this called?". Not one student could answer what it was called. . . . I wrote on the board "improper fraction".

The emphasis on terminology was brought up repeatedly by many of the teachers. For example:

They were calling apostrophes commas . . .

They had to talk about the perimeter, the altitude, and the base. . . . They had to talk about factoring, forty-five and ninety degree angles.

They had to name the different parts of the cell . . .

As one teacher put it in describing the learning demands of her favorite teaching unit:

It's definitely a lot of language words and pronunciations that have to be mastered.

Other teachers talked explicitly in terms of what students need to know:

They need to know what the differences and the similarities are between plant and animal cells. How those make up organ systems in mammals and reptiles. . . . How they come together to make up a system . . .

To conceptualize knowledge as a transferable commodity is to subject it to properties of measurement. The exercise of quantifying the known emerges clearly in the teachers' references to content coverage:

> I've tried to say to the kids, using a comparison with my hands, "this is what we have to cover this year" and I show them a metre. And "this is what we have covered" and I show them a centimetre. . .

> We have got a lot to learn if we want to cover the grade eight program.

> There are areas that we didn't cover that we should have.

Communicating Expectations

Once teachers have determined what their students are expected to know, these expectations must be communicated to the pupils. After all, if the objective, the known, is thought to exist independently of the subjective, then sensitizing the naïve to that which must be learned defines part of the role of the teacher. In keeping with a principal tenet of the second folk pedagogy, this sensitization proceeds along a route best characterized by the language of direct transmission:

> I show the kids what is expected.

> I give them some ideas as to what I am looking for . . .

> There is a model for them to look at on the sheet that I give them and they follow that model.

> I give each child a large draft-board with all of the outcomes right across the curriculum on it.

> I tell the student beforehand, "This is what I'm expecting from you".

> I hand out an expectation sheet for the presentation—what I'm looking for . . .

Measuring Outcomes

The responsibility of defining and communicating what is to be known places the teacher in a position of pedagogical authority. The unidirectional transmission of the known from teacher to student elevates the former to a position of expert. As such, the task of determining the success of student learning lies not with the student but rather with the teacher. This pattern emerged from the interviews in the form of teachers' talk about the use of traditional testing practices:

> I was shocked by my test results in math, spelling, and reading . . .

> We've got a lot to cover and the quickest way I'm going to do it is to teach those lessons and then test them.

> I had five classes all day yesterday and three of the periods were taken up with quizzes.

> If they can do well on a test then I've done my job.

Not surprisingly, learning success was sometimes quantified:

> In order to be successful they need to have at least eighty percent . . .

> I'm looking at around 750 marks for them.

> I received a call from a concerned mom who figured ninety-seven percent isn't enough.

One teacher responded to a question asking her to describe the academic abilities of her students as follows:

> Well, based on the last report card the class average was seventy-three percent.

Requisite Behavior

For the known to be successfully received, the student must adopt a particular behavioral stance. The ability to pay attention was frequently mentioned as a necessary prerequisite for receipt of an instructional message:

> It has been sit down, get quiet, learn to focus, learn to concentrate . . .

> They are able to listen to lessons now. They know how to listen with their eyes as well as their ears. They know how to put pencils, toys, and rulers down.

> We had to work on listening skills and go over the instructions.

> I find I have to repeat myself incredibly when it comes to instructions and then wait time and again. I keep telling them that there is no point in me talking unless they can hear me.

The four thematic elements of teacher practice presented thus far group sensibly under the rubric we have defined as a concern for the known. Indeed, if the story were to end here the emergent picture would be one of consistency best described in terms of the second folk pedagogy. Teachers determine, transmit, and measure what students are to know, whereas the latter enhance the likelihood of successful learning by filtering out surrounding noise that may interfere with the intended transmission. The story does not end here. A different set of features simultaneously characterize the practical context inhabited by the same group of teachers, features we may describe as reflective of a concern for the subjectivity of the student. We present shades of evidence for this—the third folk pedagogy—in the following.

CONCERN FOR THE SUBJECTIVE

The teacher interviews yielded four categories that prove illustrative of a concern for the subjective features of knowing. The first of these, *Children and their Needs*, is comprised of statements reflective of an identified need to consider student individuality. The second and third categories, *Self-Regulated* and *Cooperative Learners*, detail the ascribed student role. Finally, *Facilitator and Fellow Learner*, captures the reports by teachers of their own roles.

Children and Their Needs

Clay (1996) argued that it is not groups that learn but rather individuals. Concordant with this perspective, the teachers in our study articulated the need to acknowledge the diversity among the learners in the classroom:

> I look at meeting the needs of all kids . . .

> I believe that all kids are different and that they have different ways of learning.

> We've had discussions about meeting the needs of the children in the school . . .

> If I've got a lot of children that love to research then I need to meet their needs. I also have kids that need activities, so I'll structure the unit towards that as well.

One teacher spoke explicitly in child-centered terms:

> The whole thing centres on the child. A lot of us here have the same view of the child in mind. Some people don't really take a look at these kids and say, "Hey, where are these kids coming from?"

A successful activity or lesson was often defined as one that offered something for everyone:

> All of them try it. It doesn't matter what level they're at. They are able to do some of it. The number one concern behind it is that it shows a concern for the kids.

> It's good because all of the students can do it at one level or another. It integrates all of the different levels in the class.

Self-Regulated Learners

When pedagogy tends in the direction of the subjective, the stance of the learner becomes one imbued with images of activity. Self-regulation is said to occur when "students activate and sustain cognitions, feelings, and behaviours oriented toward attainment of academic goals" (Gettinger, 1995, p. 671). In effect, self-regulated learners take responsibility for their own learning (Zimmerman & Martinez-Pons, 1992). Such responsibility emerged in the interviews through talk about the promotion of student self-reflection:

> We modify the curriculum because that's where the kids are at. They feel successful and they are learning, although according to their marks they are technically failing.

> I have students involved in the generation of learning criteria on an ongoing basis, doing things like self-assessment . . .

> They think about their own learning. What they have been doing, what they did in the past, how they felt about it, what they are doing now, how they feel about it.

> I want them to have confidence in their abilities as learners and I want them to be able to communicate and reflect on that.

> They write down what the activity was, what they did, what they learned from it, how they felt about it, and what they'd like to do next.

As illustrated in the immediately preceding quote, some of the teachers encourage their students to assume responsibility for the direction of future learning:

> I tell them they're my little scientists. They have to go out there and do it on their own. I'm trying to teach them to be inquirers . . .

> I've given them the chance to go and investigate for themselves. They decide, "what can I go and learn from here and not have Mrs. [name] tell me that I have to learn this?"

Cooperative Learners

As we saw in the presentation of the epistemological assumptions of the third folk pedagogy, subjective belief counts as evidence for knowing and, moreover, to justify beliefs is to share them with others. Acknowledgment of the collaborative or communal features of the learning environment emerged in talk about group work:

> It has always been my philosophy to have them sit with their friends and work at cooperative learning . . .

> I encourage peer tutoring a great deal.

> They worked in companies to build pasta bridges.

> I find they learn more with groups . . .

> We were doing a jig-saw. Everybody had become an expert on one of the five kingdoms.

> They do research projects on World War II in a small group situation.

Facilitator and Fellow Learner

In acknowledging the subjective dimension of knowing, the teacher's role shifts from expositor to that of facilitator:

> I did a lot of facilitating in the unit. I tend to not like to talk very much. I try to move them along in their own learning rather than me just spouting information.

> I do less talking and let their learning "flow" more . . .

Learning becomes a partnership process, with the teacher assuming the posture of fellow learner:

> If we're trying to teach kids to be lifelong learners then we need to be as well.

> You cannot go through this day to day business without learning something yourself.

> I do not talk down to my students. I talk to them as equals.

> I learn from the students everyday.

> I learned something new from Scientific America the other day and used it in class with the grade sevens. They were as amazed as I was.

Just as we saw in the policy context, accounts of teacher practice are filled with examples that point to a simultaneous consideration of the subjective mental life of their students and that which is institutionally known. In the language of the third and second folk pedagogies, respectively, this dual concern becomes problematic in that each element maps onto a different epistemological and mental assumption. However, the problem is not one generally identified by teachers. The teachers we spoke to seemed quite content to straddle the fence separating the subjective and the objective dimensions of the known without any attempt to bridge the two.

EDUCATIONAL IMPLICATIONS—TOWARD A FOURTH FOLK PEDAGOGY

Why the need for consistency? Why the need for the bridging framework of a fourth folk pedagogy? Perhaps because pedagogical practices of all varieties communicate something about the learner to the learner. They each communicate a way of thinking about the self. They are the vehicles through which children come to think of themselves as competent on the one hand or as incompetent on the other.

Once we see that what a child knows experientially, personally, and subjectively can be clearly distinguished from the institutional knowledge taken as known, we may be in a position to sketch out possibilities of a new relation. The route proposed here is to demythologize objective knowledge by reading into it the human knower on the one hand, and to objectivizing subjective knowledge by relating it to the archival, textual tradition on the other. Thus, the need for pedagogical consistency need not imply a forced choice between both elements of the epistemological enterprise of the sort discussed earlier in connection with educational theory. Rather, the need is for a richer pedagogical theory of the sort spelled out in the fourth folk pedagogy, a theory in which the subjective and collective dimensions of what is known can be recognized and related.

A call for the adoption of a more complex folk pedagogical theory poses a substantial challenge to teachers, one of changing beliefs. Effecting such a change can be a formidable task. Kagan (1992) suggested that attempts to change the beliefs of teachers should proceed along the lines suggested by research on conceptual change. Various models of conceptual change exist in the literature (cf. Carey & Spelke, 1994; Chi, 1992; Dole & Sinatra, 1998; Hewson & Thorley, 1989; Nussbaum & Novick, 1982), although a feature common to all is that subjects are confronted with the inadequacy of their beliefs. Our current research program is concerned with explicating the conditions under which teachers are, at least at some level, aware of being pulled between the two sets of constraints—a concern for the transmission of the known and an equal concern for the subjective mental life of students. Exercises in reflective practice (Astington, 1997; Gomez & Tabachnick, 1992) centered on the notion of modifications appear to be promising catalytic candidates. By definition, modifications require a simultaneous consideration of both the child and his or her understanding, and the curriculum, a phenomenon that produces the following prototypical comment:

> I modified the program so they can be successful. Well, what is successful? Is successful 50%, 60%, 80%? When you modify for those children so that they are successful, if you have a watered-down program to the extent that these children are, on paper, a success, and they go off to high school and those modifications aren't met, you've watered it down to the extent that it's not a true outcome. . . . We're between two worlds—it's kind of like a twilight zone.

REFERENCES

Applebee, A. N. (1996). *Curriculum as conversation: Transforming traditions of teaching and learning*. Chicago: University of Chicago Press.

Astington, J. W. (1997). Reflective teaching and learning: Children's and teachers' theories of mind. *Teaching Education, 9*, 95–103.

Astington, J. W., & Pelletier, J. (1996). The language of mind: Its role in teaching and learning. In D. R. Olson & N. Torrance (Eds.), *The handbook of education and human development* (pp. 593–619). Cambridge, MA: Blackwell.

Belenky, M., Clinchy, B., Goldberger, N., & Tarule, J. (1986). *Women's ways of knowing: The development of self, voice, and mind*. New York: Basic Books.

Bereiter, C., & Scardamalia, M. (1996). Rethinking learning. In D. R. Olson & N. Torrance (Eds.), *The handbook of education and human development* (pp. 485–513). Cambridge, MA: Blackwell.

Brown, A. L., & Campione, J. C. (1994). Guided discovery in a community of learners. In K. McGilly (Ed.), *Classroom lessons: Integrating cognitive theory and classroom practice* (pp. 229–270). Cambridge, MA: Bradford Books/MIT Press.

Bruner, J. (1961). *The process of education*. Cambridge, MA: Harvard University Press.

Bruner, J. (1996). *The culture of education*. Cambridge, MA: Harvard University Press.

Carey, S., & Spelke, E. (1994). Domain-specific knowledge and conceptual change. In L. A. Hirschfeld & S. A. Gelman (Eds.), *Mapping the mind* (pp. 169–200). New York: Cambridge University Press.

Chandler, M., Boyes, M., & Ball, L. (1990). Relativism and stations of epistemic doubt. *Journal of Experimental Child Psychology, 50*, 370–395.

Chi, M. (1992). Conceptual change within and across ontological categories: Examples from learning and discovery in science. In R. N. Giere (Ed.), *Minnesota studies in the philosophy of science: Vol. XV. Cognitive models of science* (pp. 129–186). Minneapolis: University of Minnesota Press.

Clay, M. (1996). Accommodating diversity in early literacy learning. In D. R. Olson & N. Torrance (Eds.), *The handbook of education and human development* (pp. 202–224). Cambridge, MA: Blackwell.

Collins, A., Brown, J. S., & Newman, S. E. (1989). Cognitive apprenticeship: Teaching the crafts of reading, writing, and mathematics. In L. B. Resnick (Ed.), *Knowing, learning, and instruction: Essays in honor of Robert Glaser* (pp. 453–494). Hillsdale, NJ: Lawrence Erlbaum Associates.

Dewey, J. (1902/1966). *The child and the curriculum*. Chicago: University of Chicago Press.

Dewey, J. (1938). *Experience and education*. New York: Collier Books.

Dole, J., & Sinatra, G. (1998). Reconceptualizing change in the cognitive construction of knowledge. *Educational Psychologist, 33*, 109–128.

Dunbar, K. (1993). Concept discovery in a scientific domain. *Cognitive Science, 17*, 397–434.

Fenstermacher, G., & Soltis, J. (1992). *Approaches to teaching* (2nd ed.). New York: Teachers College Press.

Gettinger, M. (1995). Book review of *Toward an integrated theory of self-regulation* by D. Schunk & B. Zimmerman (Eds.). *Contemporary Psychology, 40*, 670–673.

Gomez, M. L., & Tabachnick, B. R. (1992). Telling teaching stories. *Teaching Education, 4*, 129–138.

Havelock, E. A. (1982). *The literate revolution in Greece and its cultural consequences*. Princeton, NJ: Princeton University Press.

Hewson, P., & Thorley, N. (1989). The conditions of conceptual change in the classroom. *International Journal of Science Education, 11*, 541–553.

Kagan, D. M. (1992). Implications of research on teacher belief. *Educational Psychologist, 27*, 65–90.

Katz, S. (1998). *Folk pedagogy and The Common Curriculum: An examination of alternative folk pedagogical forms in the context of a particular curricular innovation*. Unpublished master's thesis, University of Toronto, Toronto, Canada.

Kitchener, K. S. (1983). Cognition, metacognition, and epistemic cognition: A three level model of cognitive processing. *Human Development, 4*, 222–232.

Kitchener, K. S., & King, P. A. (1981). Reflective judgment: Concepts of justification and their relationship to age and education. *Journal of Applied Developmental Psychology, 2*, 89–116.

Kitchener, K. S., King, P. A., Wood, P. A., & Davidson, M. L. (1989). Sequentiality and consistency in development of reflective judgment: A six-year longitudinal study. *Journal of Applied Developmental Psychology, 10*, 73–95.

Kruger, A. C., & Tomasello, M. (1996). Cultural learning and learning culture. In D. R. Olson & N. Torrance (Eds.), *The handbook of education and human development* (pp. 369–387). Cambridge, MA: Blackwell.

Kuhn, D. (1991). *The skills of argument*. New York: Cambridge University Press.

Kuhn, D. (1992). Thinking as argument. *Harvard Educational Review, 62*, 155–178.

Latour, B., & Woolgar, S. (1986). *Laboratory life: The social construction of scientific facts*. Princeton, NJ: Princeton University Press.

Lincoln, Y., & Guba, S. (1985). *Naturalistic inquiry*. Beverly Hills, CA: Sage.

Ministry of Education and Training. (1995). *The common curriculum: Policies and outcomes, grades 1–9*. Toronto, Canada: Queen's Printer for Ontario.

Nussbaum, J., & Novick, N. (1982). Alternative frameworks, conceptual conflict, and accommodation: Toward a principled teaching strategy. *Instructional Science, 11*, 183–200.

Olson, D. R. (1994). *The world on paper: The conceptual and cognitive implications of writing and reading*. New York: Cambridge University Press.

Olson, D. R., & Bruner, J. S. (1996). Folk psychology and folk pedagogy. In D. R. Olson & N. Torrance (Eds.), *The handbook of education and human development* (pp. 9–27). Cambridge, MA: Blackwell.

Perry, W. (1970). *Forms of intellectual and ethical development in the college years*. New York: Holt, Rinehart & Winston.

Phillips, D., & Soltis, J. (1991). *Perspectives on learning* (2nd ed.). New York: Teachers College Press.

Polanyi, M. (1958). *Personal knowledge*. New York: Harper & Row.

Popper, K. R. (1972). *Objective knowledge: An evolutionary approach*. Oxford, England: Clarendon.

Premack, D., & Premack, A. J. (1996). Why animals lack pedagogy and some cultures have more of it than others. In D. R. Olson & N. Torrance (Eds.), *The handbook of education and human development* (pp. 302–323). Cambridge, MA: Blackwell.

Rogoff, B., Matusov, E., & White, C. (1996). Models of teaching and learning: Participation in a community of learners. In D. R. Olson & N. Torrance (Eds.), *The handbook of education and human development* (pp. 388–414). Cambridge, MA: Blackwell.

Ryle, G. (1949). *The concept of mind*. London: Hutchinson.

Smith, D. (1990). *Conceptual practices of power*. Toronto, Canada: University of Toronto Press.

Strauss, S. (1996). Confessions of a born-again constructivist. *Educational Psychologist, 31*, 15–21.

Strauss, S. (1993). Teachers' pedagogical content knowledge about children's minds and learning: Implications for teacher education. *Educational Psychologist, 28*, 279–290.

Tomasello, M., Kruger, A. C., & Ratner, H. (1993). Cultural learning. *Behavioral and Brain Sciences, 16*, 495–511.

Zimmerman, B., & Martinez-Pons, M. (1992). Perceptions of efficacy and strategy use in the self-regulation of learning. In D. Schunk & J. Meece (Eds.), *Student perceptions in the classroom* (pp. 185–207). Hillsdale, NJ: Lawrence Erlbaum Associates.

Author Index

Subject Index